NO SAFER KINDER HATRED

Frank Thabani Sayi was born in Rhodesia, now Zimbabwe, in the late 1960s, on the cusp of the war of independence or the Bush War, to overturn a century of racial subjugation. After Zimbabwe's independence from White rule, he bore witness to and survived the Gukurahundi massacres orchestrated by Robert Mugabe's militias in Matabeleland in the early 1980s. He came to England on a scholarship, and has worked as a nurse in cardiothoracic medicine, intensive care, and gender-reassignment surgery. And for twenty-five years as a police officer in child sexual exploitation, Black-on-Black violence, and modern slavery and child criminal exploitation. And most recently, as a lecturer at the Open University in the Law and Business Faculty. He holds a doctorate in English and Humanities and a master's in Cultural and Critical Studies, both from Birkbeck, University of London. Frank is also an associate editor on the Brief Encounters journal as SOAS. His first short story, 'Shadows', was published in *The Mechanics' Institute Review* in 2015. In his spare time, he enjoys long walks and exploring the beautiful Buckinghamshire countryside.

NO SAFER
KINDER HATRED

How Racial Hatred and Ethnic Violence
Shaped Zimbabwe

Frank Thabani Sayi

riverrun

First published in Great Britain in 2025 by

r
riverrun

an imprint of Quercus
Part of John Murray Group

A CIP catalogue record for this book is available
from the British Library.

HB ISBN 978 1 52942 730 1
TPB ISBN 978 1 52942 731 8
EBOOK ISBN 978 1 52942 732 5

1

Quercus Editions Ltd hereby exclude all liability to the extent permitted by law
for any errors or omissions in this book and for any loss, damage or expense
(whether direct or indirect) suffered by a third party relying on any
information contained in this book.

Typeset in Aldine401 by CC Book Production

Printed and bound in Great Britain by Clays Ltd, Elcograf S.p.A.

MIX
Paper | Supporting
responsible forestry
FSC
www.fsc.org   FSC® C104740

Papers used by Quercus are from well-managed forests and other responsible sources.

Quercus
Carmelite House
50 Victoria Embankment
London EC4Y 0DZ

John Murray Group
Part of Hodder & Stoughton Limited
An Hachette UK company

The authorised representative in the EEA is Hachette Ireland,
8 Castlecourt Centre, Dublin 15, D15 XTP3, Ireland (email: info@hbgi.ie)

To the future generations in my family, exiles all,
awaiting still the possibility of return.

To my grandmother and to all the women who raised me,
whose voices reverberate throughout this book.

And to the people of Mawabeni,
a boisterous little place with a big heart!

These women, alive now and sitting on the edge of the smooth wall, are the most substantial evidence of survival there is, of courage, of struggle. Alive now and looking right past their own shoulders, as though they are invisible beings, interested in the things beyond, the secret things that only their minds have known and as close to their own bodies as their more perplexed and curious minds can endure.

– Yvonne Vera, *The Stone Virgins*

PART 1

PART I

CHAPTER 1

I had this strange feeling that something was wrong. I knew that it had to be my mother. I opened the door straight into the corridor and sleepwalked the short distance to the communal phone. I punched in the number on the prepaid phonecard and dialled my mother's work telephone number. The phone rang and someone promptly answered. The voice sounded annoyed.

'Yes!'

'Can I speak to Elisabeth, please?' I asked tentatively.

'She's dead. Three, maybe four months ago!'

My throat went into a spasm. I felt my own presence, but at the same time felt inaccessible to myself. A million questions flooded my senses.

'She is my mother; how can you say she's dead?' I said rather apologetically.

The voice bellowed back: 'She's dead – that's for sure. Has been for quite some time. If you want to know more, please call her daughter.'

He gave me a number in a rapid fire of digits, before hanging up. He didn't even wait for me to check if the number was correct.

Then I realised I had felt something – only I hadn't been listening to my own body. Bodies aren't passive. If you listen to yours, it'll tell you things about you beyond pain, hunger, and thirst. That snap of the wire of the thing that connects us. As long as we remain connected to other people, we are never free from the intrusion of subliminal messages.

First came the confusion, followed by an overwhelming sense of helplessness. For the first time in years, I needed a hug, but I was alone in the corridor of a high-rise building in the middle of London. I thought about my mother. To walk backwards and retrace your footsteps is the most difficult thing you'll ever do. My emotions collided with everything, but in my heart I knew full well that there was nothing I could do but return to Zimbabwe.

A week later, I arrived in Johannesburg in the morning to catch a connecting flight to Bulawayo. As the plane straddled the border, I could see the Limpopo River cutting through the red earth's crust. The savannah sprawled out as far as the eye could see. I sat next to an Afrikaner with broad tanned forearms and a wisp of golden curly hair. We exchanged pleasantries. After a while, he said, 'I love the accent. Where is it from?' As if I and the way that I spoke were two separable entities.

'I was born here, but have been away for quite a while,' I said. That felt odd because we were in the air between countries.

And he quipped: 'This place is a fucking disaster!'

I didn't know what to say. I felt a lump of anger rise to my throat. I let it go.

★

Two hours later, we landed in Bulawayo. The immigration officer glanced at my British passport and looked at me twice, as if there was an incongruity between my face, name, and the passport. Some identities sneak up on you, imperceptibly, and a slip of the tongue can betray you. In Zimbabwe, my name carried a legacy I could not shake, and all the distortions that went with it. I focused on the space behind his head. He stamped my passport with a business visitor's stamp, allowing me two weeks in the country. I cleared customs and found myself on the other side of the world. No one was expecting me. I put my sunglasses on and walked straight to a taxi.

'City centre, please,' I said, getting in.

'Where exactly in the city centre?' the taxi driver asked, looking at me through the shards of a broken rear-view mirror. A Lonely Planet guidebook had recommended the Belvedere just off Selbourne Avenue. I instructed the taxi driver to take me there.

'*Ah, livela eGoli Mdala?*'* he probed in isiNdebele with an unsettling familiarity.

'England,' I said, trying to discourage conversation.

'Life is tough here; everything is hard!'

All the while, he was looking at me as if trying to locate me, but all I wanted was a perimeter of solitude. He bellowed out the names of the new streets. Selbourne Avenue had now become Leopold Takawira Avenue, Queen's Road subsumed into Robert Mugabe Way, and George Street had morphed into George

---

* Have you just flown in from Johannesburg?

NO SAFER KINDER HATRED

Silundika Street. And so the list went on. History rewritten, weaving street names into new narratives of a nation. I remained silent, taking in the scenery, whilst trying to work out the internal landscape of this place. As we approached the city centre, everything seemed dusty, crumbling, and decaying. I noticed dry, hungry lawns, the lack of flowers, and the glaring absence of Whites and Asians. Or Coloureds. When I was young, this used to be their undisputed domain, their playground. I didn't say anything as I didn't know who else the taxi driver worked for. I paid US$10 for the fare.

My room at the Belvedere was very small, with a single bed, a shower cubicle, and burglar bars on the windows like a prison cell. Basic but clean. If all went well, this would be my home for the next ten days.

As I unpacked, I recalled my mother's last words to me.

'*By the time you come back everyone will be gone!*'

Why didn't she tell me that she was terminally ill? I opened my rucksack and grabbed a bottle of whisky that I'd brought with me, poured a large home measure, and knocked it back. Jet-lagged, I collapsed on the bed and fell asleep.

In the morning, I sat in the courtyard under the shade of banana trees, a small sanctuary away from the hustle and bustle of the Bulawayo City Centre, a few feet away from a pot-bellied White man with predatory eyes. He asked for my name, and I gave him the sideways look of the victim of a dog bite. He shuffled his feet uncomfortably, revealing pale white skin in the glare of the morning sun.

A couple came out of one of the rooms: an older White male holding hands with a skinny Black boy with a crop of knotty, unkempt Afro hair. I felt afraid for the first time since my arrival. I couldn't call anyone as the only number I had was my mother's work telephone number. I asked the receptionist to arrange for a taxi for me, someone known to her.

A little while later the taxi drew me up outside my mother's old house. There was nothing extraordinary about my mother's last house on earth, except it was in Makokoba, the oldest township in Bulawayo, a stone's throw from the city centre. To see both poverty and the resilience and triumph of the human spirit, you needed to come here.

There were children playing outside. When I approached, they ran back indoors. My sister Gift came to the door. Time stopped as she stood there looking at me. I could see in her eyes that she was grappling with what she saw. Her eyes were hollow; she'd aged. She was all bones. I saw something was eating my sister alive. I ran towards her and tried to give her a big hug, something I'd been looking forward to since that moment in the corridor in London, but she froze. Both her arms remained by her side.

'It's me!' I said.

She twisted her neck like a pigeon trying to work something out. And then she called out my name, and her voice pierced the eerie silence in the yard.

'*Thabani!* It is you; it really is you!' she screamed. 'Where have you been? We tried, *I* tried, to contact you. She's gone; it's too late now,' she said.

My Aunt Gladys came out too. Gaunt, with eyes deep inside the cave of a face.

'Why have you come now?' she said.

I had no answer to that. I was left holding my rucksack. On hearing the screaming, Thula – my younger half-sister – emerged from the box of a house. And when she looked at me, her countenance remained at the crossroads between a smile and a cry. Although tiny, she confronted me right from the door across the yard.

'We thought you were dead. So where were you all this time? You didn't write; you didn't call. Now you come here like a celebrity – what is it you want?'

When I had seen her last, she was just a little girl.

'Mama died like a dog,' she continued. 'She wailed and asked for you. There was nothing we could do to find you and bring you here. She wanted to say goodbye and she prayed to see you just one more time. So, why come back now?'

'I have come home,' I said.

'No, you haven't! This is no longer your home!' she retorted. 'I can see the fear in your eyes. Coming with all your money, thinking you can buy us. Where were you when we needed you? When *I* needed you?'

She flew at me, and rained blows on my body. I held her tightly. It felt as if her anger was penetrating the earth like a bolt of lightning. All the while, she was calling our mother.

'*Mama! Mama!*'

I wanted to say that I was sorry. That I needed them more than they needed me, but it was of no use. I could feel her anger in my bones.

'I needed you. We all needed you! She had no painkillers. It was me who saw Mama's last gasp for air because everyone left, including you. All of you!'

She pointed at my older sister, who looked away in guilt.

I felt exposed and ashamed. Life doesn't teach you this: your own betrayal is the hardest thing to swallow.

After rage was exhausted and everyone had calmed down, Gift decided that we should all go to our grandmother's village – Mawabeni.

My aunt, sisters and their children took the bus. I took a taxi. We left just before dusk. As we drove further away from the city, the landscape became mean and broken, with tufts of bleached grass clinging to life on top of lumps of red earth. The road glided on the back of mountains, down small hills, and wound its way through a landscape interspersed with acacia trees and goats. The sun sprinkled its rays against the horizon as flocks of birds traversed the sky westwards. On each side of the road, golden thatch grass waved gently in the silent wind. Apart from the occasional settlement, there was nothing to see except women with loads so heavy their necks were bent to the side.

I arrived just after sunset. Aunt Gladys, my sisters, their children, cousins, and distant relatives were already there. My grandmother was now in her eighties. It had been agreed that by way of introduction they'd tell her that I was my younger sister's boyfriend, to prevent her going into shock. When I was introduced to her, she looked at me with an out-of-season storm on her face.

'Come closer,' she said, 'I cannot see you.'

There was something in her voice that brought words to life. I moved closer to her, and she felt the contours of my face with her fingers.

Her rough fingers fell into the crevice between my lips. I tasted salt and smoke from the firewood.

'Child, why are you crying?'

Somehow, she felt my presence and instantly recognised me. She started ululating and wailing. She rocked from side to side and howled. Despite what my sister had said earlier, *I was home.*

'I knew you'd come!' she said. 'I have prayed and waited. Lord knows, I prayed and waited. God kept his promise! After everything that has happened, I knew you'd come. Your mother is gone. Your uncle too. God has listened to my prayers.'

As we sat by the fire, she continually rubbed my arm with a tenderness I never knew she was capable of. The voice and hand that tormented me as a child now soothed me. I had scars caused by her still, but she was no longer bitter or angry, just old, partially blind, and waiting for God.

That night, she wouldn't let me go to sleep. No one in the spirit world knew that I was there, because I was a stranger now, but, with her right next to me, I felt the power of her centuries-old wisdom. For the first time, I felt what it meant to be anchored. I kept stoking the fire with small pieces of wood. The smoke was unbearable, but useful too: I needed to cry, let it all out.

At dawn she took me to my mother's grave, just a red mound of earth. As we got closer, she started clapping her hands, calling my mother's name and all the names of our ancestors. She was old and frail and yet she remembered all of them. It suddenly occurred to me that I did not know any of this. What would happen to us when she'd gone? Grandma was the tar that bound generations together. Without her, everything would fall apart.

As the sun came up, she introduced me to each of Grandpa's, Mum's, and Uncle Sami's graves. She gave me three small rocks, one for each. She said things I never knew. For the first time, I felt connected. My heart opened up, and I surrendered everything I had to my mum's grave, and everything fell into place. My grief had finally found a home. The pain and confusion that I'd carried with me all the way from London poured out and I wept, gasping for air, first holding the world in, and, in the end, I let it go. When it was all over, I knew what it felt like to be free from pain, from the fear of not knowing, and from being afraid all the time. We sat in silence and listened to nothing but the essence of the place.

Dawn gave way and sunlight's morning golden glow emerged from behind the Waba mountain. Grandma sang a song that made me feel that something bigger than me had brought me home. I surrendered to its spell and let her guide me to the places I hadn't been before. It was a comforting feeling. I suspended everything that I thought I knew about life and kept silent in all the languages that I spoke, because of what had happened to me in that small room in London. I hadn't known how connected I was to this place, to these people, until I'd felt the ache in my bones.

I left Grandma's place just before sunset. She limped with me to the wooden gate. There she held my hands: 'Go well, my child. Now I will die in peace having seen your face again!'

It would be the last time that I'd see her alive. Her burden was all mine now. Because there is no safer, kinder hatred.

CHAPTER 2

My earliest memory of being in the world is of my grand-mother's voice soothing me to sleep and waking up next to her, snuggled up in the curve of her spine, ensconced between her, my two sisters, and the wall. We slept on a straw mat, *icansi*, made by Grandma from soft river reeds held together by parallel rail tracks of thread, whose meandering and unequal dimensions at various points, due to her myopia, were enough to derail real trains.

There were five of us: Grandma, Uncle Sami, my two sisters Thoko and Gift, and then me. Thoko was the eldest, I was the youngest. Gift was wedged between us. We lost a brother, too, Ma's firstborn. I inherited his name, Thabani, which means Joy. My mother was thrilled that, finally, she had a boy. There was a grave hidden somewhere, but my brother's baby things were still there: white reusable cotton nappies, soft woolly hat, and tiny cotton boots, blue.

There was only one photograph of my grandmother and me. But none of us as a family. It was staged; I am not sure how old I was in the photograph. Just under two years old, maybe. I have

NO SAFER KINDER HATRED

no recollection of what happened immediately before or after that photograph was taken. Or where or why Grandma had it taken. An instinct perhaps, to curate memories. It is all I have of her and me, frozen in time.

I was born in Rhodesia, now Zimbabwe, in the late 1960s, on the cusp of the war of independence, or the Bush War, to overturn a century of racial subjugation. I have memories of two worlds: our world – poor, wretched, constrained behind the barbed wire of the Native Reserves; and the other world – occupied by White people: prosperous, inaccessible, closed.

Our village, Mawabeni, was located forty kilometres south-east of Bulawayo. A few kilometres east of the Matobo Hills, home to the graves of Ndebele kings, and, controversially, Cecil John Rhodes, one of the architects of colonialism in sub-Saharan Africa. Rhodesia was named after him; his grave was carved out of granite rock in the most serene, sacred, and beautiful place on earth, next to the spiritual shrines of our people. For all the pain that he caused, there was no one angry enough to desecrate his grave, fling his bones to the wind, and erase his name from the annals of Black African history. As Grandma would say, everywhere they went, White people erected monuments, as if they had a fear of being forgotten.

To the east, the horizon was dominated by a whaleback of a mountain, the Waba. Its countenance rose into the clouds. And on its back rested unsightly barnacles of grey concrete water tanks. The mountain was where the name Mawabeni came from – it simply means 'the Place of Hills'.

It was a land wedged between mountains. During hot summers, wildfires ignited tonnes of bone-dry tinder and grass

14

spontaneously. And, at night, intensified by the darkness, you could see the scale and ferocity of the flames. As the god of mountains rained fury, tiny specks of burnt-out tinder fell from the sky, a kind of black rain, soft, delicate, without moisture.

Mawabeni was held in suspension by two competing but unequal forces: Bulawayo to the north-west and Johannesburg to the south-west. Although hedged in by mountains, it was a boisterous little place. Its soils hosted hard-packed clumps of shrub land, thorn bush and a scattering of mopane trees. Mostly, it was rugged terrain full of stones and nothing else but undulating hills. A permanent layer of dust had settled on everything: grass, trees, road signs, buildings, old newspapers, and plastic bags. There was barbed wire, in every direction, as far as the eye could see. Much land and its residents had been displaced to give way to White farms. Their homes rested precariously on the side of the hills. Mawabeni, like all Native Reserves, served as a containment, intended to discourage deeper roots.

But people did stay because of a deeply held conviction that, should they find another place – watered, with fertile soils – that, too, would be taken away from them. So they embraced this inhospitable terrain as a respite from an advancing, violent, insatiable White greed. And, through dogged determination, turned it into the region's heartbeat. It became the intersection through which every significant connection must pass. Places are, after all, about their people. The people of Mawabeni were renowned for their commerce.

Our lives revolved around the Mawabeni Business Growth Point. An aerial view would reveal a tapestry of dusty roads, a starburst of different directions from its epicentre, towards Nsezi,

Gongo, Diana's Pools, Umzinyathi, and Matobo. Each road brought back people, goods, strange fruit, and other surprises.

Upon arrival at the Growth Point, passengers would disembark as soon as the bus doors opened. Men, too desperate to hold on, clutched the front of their trousers and scuttled, crab-like, until they disappeared into the bushes. But many journeys began there too: buses destined to travel to the various corners of the country – Ncenga-Ncenga, Godlwayo, and Shu-Shine. But the Whites-only omnibus, with its sombre cream colour and green sash across the middle, never stopped. It took the curve past the Growth Point at hair-raising speed. There was nothing they wanted to see of us.

In the rainy season, trucks from the eastern highlands would arrive laden with wild guava, papaya, mangoes, and overripe tomatoes. When it rained, a red mud abounded; buses, lorries and cars would skid, creating deep furrows of water where birds, bees, wasps, dragonflies, and small lizards would drink unperturbed by the humdrum of commerce.

Seasonal rains presaged a time of plenty too: charcoal-grilled corn on the cob, sweet reed, steamed sweet potato, salted monkey nuts, and sugar cane. But there was also the welcoming aroma of charcoal-roasted meats, roasted peanuts, oranges, and the intoxicating fragrance of the marula fruit*, which lingered in the air, counteracting the smell of diesel and petrol fumes.

---

* Marula trees are found mainly in woodlands across Africa. They are deciduous trees, and they belong to the same family as cashew nut and mango trees. Their seeds can be consumed as nuts and the fleshy pulp used to make different types of alcoholic beverages and liqueurs such as Amarula Cream.

Women's and girls' necks would bulge, compressed under the punishing loads on their heads of bananas, boiled eggs, steamed sweet potatoes wrapped up in old newspapers and ground nuts in small funnels, arranged neatly in rows inside river-reed baskets. As they got closer to the buses, they'd swivel round, so the customers could view their wares from the bus windows. There were many unwritten rules, but intuition served them well. Hard bargaining saved the day, and rude customers dealt with in kind.

'*Hayi wena!** Stop squeezing things you haven't paid for. This is not the city – either you pay or stop wasting my time!'

And how the women detected the slightest of changes to the weight of their load remained a mystery.

'No, I said put it back! You only paid for one, not two. This is not a buy-one-get-one-free bonanza!'

'Sorry, *malukazana!*'†

'Yeah, I hear that all the time – do I look like I cook for you? And don't even try it. You think I was born this big, hmmm?'

'Cabbage! Cabbage! I said come over here!' a fat man might call, gesticulating as he squeezed himself through a small window aperture, risking strangling himself. There might be a tussle between the women as they made a beeline for his window. They would viciously elbow each other out of the way, their tongues lacerating those suspected of the infraction of the market's rules.

'Don't get too friendly – keep your smelly armpits to yourself, thank you! And, as for the horse breath, it is bound to kill customers, that's for sure!'

---

* Hey, you!

† Daughter-in-law

NO SAFER KINDER HATRED

'Next customer, next! Tomatoes! Tomatoes over here!'

'Tell you what, you look like a potential son-in-law. Buy a big bag of oranges and I'll throw my daughter on top!'

'And where is she?'

'At home waiting for you!'

'*Awww,* you see, I need to check the merchandise before I buy!'

The fat woman laughed; her body shook in small but noticeable ripples. 'One thing at a time. Buy now and we'll talk about *lobola** next time we meet!'

Her customer kept squeezing the oranges until she decided that he wasn't serious enough to buy anything. And she quickly moved on to the next potential victim.

'How much?'

'*Me,* or the oranges?'

'What? Are you looking for a husband as well? Who would marry a woman from around here? Now turn round. Let's see what you've got!'

'Darling, stick to the oranges because you can't afford me!'

In between bouts of market traders jostling and shouting at each other, the man known locally as Msunduzwa or outcast would play his single-stringed *berimbau*† for his lost love Maybeline, interrupted only by the sting of lice that colonised his hair and clothing, and the untimely tics that disfigured his rhythm into an ill-tuned rasp of the violin. Except when he sang, nothing ever came out of his mouth. His legs were swollen with elephantiasis, his face was pockmarked, and his skin darkened like shimmering

---

* Dowry
† A kind of violin.

tar. Daily, he'd sit on the same spot, and he'd leave when the sun went down. Nobody knew where he lived, but somehow, when the sun rose the next day, we all expected him to be there outside MaMampofu's store. People embraced him as part of the landscape. Like many, he had arrived out of the blue and stayed. As Grandma would say, home is where people miss you when you're gone. I guess he was at home too.

Apart from MaMampofu's store, there was Bambazonke's, Mbuyazwe's, Ngenisa's Bottle Store, and Marramane Fish and Chips, and of course the grinding mill. But you could never get credit from any other store except MaMampofu's. At Ngenisa's you could buy the coldest beer straight from a refrigerator, which purred continuously like a sleeping cat. At Marramane, chips with no fish. Besides, Grandma said that no one in their right mind would pay for a palm-sized tasteless fish! Or you could opt for the flame-grilled offal at Mbuyazwe's Butchers. But, of all the grocery stores, Bambazonke's was by far the largest. As the name suggested, it was an Aladdin's cave of merchandise: hardware, homeware, school uniforms, cakes of soap, bread, and soft drinks – Krest Lemonade, Fanta, Stone's Ginger Beer in brown bottles, Schweppes Lemonade, Coca-Cola, and Sparletta. Those with extra cash would also buy various cold meats as an accompaniment to their cold beers – hunks of beef covered in an embroidery of yellow fat, enticing to the eye, but not good for the heart. But life in the reserve was a lottery; there were no guarantees.

CHAPTER 3

Our home was perched a stone's throw from the Business Growth Point. When Grandma sent me to the store, she'd spit on the ground and warn me to be back before the spit was dry. Which of course was an impossibility. I dawdled on the way there, getting carried away in a dreamy world of red and white swirls, powdery-pink fish marshmallows, and gobstoppers – colourful spherical sweets, solid on the outside with a delightful soft middle. I pinched many pennies of Grandma's money just to sample sugary treats.

Grandma's four mud huts sat under the shadow of a small hill or *kopje** dominated by tall, barren fig trees. The huts were simple structures built from mud bricks, and their roofs were made from thatch grass. A wooden fence divided the living quarters from Grandma's Garden. And, beyond the fence, near the secluded corner of the garden, lay Grandpa's grave, Grandma's cornerstone of silence.

Of the four huts, three served as bedrooms: Ma's, Uncle Sami's, and Grandma's. In Grandma's bedroom, planks of various sizes

---

* A small rocky hill on the African veld.

and measurements had been corralled into a rickety door, lopsided and heavy. To close it, we had to lift it up and drag it across. The locking mechanism was a hole drilled into the frame, into which we inserted a small cylindrical piece of iron to hold the door in place. It was all that stood between us and the outside world at night.

The floor was smothered in fresh cow dung. My sisters collected it from the *kraal** and mixed it with water into a thick green paste, which they spread from the deepest point in the room. They worked backwards on all fours, creating a beautiful mosaic of shapes: small interlocking circles, random squares, and faces. Once the floor had dried, they swept off the excess, leaving behind a fragrant smell of green grass, leaves, and shrubs – better than that of urine, stale sweat, Grandma's concoctions, and her tobacco.

Occasionally, accidents occurred in the night. It was always the same vivid dream. I was out playing with friends and suddenly felt the urge to urinate. I ran and hid behind a tree and let go of the tap. A jet of urine landed on Grandma's back, prompting an instant backlash.

Sometimes in the morning there were arguments over disowned and inexplicable patches of urine in the area where my sisters slept. And at other times one of us tipped over *turu*, or chamber pot, in the dark, dousing a flood of stale urine over pillows, blankets, and straw mats. As a result, Grandma's bedroom had a very distinct ambience, infused with smells of camphor, home-made potions, kerosene lamps, and Grandma's unique body odour of snuff, sweat, and smoke. The smells had a

---

* In this context: a cattle pen or enclosure for livestock. But it can also mean a village, typically consisting of huts surrounded by a stockade.

homely mustiness to them. In the darkness, and in the pervasive fear of war, it was soothing to fall asleep to familiar sounds and smells. Grandma's guttural and deep-throated snoring, my sisters' random coughing fits, the occasional gasping for air and, of course, the intermittent sounds of gunfire throughout the night.

The only item of value in Grandma's rondavel was a big metal trunk with all our clothes, everything smothered in mothballs. The trunk was kept under lock and key; apart from our clothes, it housed a motley of documents: ink-stained, crumpled birth certificates, BCG vaccination certificates, livestock certificates, identity documents, and three political party membership cards. One for each party: ZAPU, ZANU, UANC. In Grandma's eyes there was no such thing as allegiance to one political party. She was very shrewd and well versed in politics. Politicians were all thieves, she said. They were only ever after one thing: *money*.

On top of the trunk there were blankets of various sizes and descriptions, and hard home-made pillows stuffed with rags and old clothes, heavily stained. And hidden behind the door was *turu*. *Turu* was an institution: a five-litre plastic beer-container-turned-chamber-pot. Grandma acquired her from the beer garden in the city. Quite how, I had no idea. The onomatopoeic name derived from the sound one made whilst urinating into the improvised chamber pot. Fear of the dark was so pervasive that any thought of venturing outside at night was inconceivable and so we took turns to urinate into *turu*. Crude noises punctuated otherwise uneventful nights, besides barking dogs and delusional cockerels announcing a false dawn. Transgressions of this kind often necessitated the death of the culprit.

Grandma's small kitchen was a proud display of poverty. Inside, it had two small pots, one big black cauldron, or *potjie*, a collection of enamel cups and plates. There was no furniture except for an iron cooking tripod with a hearth in the centre of the kitchen. A rectangular mound ran along the bottom edge of the inside wall, from which tiny, ferocious black ants, *iswintila*, emerged. Their sting, mostly unprovoked, was excruciating. When my sisters cooked thick porridge, *pap**, the cauldron fitted snugly within the confines of the tripod and stopped it from rocking. Cobwebs hung from the rafters, small threads of smoke, fluffy as black snow, amongst which the scorpions and cockroaches sought refuge. In the winter, a cold draught entered unhindered, through the spaces between the wall and the rafters, forcing us closer to the fire, where our bodies absorbed its radiating warmth. But thick smoke billowed from the wet firewood, making it harder to see or breathe. When its intensity became unbearable, we ran outside and took in gulps of fresh air. Smoke, after all, was the biggest cause of respiratory diseases and blindness in the reserve.

The rest of the yard was barren save for the peach and guava trees. The peach tree was the bane of our lives. When Grandma was angry, which was often, she'd force us to harvest our own switches from it. Size meant everything; her sadism knew no bounds. Those switches from the peach tree were unbreakable. When she assaulted you, the flexible branches would wrap

---

* A type of thick cornmeal porridge, similar to polenta, made from maize or cornflower, and is a staple food in several sub-Saharan African countries such as Malawi, Mozambique, Namibia, South Africa, Uganda, Zambia, and Zimbabwe to name just a few. Known by its various names according to region: isitshwala, nsima, posho, sadza, and ugali.

themselves around your body like numerous, lacerating tentacles, and it felt as though you were dying with a rib cage full of air.

Grandma's life revolved round her church. Like her God, she was petty, unforgiving, vengeful, cruel. I had night terrors in which the devil, the scariest creature that I could conjure up in my mind, from numerous hell-raising sermons at Grandma's church, guarded the gates of hell, armed with a trident, in which an eternal depthless fire raged. I woke up when he was about to throw me in there. But a nudge from Grandma's elbow brought the nightmare to an end.

Grandma was a widow; Grandpa had been gone for a while. I still had vivid memories of him: the smell of tobacco in the evening just after dusk, his pipe glowing intermittently like a firefly in between puffs of smoke. Once he took me to a secret wild cherry tree, pregnant with big round cherries the colour of sunset, with raindrops dangling on the leaves like pearls. It had rained that day – snails and millipedes were out in numbers. Grandpa was tall and fragile, and each time he picked up a cherry he'd look at it and turn it over before carefully placing it on his tongue. Then he'd spit out the stones carelessly as if annoyed by the whole thing.

Another time he took me to the snot apple or *kaffir* apple tree, with hard spherical fruit capsules divided into small sections. When ripe, each section would split at the seam, exposing its seeds and a sweet golden honey, which stuck to the fingers. It was easy to carry the fruit in your pocket – boiled, salted, and preserved, it was a perfect accompaniment to Grandma's perambulations.

But what I didn't know then was that Grandpa was seriously ill.

As his illness ravaged him, he was taken to Mpilo Central Hospital in Bulawayo. Although I have a very hazy memory of that time, I do remember the comings and goings, hushed voices, and the sense of an impending calamity. And, of course, Grandma's prayers: intense, relentless.

After he was gone, Grandma continually regaled us with stories of how they met.

'Your grandpa was the smartest man I ever knew. I can still smell the lavender ironed into his clothes, *mh-mmh*! Every Sunday night I'd wait till I saw the beam of his bicycle light in the distance. He cooked for White people, you see. And not many people, even to this day, can do that. You know how fastidious they are about who touches their food!'

And then she'd brush her hands against each other as if we knew what she meant. Subconsciously, we were being socialised to always put White people's needs first. To always think of their needs as more important than ours.

'He was clean and smart. The seams on his khaki uniform could slice a fly in half! And don't laugh, because this is so true!' she exclaimed, briefly exposing her big tobacco-stained teeth. 'See, the way you create beautiful creases is to lay the trousers flat on a blanket. Are you listening?'

She cajoled us into paying attention.

We'd heard this story before many times, and each time it was embellished with new additions like a stew in the pot: a bit of salt, pepper, chilli, till she got the balance right, depending on her mercurial mood.

'Make sure everything is aligned properly, otherwise you'll have creases everywhere. And then you rub a bar of soap along the edge of the seams on both sides, and afterwards press hard with a very hot iron. You can wet the bar of soap a bit if you want a better shine.'

She dipped her fingers into an imaginary cup filled with water and flicked droplets of water along the seams of Grandpa's imaginary trousers.

'And you should have seen him on his way to work. Such a proud man!'

Grandma would say, 'He'll come back stronger!' but there was an incongruity between her feigned optimism and her sad, sad grey eyes.

Those days in Mpilo Hospital would be the last we'd see of him. Months later, a man arrived with a telegram from our ma in the city and gave it to Grandma, who passed it on to my sister Thoko, who read it out loud. In a single sentence, written in big, bold red letters, came Ma's announcement: 'Father died today.'

As Thoko read the note, Grandma clutched her belly with both hands, and wailed as if she had unbearable pain. She swayed and swayed as if she was moved by the wind until the pain in her stomach planted itself on her face, and from that day onwards she walked around with an expression as if she'd stepped on thorns. For the first time, I registered red as the colour of death, grief, and bereavement.

But Grandma already had a wound of her own, a keloid scar on her back that ran from the bottom of her ribs all the way up to the tip of her shoulder blade. She didn't explain or talk in any depth about it, save to say that when she went into hospital with a severe headache, she'd come out with one kidney missing – it was more likely than not that unscrupulous doctors had harvested her kidney and sold it, without her knowing it at the time. Grandma was teetotal, she didn't smoke (though she chewed tobacco) or have any major illnesses. Apparently, doctors had told her that she had a frog where her kidney should have been, whose growth could have led to her death just like Grandpa. She said that a haustorium, the kind we saw on trees, took over his lungs until he couldn't breathe. You see, she had no words for cancer – to her, illnesses were comprehensible only as metaphors.

The weather, especially when it was cloudy and damp, played havoc with her. She'd look at the sky and simply say: '*It's coming!*' The pain augured tough times ahead. When it got too much, she'd stay in bed for days, during which time she remained inaccessible. She withdrew into this dark, dark place and left us outside, bereft. To us, it was just an old wound, healed. To her, it was as raw as when they'd first cut her open. She kept the bandage, reams of it. But when she came out the other end she had fire in her eyes, a red anger that propelled her. 'We must go on,' she would say. Moving forward was an act of courage; it was all we could do. And, true to her word, she never remarried.

While Grandpa was ill, she had collected cut-offs from dress-makers and, using corn sacks as a base, and with a specially designed crochet hook, pulled each tiny piece of cloth, from a multitude of colours – blue, black, mauve, yellow, purple, red, green – halfway through the sack into a loop, and joined them in a symmetrical alliance to create a miniature quilt, resembling a beautiful flower bed, which she would place inside the grave when Grandpa was later laid to rest. Because, to her, grief was the thing with many colours and textures.

Losing Grandpa crushed her. From then on, everything in our lives would radiate from grief. There were no universal family milestones. No birthday celebrations or anniversaries. But we always remembered the end of our grandfather.

A few days after the telegram, we watched the grown-ups as they dug a deep hole in the ground. As the hole deepened, we could see the rise of the shovel in the air. Whilst the men dug, women gathered stones. They delicately placed them into a pile right next to the mound of red soil. At dusk, they brought Grandpa's body out, wrapped up in a grey blanket, tied with a string at both ends, and lowered it into the grave, on top of Grandma's quilt. As children, we were not allowed near. So we stood and watched from a distance, and listened to the funeral dirge as the adults piled stone upon stone on top of Grandpa. Gift said the stones were intended to stop wild animals and dogs from digging him up.

Towards the end, it started to rain. Rainwater travelled down each strand of the soot-stained thatch grass, forming a ring of small dots round the perimeter of the hut. We sat quietly on the *stoep** and watched the proceedings through a curtain of black rain. We extended our arms, and felt the rain slide between our fingers, and the salty, smoky water fell on our faces, then into our mouths, which left behind a bitter, lingering aftertaste. And that, too, was the memory of Grandpa.

That night, violent thunder tore the curtain of the sky. A sudden darkness enveloped everything. As heavy hailstones fell, we huddled in the corner of Grandma's kitchen. The ground shook as if an irate monster was pounding it. Grandma said that

---

* Small veranda or porch around the outside of a building.

the rain was a sign that Grandpa had a good heart. But even she was afraid. Normally she had three tongues in her mouth, and yet that night she was silent.

It took a few weeks for things to get back to normal. God had decided not to end the world, after all. Grandma's prayers returned to the usual litany of complaints against God's negligence – now fearless, less humble, and more bilious, just like her ransom letters to our ma.

As a child it was harder still for me to register Grandpa's death as something permanent. I still expected him to burst into the room and take me out for our usual walks. But, with time, it dawned on me that he wasn't coming back. His death was my first real experience of a crushing loss. But the gift of childhood was that something else soon took over my life and I soon forgot all my sorrows.

But for all the rain, the storm, the wailing, and the people surrounding Grandpa's funeral, I don't recall my mother being there. A photographer came and took a photograph of us as a family, but when it came back, outlines were blurred, just as when you gaze at the sun too long with your eyes closed and your eyelids transform into a dull red blanket. But she had always been there, our ma.

CHAPTER 4

Our mother was born and raised in Bulawayo. She worked in the city at Toppers, a shop selling clothes and school uniforms. She'd stand outside on the pavement to entice customers in whilst the Indian owners stayed inside in the shade. To subsidise their meagre wages, she and a group of her friends formed a syndicate. Each member would make a standard contribution to a common fund, and each month the total contributions were disbursed to a single member of the syndicate. Since there were four of them, she was able to come home at least once every four months.

On Saturdays, she finished work at noon. By the time she finished her grocery shopping – sugar, bread, flour, Stork margarine, strawberry jam, sweets, and Grandma's tobacco – it would have been late afternoon. To get home, she hitched a ride outside Mark's Garage on Selbourne Avenue, where drivers stopped to refuel before heading south along the Bulawayo–Beitbridge road. Sometimes, she hitched rides with Coley Hall or Swift truck drivers. Or took a bus, which, for her, was a last resort. But when she arrived at the Growth Point, before she came home to see us, her first port of call was always Ngenisa's liquor store, where she joined a coterie of friends, and they'd sit on the veranda and drink bottled beer and spirits. She'd send the groceries with friends or any of our neighbours.

At Grandma's behest, I would go to bring her home, but never succeeded. As I waded through the crowds, a cacophony of strange languages assaulted my ears: Venda, Kalanga, Tswana, Chewa, Chibarwe, ChiNdau, Shangani, Tsonga, and Xhosa. This discordant chorus was broken by the intermittent drum of the mill and the belch of the haulage trucks on the main road.

By then, late afternoon, Ma would be behind Mbuyazwe's Butchers, because at the back of the butcher's there was a *braai** area. A rusty old oil drum, halved lengthwise, rested on four pillars of concrete. On top of the oil drum was intertwined wire mesh, divided into small squares, big enough to let the occasional piece of meat fall through into the flame. This is where Ma and her friends congregated to grill meat.

On seeing me, she would look at me as if disappointed, but she'd nonetheless signal for me to come closer.

'Come here, son!'

And then she'd turn to her drinking companions: 'This is my only boy. He'll be a man soon and I want to send him to art school,' she'd announce.

The men responded with indifference and the women were not even vaguely interested. And I was not interested either, except in the meat on the grill. Ma would fetch her small purse from under her brassiere and give me loose change.

'Here, go and buy yourself a soft drink and cherry cake!'

---

* Braai is an Afrikaans word for grilling meat on an open fire.

Every Saturday, from dawn till dusk, people gathered around the grill to drink beer as chunks of meat contested for space. But in the haze of the smoke and beery eyelids, whole pieces of meat were swiped from right under the noses of the distracted drinkers, and bigger ones swapped for smaller pieces.

'Why are you ogling my meat like someone else's wife?'

'What do you mean *your* meat?'

'There, that's my meat! Oh, I made sure that mine had a bone in the middle; see that there, the smaller piece in the middle? That's yours. In fact, you're the one ogling what you can't afford, my friend!'

To the discerning eye, striations of fat, a small bone here, cartilage there, or the cut and the thickness of the meat, were all features that made one piece of meat distinguishable from the next.

With that, they all burst out laughing. But, despite the laughter and ease of tensions, Ma, like the rest, still guarded her meat diligently.

As it got darker, the guttural laughter continued and people relaxed. And, as the beer continued to flow, everyone became sloppy. I managed to evade beery eyes and snatch small bites of meat, here and there, to my absolute delight. I would be sent on errands. First, to Ngenisa's to buy Black Label, Lion, Castle beer, and Smirnoff, which they drank neat, only for their faces to contort as if they'd just taken bitter medicine.

Afterwards, I would collect the empty bottles, and take them back to Ngenisa's in exchange for money. And, since the drinkers had forgotten to ask for their change back, I hid the coins inside the secret lining of my shorts. Then, when the meat ran out, they'd send me back to the butcher's for more.

After dark, they wandered to Kiki's illicit liquor bar, Ma included. Many went there to imbibe *tototo*, a lethal moonshine distilled by Kiki, a no-nonsense Xhosa woman. She concocted the liquor from stale bread, potato peels and fermented fruit salvaged from the market. Its name was derived from the sound of the distillate as it slowly dripped into a metal container – *to to to to to*!

Drinking *tototo* was a calling; seasoned connoisseurs drank it neat. Its major attraction was that it was dirt cheap. Kiki provided a fool-proof in-house credit system in which she kept the tab, however exaggerated. Besides, her mostly inebriated clientele could hardly remember anything of the night before since they existed inside a *tototo*-induced haze. You only ever saw them upright once a day – on their way there! The potency of the pure liquor was such that many never even made it home. *Tototo* connoisseurs were distinguishable from ordinary drunkards by the discolouration of the skin on their faces and extremely red lips. It was said that if you poured the pure liquor on raw animal liver it would cook instantly. The discolouration of the skin was a sign of the deterioration of the liver and other vital organs. But, when they died, witchcraft was always blamed. Or speculations would abound that they'd been poisoned, usually by an old woman. And both of those things were true in a way. Concocting moonshine was witchcraft; alcohol was poison. And Kiki was an old woman who poisoned people over a long period.

When Ma and I got to Kiki's, the hostess was seated right by the entrance, perched on a wooden stool, legs wide apart, with her dress thrown in between her legs. She was short, unusually wide round the waist and her colourful headdress tilted precariously forward, towards her forehead, as if it was about to fall.

Her light-brown skin glistened in the glow of the subdued light. And when she saw Ma she jumped off her stool and embraced her like a long-lost daughter.

'Lisabeth, I have just been talking about you!' she said as she tilted her head backwards and filled each nostril with snuff. She then extended her snuffbox towards Ma, who snatched a pinch and clumsily tried to bring it to her snout, as she desperately tried to steady herself.

'Wasn't I just talking about her?' Kiki turned to a drunk, slovenly dressed man, sitting right next her.

The hum of voices rose and fell as sporadic laughter interrupted the slow drift into oblivion. After all, many came there to forget, to get wired on the vine.

Kiki, still excited, continued unabated: 'Look at you? City life has been good to you. Sit down and don't just stand there!'

They shared in this moment. Ma fell into a heap, took off her stilettos; she laughed as if free.

'Things are tough in the city! You know those Indians are worse than Boers!' she announced, unprompted. 'They demand more, pay us less and exploit us with impunity. Sometimes they run you ragged for a whole month – and I mean a whole month – before they tell you that you haven't met your target! What target, I say? See, they never tell you right from the beginning what that target is. Only when they don't want to pay you, this thing called target is mentioned. Then its target this, target that! They are worse than Boers! Even *they* are leaving in droves. There are signs everywhere saying *property for sale, business to let.*'

And she elaborated.

'Those left behind know full well how desperate we all are.

And they treat us like donkeys. I have three children and their fathers are nowhere to be seen. These men are not good to us, and I sometimes wonder how we're going to survive. I have been working all my life and I have nothing to show for it! And now with this war raging on and on, and the Whites fleeing in droves, how are we going to survive?'

Kiki said, 'Here, drink this and don't upset yourself. I hear you! Nantu over there was sacked from her job last month. See her with a cheap wig? She comes here every day to drown her sorrows. Judging by the amount of time she spends in the bushes; I don't even think that these men give her enough money for what she does for them. But, as they say, there is no room for a heart in this world. A body is just a body; there is no need to be precious about it. But if you ever need anything, come to me!'

And then they slapped hands mid-air and drank some more.

There was a fire in the middle of the rondavel. Small sparks threatened the thatch grass and provoked a cough here and there. Men and women sat on the raised structure along the wall.

Outside, men sat and drank from the same calabash. Each person gently swirled the contents, followed by a gentle blow, took a big gulp of the golden liquid, and passed it on. Whilst waiting, the others sang songs that no one could sing alone. Voices rose, evoking the memory of their youth, and the mineshafts, deep inside the gold mines of Johannesburg. But this was a kind of performance too. Voices competed for prominence, whilst the sharp piercing whistle, *ukhwelo*, funnelled air through curled tongues, producing a haunting melody. And the synchronised light shuffle of the feet, the call of the lead singer, the smooth tenor of the accompanying voices, made the rhythm feel like an unstoppable train in motion – *Is'timela!*

So, it went.

Someone stirred the fire. Small sparks landed on the arms and faces of unsuspecting revellers in a *tototo*-induced stupor, and they'd suddenly jump up, back to life.

In the darkness, illicit alliances formed, however treacherous. Small paths led away from Kiki's and forked into small rocky alleyways. Way past the slaughterhouse stench, on the edge of the knoll, shadowy figures sat on the rocks in the dark a metre or so away from the gravel road. Bright lights from the haulage trucks penetrated the fog that fanned out into the woods. Nearby, mopane woods bristled with activity: men unbuckled their belts as women undressed. When they'd finished, they walked straight back to the path that led to Kiki's. As the night ended, the embers in the fire dimmed and the shuffle of the long, slow mine song meandered back whence it came.

Ma was drunk. She continuously sniffed snuff.

'He is my only son, you know, my last-born boy. See, he's already looking after me!' she announced, as if seeing me for the first time.

And she paraded me shamelessly: 'Go on – stand up. I want them to see you.'

But no one really looked at me. I hinted that we should go home. Grandma and my sisters were waiting for us.

But, undeterred, Ma continued: 'He's very talented. I am already saving money to send him to art school. See those beautiful artworks above the shops? That's what I want him to do!'

And then she suddenly burst into tears as if something had terribly gone wrong.

'Come on, Lisabeth,' said Kiki. 'It's time to go. You could sleep here tonight, but Muvu won't have it. You best go and see the rest of your children, huh?'

Kiki then turned to me and said, 'Young man, your turn to look after your mother. Make sure you take her straight home, okay?'

I gave her a nod and said nothing. If anything, I dreaded to think what Grandma would say or do, given that Ma had arrived late the previous day and it was now the early hours of the morning.

A brown liquid trickle escaped Ma's nostrils. She caught it with her tobacco-stained handkerchief. She gathered herself from the ground up. After a few failed attempts, she finally succeeded.

We left Kiki's and walked straight into a forbidding darkness. The way home was hilly and rocky. Ma was wearing her stilettos. She stumbled and almost fell into a ditch by the side of the road. And then she giggled as if there was something amusing that only she knew. She spoke to me, talking to herself, talking to Grandma. She was practising what to say once we got home.

'The bus broke down and I—'

'Grandma won't buy it,' I interrupted her. 'Besides, Salani's ma was on the same bus as you. She came by to say hello to Grandma and to drop off your groceries. Grandma said unlike you she doesn't drink!'

And Ma completely ignored me.

'As I was saying before you interrupted me, the bus broke down and I—'

'But Grandma heard you laughing all the way from the Growth Point – that's why she sent me to come and fetch you!'

We walked through the dark as Ma continued to make threats to whoever was out there. She encouraged me to throw stones, randomly, which I did, rather too enthusiastically, creating sparks of light in the dark when they smashed against rocks.

Ma continued to advertise her drunken, empty bravado: 'Whoever is out there, come out! There are four of us and we are not scared of you!'

And then she tried, unsuccessfully, to suppress her laughter.

On our approach, our dog Sport barked excitedly. She spun round and jumped on to me. But the joy was short-lived; Grandma was ready for us. She welcomed us with her drowsy cockerel routine, but her claws were already out.

'So you've finally decided to come home? Everybody else, especially decent mothers, came home last night. And you come home drunk a day after you arrived, expecting me to applaud you?'

And with an irascible scorn and utter contempt she swept Ma with a look up and down and then pointed at me.

'And you, what did I ask you to do?'

I didn't answer. We sat, Ma and I, right on the edge of her rage, within reach. But I was comforted by the fact that while Ma was there Grandma would never touch me. But the tension remained.

In the morning, Grandma sacrificed a cockerel to satiate Ma's hunger for meat, the ultimate cure for her hangover. She tried to entice the whole brood of chickens under the pretext of feeding them corn. Dozens gathered around her as she dispersed corn kernels, whilst keeping an eye on her target, the intransigent cockerel who'd been firing blanks, hence the dwindling population of chicks.

'*Kikiri ki, kikiri ki, kikiri ki.*' Grandma desperately tried to entice the chickens to feed as she edged closer and closer to her target. But when she dashed forward to grab him the cockerel immediately flew over the fence, over Grandpa's grave, with his claws out, into the cactus enclosure, well beyond reach. A mother hen squeezed through the gaps in the wooden fence as her chattering of chicks dived under the pile of firewood, a well-rehearsed manoeuvre for when hawks struck.

My sisters and I went after the cockerel. Since his slaughter was imminent, there were no holds barred. We threw stones at him, probed him with sticks, and harangued him out of the cactus enclosure. He flew halfway up in the air, claws drawn, nearly taking Gift out, before he landed and ran straight into Grandma's kitchen. Grandma promptly shut the rickety door. Cornered, he went berserk, and flew over our heads, tearing into us with his claws, as enamel cups, pots and pans were dislodged from their moorings on the wall, until, finally, covered in feathers and chicken poop, we managed to wrestle him to the ground. Grandma tied his feet together and walked hastily towards a horizontal log. She stepped on his wings, grabbed his head, stretched his neck over the log and decapitated him with an axe. She let him bleed to the ground till he stopped twitching.

The squawking amongst the chickens continued long after the cockerel had been decapitated. The outraged mother hen retreated with her chicks right underneath Grandma's barn, where a new battle ensued between her and Sport who protested vehemently against the unwarranted intrusion and the related risks to her still-blind puppies sharing space with chickens. In the end, Sport won. Mother hen and her brood relocated to the shaded area behind the wooden fence.

By the time Ma woke up, Grandma had already fried the cockerel in Ma's favourite clay pot and cooked soft *pap*, just the way she liked it. But Ma's demeanour suggested that she was in no mood to talk. Grandma, keen to assuage tensions, placed a plate full of Ma's favourite cuts in front of her: deep-fried wings, back, and neck. But Ma simply washed her hands and ate silently, the echo of last night's laughter at Kiki's shebeen now a distant memory. Her eyes spread a sadness that led us into anxiety, which forced Grandma to engage in small talk.

'How's work?'

'Work is work. What else is there to say?'

Ma rebuffed Grandma's fake civility. From the looks of it, she intended to stay inside this foul mood. I could see that something didn't connect between Grandma and Ma, who in fact was her aunt. Ma had never spoken to us openly about the death of her own mother, Grandma's younger sister Annie. There was a wound somewhere, hidden. Grandma's unwarranted animosity, compounded by a terrible hangover, and unresolved grief, triggered Ma. Just then, she became tearful and started to hyperventilate. Her lips quivered and her body shook uncontrollably, and she became apoplectic as if an invisible hand had a grip on her throat.

Eventually, Grandma retreated and let her be. Meanwhile, my sisters and I dipped lumps of *pap* into the chicken gravy. As they bit into the gelatinous and sinewy feet, I tussled with the cockerel's head, chewed through its comb, ravished its wattle, and afterwards ripped opened its beak, exposing dead ants it had swallowed whilst it was alive. I discarded the ants and chewed my way through the soft bone and cartilage until, at last, I reached the delicious soft brain.

In the early evening, just before sunset, I walked Ma to the bus stop. When the bus arrived, she took a seat by the window, and waved, silently. She'd be gone for another four months.

In our family, as in the rest of the country, everyone was all stitched up, silent about the past. But my grandmother, like most adults who raised us, had this sense of dignity, a mulish stubbornness. In isiNdebele we call it *ubuqholo*: the silent, restrained anguish and strategic sluggishness, the refusal to follow rules.

As children, we were very happy in our own way: nothing was out of bounds; our world was full of wonder. Right on our doorstep lived the most venomous snakes in the world: cobras, mambas, puff adders. And we treated them with the same disdain reserved for unwanted intruders – we just threw stones at them. Or, in extreme circumstances, killed them.

We watched cows birth calves, dogs lick their blind newborn puppies and animals being slaughtered. We understood perfectly well the circle of life. We never really thought about White people, except when they were there in front of us, like aberrations. Perhaps that was our saving grace. But we also lived in a world corrupted by the dislocation of truth, in which adults unwittingly became the conduit through which the idea of white supremacy entered our homes. They marvelled at how blessed White people were, how kind, how well educated, how prosperous, how clean, how civilised, how loving, how gentle – how innocent, how very forgiving. Which was why we called them *abelungu*, a people with gracious souls. We could see this for ourselves. Whites seemed to have it all – good-quality lives, better schools, living in much more affluent and beautiful places than we could ever imagine – but there was never a valid reason why. In our minds, each of these images cemented the idea of our own inferiority. And there was a phrase that adults often used to express disappointment: 'What do you expect from Black people?'

It has been said that when someone calls you something for long enough you start to believe what they call you, because words are very powerful; they have a magic of their own. And they bewitch. Whites could touch us inside without ever getting closer to us; self-love for us became the hardest thing of all. As we accepted what harmed us, we memorised the dimensions of a grave by heart, and yet we did not know those of a farm. We embraced self-hatred in our daily conversations too and spoke disparagingly of our own people. And when we lost faith in ourselves, we underestimated the oppressor's capacity to harm us.

All Whites could say was: 'It's just the way things are!'

Racism, like fear, worked in extraordinary ways. Everything was purest white. In the end, whenever we saw White people, we expected them to give us something. A little of what they had – a gift, however small – that would transform our lives. After all, they seemed to have much more than that of which we could only ever dream. They moved freely, without the hindrance of the barbed wire and the invisible laws.

Sometimes, they threw things at us from fast-moving cars: chicken bones, soiled nappies, aluminium foil, empty bottles, and cans from exotic drinks. Occasionally – pencils, pens, and other things for which they had no use; neither did we. But to us even their casual throwaways were the best gifts.

As Grandma would say, our country was a country of extreme sentiments. Those who professed to love it, sacrificed others for it. To Whites, every grown Black man and woman was a half-child. They feared we might grow beyond their distortions.

Our saving grace was that the only White people closest to us lived one kilometre away from Grandma's home, within the confines of the Ministry of Transport compound by the river basin. Naturally, the area was fenced off, because in the White world fences made good neighbours. Their house was the biggest I'd ever seen. So big, in fact, that in my child's mind I could only compare it to a small hill. And there were just five of them: two adults, a teenage boy and two small children my age. The mansion was shrouded under tall trees, its walls and chimney choked by red flowers.

At the weekend, my sisters and I watched the White children as they rode their bicycles within the expanse of the compound and played with a real leather football, unlike our home-made plastic ball, or as they fished by the river with proper fishing rods. But every time we made efforts to engage with them they were standoffish, very aloof. See, as children, we hadn't the slightest idea of racism. In our minds, we thought that the problem was simply that of language – with time, we would find common ground. But it wasn't just the fence and vicious dogs that separated us.

It was with that same family that Grandma's son Uncle Sami got his first job. Despite his standard-six education, the equivalent of two years of secondary-school education, he ran errands for the family.

Every night, I could hear him yelling at Grandma, *'Baas** hits me, you know. Or *Baas* keeps calling me a useless *kaffir*†. And I can't take it anymore, Mama!'

Baas was a fifteen-year-old boy; Uncle Sami was on the cusp of manhood. *Kaffir*, like *nigger*, was a catch-all derogatory word used by Whites to refer to Blacks of all ages. But they reserved the worst for black women: *oil drums*. In their eyes, Blacks were all the same, tainted by the stigmata of blackness. We were there to make others shine. Always on the periphery, shadows who left no trace.

And yet Grandma, and many others like her, saw our condition as purely existential.

For a while Uncle Sami endured and persevered. As compensation, he brought home broken fountain pens, damaged fishing lines and ink-stained exercise books. One day he brought home a small brown book; I had the feeling that he had stolen it. He read it obsessively; the more he read it, the angrier he got. It was called ominously, *The Mind of Man in Africa*.

But all Grandma could say in response to his anger was, 'A

---

* Dutch/Afrikaans word for boss. Used during both Rhodesian and South African Apartheid by Black employees to address mainly White (sometimes Indian) males and to acknowledge their presumed superior social status over Blacks.

† *Kaffir* was first used by Muslims in Africa as a way of referring to non-believers. Over time it evolved and became firmly entrenched in the racist lexicon. Under apartheid in South Africa and Rhodesia it was used by Whites in a way that was consciously offensive and demeaning towards Black people.

word is just a word, son – no more no less. Besides, if you touch that boy, they'll send you to prison; worse still, they'll hang you!'

But the stifled rage finally spilled over.

One night a Black policeman and White man came to our home. The White man was tall, gangly, stern. Like an apparition, he did not fit into the order of things. Whites generally brought a sense of foreboding. But a White man, with a gun, at night, meant nothing but trouble.

Grandma looked as puzzled as we all were. I went through the list of possible transgressions against White man's rules. Had we not paid the hut tax? Had our head of cattle trespassed into a farm? Had we forgotten to pay our dog tax? In the end, I went right back to being afraid. When all else failed, fear was our default position.

The Black policeman was Mr Dube, who lived down the road. It was he who addressed Grandma; he could not look her in the eye.

Grandma was becoming increasingly agitated. When she became very angry with anyone who imposed themselves on us, or became far too officious, she just took off her clothes. It was a simple but defiant gesture. Men in positions of authority did not know how to deal with the wrath of an old woman. But this time she did not take her clothes off.

The White policeman was holding his camouflaged FN rifle with his right hand. It was down to our neighbour, the traitor, to explain to us what was wrong.

To us there was no difference between soldiers, police officers, auxiliaries, district assistants, and guerrillas. Their uniforms might have distinguished the differences between them, but to us they were all men of violence.

The Black policeman explained that they'd come for Uncle Sami. Apparently, he'd assaulted a White boy, broken his jaw for calling him a *kaffir*.

Grandma had said the molestation of the body of a White person was sacrilege. Black people hanged for it. And the law favoured White men – always.

The Black policeman handcuffed Uncle Sami, with his arms twisted to the back. He smiled, gripped the handcuffs tighter. We watched them leave.

We didn't know how long he would be gone for. All we could do was wait and pray.

Uncle Sami was Grandma's only child. He was tall, slim, and very dark-skinned. Grandma called him Mathambo or Bones, because of his lean physique. My first memory of him was of a ghostly presence. An old fountain pen, a dry inkwell, and the smell of books stacked up high in the corner of his room, disconsolate. His room felt stuffy, lived-in, even though he wasn't there most of the time. Maybe because I was afraid of him, the way a dog is petrified of the smell of its secret abuser, I could always smell his presence. I don't remember him growing up, except one day he was there: tall, skinny, angry, violent. We thought he was our brother, and that's what we called him.

Grandma told us she'd had such difficulty conceiving that it was a miracle he'd been born. To her, he was the most precious thing in the world. So, when he was taken away, she was very distraught. In the days and weeks that followed, she was engaged in a frantic search for him.

For the very first time, she left us with the neighbours. There was an agreement between White farmers and the Rhodesian government, since many Blacks were reluctant to work on farms, so she visited the prisons, detention centres, farms, and all the places she could think of where Blacks could be arbitrarily detained and used as indentured labour. When she couldn't find him, she visited mortuaries; given the magnitude of the crime, Grandma feared the worst.

Mr Likwa, the neighbour we stayed with, had a small wireless radio, sky blue, with a cream belt-like handle, like a tiny suitcase. The speaker was round; brown silky threads criss-crossed its facia, tight as strings on a newly tuned guitar.

Right above the speaker was a dashboard, with a thin red needle behind a small glass screen. The thin needle moved across the screen as he turned the round knob backwards and forwards. At first, the wireless whistled like a kettle about to boil, and then it made swooshing and crackling sounds like big trees caught up in the wind. Then, suddenly, there was the voice – deep, contemplative, unsettling.

This is the voice of Zimbabwe. Our victory is certain!

Although the voice brought the sadness of the war into our world, for the first time I understood, even as a child, the power of a coherent narrative. Before this voice, we only understood the war from the perspective of the Whites, whose interpretation was brazenly reductive, and neglectful of our grievances: we wanted the return of our land, the restoration of our dignity and freedom. Up until then, I really hadn't grasped what the war was about. And, even then, it was still hard for me to see Whites as our enemies, given what I'd grown up to think of them.

When Grandma came back, she visited Grandpa's grave even before she unpacked. She sat in a thoughtful repose, as if in prayer, and spoke softly with the voice of someone who had lost everything. First, she clapped her hands for what seemed an eternity. Then she addressed herself to Grandpa, her knees folded at the seam, striking a lonely figure in the darkness. When she came back, she said, 'Your grandfather says hello.'

CHAPTER 5

From then on, Grandma's prayers intensified. She prayed for the end of the war, for Uncle Sami's return, and the end of pestilence. She regaled us with the biblical story of Shem, Ham, and Japhet, three brothers who came home one day to find their elderly father, Noah, drunk, naked, and exposed. Ham laughed out loud and derided his father's nakedness. Shem and Japhet took a blanket, walked backwards, and covered their father's nakedness, for which they were eternally blessed. In Grandma's retelling of the fable, Ham and his descendant Canaan were Black. Shem and Japhet were White. Grandma said that it was because of Ham's disrespect for his father's nakedness, that Blacks would dwell in God's disfavour for all eternity.*

But somehow, she could never explain how and why we became the descendants of Canaan. Nevertheless, we had to accept that our domination and exploitation by Whites had been ordained by God, because God was good. All the time.

And so every Saturday, without fail, Grandma and I went to

---

* See Genesis 9: 23-27

church. Although Pentecostal in outlook, Grandma's church came under no specific denomination. Its congregants were simply an eclectic collection of lost souls, less constrained or hidebound by rules of worship. Grandma wore her pleated pink Terylene dress. It seemed to abandon her thin frame at the waist. Her grey hair was neatly tucked under a red tight headscarf. Nothing was out of place, save for the diastema between her teeth, and her black skin looked much darker than it normally was. But I could see that she felt extremely holy, and she was no longer labouring under the Curse of Canaan.

Slowly, as we climbed up the small hill, she placed her hands across the small of her back. Although she could not read, her bible was in her hand. We walked, carefully placing our feet between sharp granite stones. A hymn was in the air, and the din of the church bells in the background. When we arrived in church, Grandma knelt by the entrance. I stayed right next to her, like her skin, clinging to her bones, a dark ebony, the texture of worn-out papyrus.

When she'd finished her brief prayer, she rose to her feet. We made our way forward and took a seat on the pews not too far away from the pulpit. There was a tension in the air; everyone was on their best behaviour. Even coughing was frowned upon because God was a very serious man. Old women lacerated unruly children with disapproving looks. When I kept looking around me, Grandma nudged me with her bony elbow. I sat still, only for my eyes to wander off before being reined in yet again by Grandma's nudge. Thela, the preacher's son, and Lala his nephew, mounted the podium. And for some reason they started preaching in English. Thela was the orator, Lala was the interpreter.

Grandma whispered, 'What's that silly boy doing snatching words from the preacher's mouth? I can't hear a thing but the echo of his voice,' as the interpreter followed the preacher around the pulpit, and imitated his every gesture: punching the air, smashing the bible against his open palm, thrusting a pen through a piece of paper to demonstrate spiritual breakthrough, opening his arms wide to welcome the spirit of the Lord.

A woman started jumping up and down and shouting, '*Hallelujah! Hallelujah!*' She threw her red headscarf to the floor, exposing a crop of grey hair. She stamped hard on the floor, lashed out with her closed fists. Her face was twisted in a knot of pain. With tears pouring down her face, she worryingly kept edging closer and closer to me. From the way she was lashing out, I thought it would not be long before she knocked me out. I dived under the pew to avoid the sweep of her arm more than once. By now, everyone was singing. There was the violent clash of cymbals, the accordion, and tambourines, which added to the already tense atmosphere. Grandma's eyes were closed; she was facing heavenward. I closed my eyes too, focused, and waited for the blinding light and for Jesus to burst through the ceiling.

To escape the impending apocalypse, I crawled out from the church, sought refuge under the foliage of the mulberry tree and feasted on its berries. When the contest for God's attention ended, and all the demons were exorcised, sins forgiven, Grandma found me covered in black mulberry-juice stains.

'What have you been up to?'

'Nothing,' I said, looking at the ground.

'What did I say about this?'

'To make sure not to ruin my church clothes,' I responded, feeling scrutinised.

It was too soon after prayers for her to even indulge the idea of whipping me. At least that was my hope.

'So you knew exactly what I had instructed you not to do, huh? Now look at you. You are covered in stains like you live up in the trees. Sometimes, I wonder who you belong to, because there is no one like you in my bloodline. God only knows what I'll do with you!'

I stood still as she inspected me with her moist red eyes without touching me, yet.

'And why did you leave church before the service was finished?'

'It was taking too long. And that mad woman was scaring me.'

'What mad woman?'

'The one who kept screaming, *"Hallelujah! Hallelujah!"* and rolling her eyes like she was dying!'

'I see, you are bored with God. Who told you that you can get bored with God? Tell me this, does he ever get bored with you? The reason why you're still breathing and feasting on mulberries is because of his grace. And you should be grateful, instead of climbing trees like a feral child.'

'It wasn't just me. Marko, Manager, Salani, and Sicelo were all there!' I responded by way of mitigation.

'Did I bring them to church?'

'No.'

'Then they are not my concern, but you are. Come here,' she commanded.

I wasn't sure what she was up to, so I kept my distance.

'Come here – let me have a look at you! What do you take me for? A monster?'

I moved closer.

'Now look at you! You've ruined your clothes; I don't even know if those stains will ever come off!'

I dropped my guard as I looked at the stains on my trousers, and the mercy of God was forgotten. She grabbed me by the ear with her claws of fingernails and twisted and pulled my ear until I started to levitate.

'When I tell you something, I want you to listen, and do as I say. Don't even think about crying! I don't want people to think that I haven't done my homework like any God-fearing woman should!'

Then she dropped me. As I regained my balance, and as she removed bits of my skin from underneath her nails, she said, 'Now listen very carefully! We are going to visit your grandmother, MaChuma, and I don't want any trouble from you now, you hear?'

I nodded, still feeling hot around the ears.

'Any trouble from you, I'll deal with you when we get home, you hear?'

'Yes, Grandma,' I said, still holding my ear.

Mrs Chuma was not a blood relative. She was one of my many grandmothers in Grandma's complex web of kinship, and I had yet to decipher the exact nature of these relationships. But if one thing connected them all it was their ability to brew the best Tanganda Tea*.

'When we get there, I don't want you to embarrass me by

---

* Tea brand in Zimbabwe.

behaving like a hungry orphan. I've instilled enough good manners in you. And, just in case you've forgotten what the rules are, I want you to politely decline all offers of food, unless expressly authorised by me!' And then she shouted in my ear. 'Because I know you, you greedy little swine. As soon as you see food, you start to salivate like a dog. If you cross me once more today, God help you!'

A certain look was enough for me to know whether express permission had been granted or not. She demonstrated both so there was no confusion: a frown and a squinting left eye was a definite 'NO'. A broad, toothy smile meant the road was clear.

'*Ekuhle!*'* Grandma yelled as soon as we entered the homestead, because in our culture it was frowned upon to just sneak up on people's doors just in case they were gossiping about you.

'Who is it?' bellowed a voice from behind a partially closed door to the kitchen.

'It's me,' Grandma replied.

Then, 'Come in, come in,' said MaChuma as she pushed the door wide open, wearing the same blue dress she had been wearing in church.

Grandma collapsed into an untidy sprawl and feigned exhaustion.

'Such a marvellous service today! The preaching was inspirational. It was wonderful to see how committed our children are to spreading the word of God in different languages,' said

---

* According to IsiNdebele tradition, a guest must announce their arrival at the gate before they enter private homesteads. Such an open declaration of one's presence reassures hosts that whoever is at the gate has no evil intent.

MaChuma with a palpable pride. Thela, the preacher, was her son, and Lala, the interpreter, her grandson.

'It's there in the bible,' lamented Grandma as she jabbed the cement floor with her forefinger, as if there was an invisible bible sitting there. She was a very dangerous Christian who chopped up the bible as she went along and chose only those verses that provided her with enough ammunition to pummel my sisters and me to hell and back.

'Doesn't the Lord say that towards the end of the days people will speak in tongues?' replied MaChuma. 'Think how lucky we are to be witnessing all these things in our lifetime, Muvu. In our lifetime! True to his word, God is sending us the signs for us to prepare for the ending of the world: war, pestilence, incurable diseases, widespread immorality, you name it, we've seen it!'

'I agree, MaChuma. Your children are wiser than they look. I mean, who would have thought that they could preach a whole sermon in the White man's language, huh? How things have changed! I wish White men were here to witness this with their own eyes; that we are not as stupid as they think we are!'

'It's with the Lord's blessing that we have these children. To see them standing there in White men's suits, preaching the word of God in his tongue, is such a revelation!'

'On that note, did you see the madness of that woman?'

MaChuma leaned forward, conspiratorially, eyes wide open. 'Do tell, which one? I was too busy listening to my son preaching to observe all that foolishness!'

'I, too, was enthralled by the preaching, but I only noticed her because she was making a fool of herself, jumping up and down like a lunatic! There is praise, and then there is devil worship right under the house of God. When are these people going to learn that God does not approve of such madness?'

'Hm-mmh, God is good; he has immense power!'

'He has an amazing grace, and he blesses us every day!' said Grandma, eyes cast upon the bubbling teapot. And I was salivating over a mound of cakes hidden under a tea towel.

'He lets us live, and we've survived so much with his blessings,' MaChuma continued.

On our way there, Grandma had been complaining about the stupidness of people praying in English. And now she was sitting there going *mm-hmm, awww, ahaa* to everything MaChuma was saying. Conversely, her stern look forbade me from uttering so much as a single word. So I kept my mouth shut, my eyes on the cakes.

MaChuma leaned forward and whispered, 'You know, this is a time of great trepidation. These monsters are now coming out of hiding, and they are brazenly walking around with their guns in broad daylight. Not too far from here, they are doing terrible things to people, all in the name of freedom!'

I surmised she was talking about guerrillas because the church did not approve of freedom fighters. I sensed a slight unease in Grandma's demeanour.

As always, Grandma brought the conversation back to the bible: 'Doesn't the bible say that we will hear of wars and rumours of war, and that all this will come to pass? We must believe that the Lord has plans for us. I mean, look, we would have perished a long time ago without his grace.'

Even I was beginning to lose hope of ever drinking any of the tea.

'Any news about your son?'

'He hasn't written for a while; perhaps he is in the mines,' said Grandma. 'We can only hope that he comes back intact. Many aren't so lucky; they are buried alive deep in the mines. The Boers let them suffocate with dust because it's too dangerous to bring up their bodies. Can you believe the callousness and heartlessness of these people?'

I discerned from the lie that Grandma had not yet disclosed that Uncle Sami had been arrested. Adults had the trifling habit of lying about uncomfortable truths.

'Muvu, hasn't the good Lord amply warned us that money is the root of all evil? People will do anything just to make money. And to what end if all it does is make the world a much darker place? See all these wars? They are about money and greed. And when will it ever end?'

'It is heartbreaking to witness mothers mourn without their children's bodies. Not even a strand of hair, fingernail, or shoe with bits of skin to bury. Such heartache!'

Grandma grimaced and planted her hands, one on top of the other, on her lower belly, as if there was pain there, and continued, 'Nobody wins. They send our sons to fight endless wars, or deep down the mines to dig their gold. Either way, they perish, and for what? So they can buy a pair of shoes? And for all the amount of blood spilled over it, death still hasn't tarnished the lure of gold. People still wear it as if it has no taint.'

'Never a truer word spoken,' said MaChuma as she bit into a cake and took a sip from her tea. A small bulge appeared on the side of her mouth as she chewed slowly, as if in contemplation, like a cow chewing the cud.

I deliberately and loudly swallowed air, made some funny noises, just to remind them that I was still in the room.

'Would you like some tea and cake, young man?'

Before I answered, MaChuma turned to Grandma. 'Your grandson has grown so quickly. What do you feed him? He was only a tiny thing, the size of my thumb, when his mother dumped him on you not so long ago!'

'Hasn't he just? The Lord works in wonderful ways. Can you believe that now he talks back to me and gets involved in all kinds of mischief? He keeps me busy all right!'

And then Grandma threw a grimace at me. The first warning that the tea and cake were a no-go area.

I ignored her and instead cast a broad, sycophantic smile at Mrs Chuma, lest she forgot about her earlier offer.

'And how is his stomach?' MaChuma enquired as she poured tea into a cup. She refilled Grandma's cup for the third time. And all along I'd been swallowing air, and the inside of my ears began to itch. My stomach was rumbling all right, but there was nothing wrong with it.

'I am fine,' I said, without any prompting from Grandma, but before I could say anything further, she barred me with a stern look from the corner of her eye again!

The caramelised-milk fragrance assaulted my nostrils as Mrs Chuma unveiled a mound of greasy *vetkoeks**, or heartbreakers, sprinkled with sugar, and then smothered in a thick paste of Stork margarine and strawberry jam. When I looked at Grandma, I

---

* A crispy and fluffy deep-fried yeast bun or 'fat cake' filled with jam or margarine.

met definite disapproval. There was no mistaking the prominent squint right at the corner of her left eye, and the deep, corrugated furrows across her forehead. It was the look she wore just before she went to war with anyone. Mrs Chuma was none the wiser that Grandma and I could carry out a whole conversation using eye language.

Mrs Chuma grabbed a *vetkoek* and gave it to me. And I accepted it with cupped hands. She slid a mug of tea towards me, and I quickly grabbed it and retreated to my original position slightly behind Grandma.

Grandma watched me with disdain, and before long she started faking unnecessary coughs, the way she often did when she couldn't wait any longer to clobber someone. I could see she was about to eject herself off the mat, which suggested that we should leave immediately.

'Thank you, MaChuma. God bless you. I must take him away before he finishes all your food. It is not as if I didn't feed him this morning!'

'*Awww*, don't worry too much. These little ones are still growing. They need all the energy they can get! It's all the running around, see?'

Then Grandma started to talk about me as if I wasn't there.

'He has no manners, and he should know better, really. He is lucky you are his favourite grandson otherwise I would have ripped off his ears and cut out his tongue. I can't stand children without manners!'

'Leave him alone,' MaChuma interjected as she rubbed my head with her soft hands. 'He is a little rascal. He'll grow up to be a teacher one day!'

Grandma snarled, glistening in her poisonous armour, as she peeled herself off the mat. As soon as we left, the inevitable happened.

'What did I tell you?'

'When, Grandma?'

'Today just before we left church?'

'Mm-mmm, nothing that I can remember!'

'Am I hallucinating?'

'No, Grandma.'

'Then what did I say? You know full well what I said, you greedy swine! Now answer me, what did I say?'

'Not to drink tea.'

'And the cake? Answer me, you greedy little swine!'

'But I looked at you and I saw you eating cake and drinking tea.'

'Never mind what you saw me doing. Have I not told you not to accept food from strangers? Not so? And what did you do? Hmm? Tell me?'

'I was hungry – besides, she is my grandmother. You said so yourself!'

'I'll kill you. You must learn to say NO.'

'But I saw you drinking tea and took it . . .'

Wallop! Followed by another wallop, and then another.

I understood that this was one argument, like many before, that I was never going to win.

As fate would have it, later that night, a neighbour's hut caught fire. The flames lit up the sky and people from across the village gathered to watch the spectacle. My sisters and I rushed there too, including Grandma. When we got back, Grandma excused herself, saying she was desperate to use the toilet.

I heard her dragging the bedroom door open and immediately thought something was afoot. Normally, after using the toilet, Grandma would come to the kitchen first to wash her hands. Worryingly, when she finally came back, she did not, and said nothing. Grandma had different ways of being silent; these were not silences at all but a mode of communication, in which each type of silence preordained what was to follow.

That night's silence presaged nothing but doom. I feigned sleep right next to the hearth. Reassuringly, I heard her muttering to herself, 'Poor thing, he must be tired.'

When I woke up in the morning, however, I saw, right above the door, wedged between the wall and roof, a bundle of neatly pruned switches. Somehow, Grandma had changed her mind.

CHAPTER 6

Besides working her land, and going to church, one of Grandma's chores was to replenish her stores of thatch grass. She used it to repair the roofs on her huts and sold the surplus for cash to buy things that she desperately needed: sugar, jam, cooking oil, flour, and salt. She had a small granary perched on raised stilts where she kept grain, black-eyed peas, and seeds for the following seasons' crops. She kept it sealed, airtight, to prevent the black weevils from destroying the corn kernels and the seeds. And, underneath the stilts, she kept pumpkins out of season.

But there was no good-quality thatch grass around her fields – she could only get it deep inside Mr Coulson's farm. Mr Coulson was a White farmer with the longest beard I had ever seen. He wore a khaki uniform like a schoolboy, and *veldskoens** with thick socks pulled up to the knees. Grandma said that the land he now owned had previously been our ancestral land, where she'd

---

* Handcrafted shoes made from tanned rawhide leather uppers with rubber soles. The word is a portmanteau formed from veld (open grassland) and skoen (shoe). Also commonly known as Farmers' shoes.

spent her childhood looking after Tata's animals. That's why she couldn't take me back there to show me the rivers and the streams where she used to swim as a young girl. She said that if you wanted to see the magnitude of our land, or Mr Coulson's as it was then, you must climb to the top of the Waba, the highest mountain in the area. From its pinnacle, you could get God's eye view of our land.

She woke me early, just so we could reach the mountain before sunrise, which meant we had to break the curfew. She asked what men in their right mind would shoot an old woman and innocent child. With that, she balanced her sickle on the curvature of its spine right on the middle of her head, and it swung like a pendulum.

Coulson's farm lay behind the Waba mountain. When you climbed it from the back, its gradient got progressively steeper till you reached the dizzying pinnacle. From here, as far as the eye could see, was a sprawling, undulating terrain. Lone trees and elephant grass swayed gently to the rhythm of an invisible wind. On clear, sunny days, and if you were lucky, you could see kudu, antelope, and baboons out in the open as if there was nothing wrong with the world.

To the south-west there was a constellation of granite outcrops. To the north, the majestic Malungwane hills sheltered under a bluish haze. In the dry season, lighting strikes on dry tinder set it on fire, which was a marvel to watch at night. The fire could go on for days. Nothing could extinguish its voracious flames except for rain. We knew that it was going to rain when angry clouds churned above the mountain range followed by an intoxicating smell, a heady mixture of soil, dry grass, and leaves carried by the wind. There was always a frightening stillness just before the rains. A vicious thunder would tear up the sky, animals sought shelter and we'd withdraw indoors for fear of lightning.

Once the thunder receded, heavy rains would follow. There'd be a thunderous rupture, now and then, like a drunken drummer beating his drum out of sync. In its aftermath, impala, kudu, and antelope grazed on the offshoots of the new grass and shrubs that sprang up from the ground within days of the first rains.

The mountain itself was no longer sacred. Soldiers used it as a vantage point to scan the area for guerrillas, and it was now littered with discarded military radio batteries, empty cigarette packs, empty cans of pilchards, used condoms.

A dusty road ran along the perimeter of Coulson's farm. It allowed him to survey his land and to instruct his men to secure any points of intrusion. In between bouts of gunfire from the Shaw Barracks, you could hear the whining of his jeep, and you could see a cloud of dust as it rose in the distance.

I thought Grandma came here, not just to cut grass, but to listen to the secret language of the mountain and forest: the crushing and flapping of the wings, and the sudden yelp of the male baboon. We climbed halfway up the mountain to get a better view.

She called our perambulations memory walks. 'See that there?' she'd say, pointing to a cluster of tall trees. 'That's the beginning of our land. Right up to the stream and over the gorge. Are you listening? You're the man and this is your great-grandfather's land. Remember,' she'd say, her grey-black skin wrapped around her thin bones like branches on an old, dying tree, 'remember, this is your land. One day they'll take it all from you. I know they are stealing our land from us,' she'd repeat to herself quietly, the red of her eyes still, impermeable. And I memorised the rivers and the streams on our land like the raised veins on the back of her hand.

She had every reason to be worried. It wasn't just White people who'd stolen our land. Mr Chuma, Mrs Chuma's husband, owner of the church and local businessman, had already asked Grandma if he could use some of our land. As soon as she agreed, he erected barbed wire around it. He hoped that when Grandma was long gone, we wouldn't remember the exact coordinates of our land. In exchange, he ploughed Grandma's fields with his tractor. My sisters and I would run behind the tractor, feeling the warmth and softness of the soil between our toes as Grandma scattered her seeds – maize, sweet reed, melon, and gourds – with a remarkable accuracy.

The seeds fell on the edge of the mound, not too deep, otherwise they would fail to push through. At the bottom of the field, the soil turned into a dark, impermeable clay. There she spread sorghum and *rapoko** seeds. They thrived better on dry ground and survived droughts. After all, it was the hardiness of our crops, our animals, and the resilience of our people that made life bearable in the Native Reserve.

But the soil was shallow and malnourished. It needed copious amounts of fertiliser, which she could not afford. Under White man's law, each field needed a contour and run-off to prevent soil erosion. To avoid going to prison or losing her land, Grandma dug the trenches herself. She never complained. She just picked

---

* Millet

up the pickaxe and we followed behind, scooping up mounds of soil with small buckets.

At sunrise, troops of baboons sat on the precarious slopes of the mountain, grooming, yawning, and looking at the world with an unyielding baboon-like inquisitiveness. It thrilled at first, but also terrified: you were just never too sure of what they'd do next. They sat still in an ordered equanimity.

Now that there was a military camp nearby, each morning, after sunrise, all you could hear was gunfire. On such days, baboons went deep into the forest, away from the maddening noise. Besides, people killed them to feed their meat to dogs, and kept their skulls to capture the magic that kept baboon families together. Sometimes, the baboons ate poisoned wild fruit, and drank water from poisoned springs. They, too, had succumbed to the war.

Grandma would say that they must have longed for peace, which was why I think she disrupted my sleep just to come and watch these creatures. She'd say that we wouldn't be free unless the baboons, too, were free. After all, they had never done us any harm. And when they were gone, all that would be left would be their bones, and no trace of their massacre. And there'd be no retribution against those responsible for it.

On rare occasions, Grandma and I watched the secretary bird, its distinct black feathers protruding at the back of its head. Its beauty far exceeded that of its cousin, the black vulture, whose ugliness banished thoughts of ever eating it.

As the wispy light cloud lifted off the canopy of the forest, it unveiled a resplendent spread of green. When Grandma was ready, we would crawl along the slippery side of the mountain, till we got down to the base.

We walked over dull, barren, and hard-worn soil, and jumped over circles of flattened grass where guerrillas slept at night. The early morning fog warped perspective as figures dressed in grass suits disappeared in the distance.

When we exited the mountain pass, it was a short distance to the Coulson's farm. Barbed wire was the most dependable feature of the landscape. Alongside tall eucalyptus trees, it heightened the farm's desolation. If you were lost, you could follow it. Like a river, it took you somewhere.

Rusty pieces of metal hung loosely on the barbed wire. The signs displayed a human skull and crossbones, juxtaposed with a warning: TRESPASSERS WILL BE SHOT! And yet we were the custodians of the land.

There was a symmetry and precision along the wire, and a tightness matched by the viciousness of its barbs. We followed it until we found a spot where it slackened, evidence that it had been used before, and that it was safe to cross. First, we sat still on the grass and listened out for the sounds of Mr Coulson's Land Rover, preceded by the sudden rise of dust in the distance. Once clear, Grandma went in first. I placed my foot on the bottom wire and pulled the rest higher up, until she squeezed through. Sometimes, her clothes got caught in the barbs and it took a while to free her.

Once inside the farm, Grandma wasted no time. With her sickle in her strongest hand, she bent over, closer to the ground, as if she was searching for a gold nugget. She clutched a clump of grass and pushed her sickle forward and hacked backwards, as if starting a stubborn generator. Her frame swayed, and she moved with such speed as she gripped and ripped into clumps of grass, here, there, and around her.

She called herself *umavuka azenzele*, which meant simply someone who did things for themself if they needed something done. Her hands were dry on the inside, and thick calluses nestled in her palms from chopping firewood, plastering adobe walls with mud, and weeding.

The wind whistled, as the golden thatch grass swayed, its stems bending gently. But she cut it, mercilessly, leaving behind nothing but sharp stubs for next season's growth. She placed it into small piles and spread it so that it dried while she cut more. Every so often, she rose and scanned the area for any signs of movement, but her eyesight was not so good. So, as soon as we arrived, I climbed up the tallest tree and kept watch while she worked. At the first hint of trouble, we had to run and leave everything behind.

I crawled right under a tree, occupied myself with mindless play, and watched her work. I played, alone, with defrocked locusts. It was easy to catch them in the morning – frost paralysed their wings. In the afternoon I could never get close to them. They spread their brightly coloured plumage, the colours of the rainbow, and glided higher and higher up, only to land on branches too precarious for me to climb. But when I caught them, I'd remove their wings so they could no longer fly. A thick green gelatinous liquid oozed from their joints; it had a very pungent smell.

I caught only the females, with their distended bellies full of nutritious eggs. When we got home, Grandma lit a fire and I would toss them on to it, including her own batch. They kept hunger at bay whilst she prepared *pap* with pumpkin leaf and sour milk.

My other job was harvesting flexible tree bark. I peeled it into small strands to make rope for Grandma. She used it to tie the thatch grass into big bundles. Before we headed home, she'd throw the heavy bundles of thatch grass over the barbed-wire fence and hide them under the trees, further away from the perimeter of the farm. When the pile was big enough, she'd hire a scotch cart to ferry it home.

But sometimes I was so caught up in this mutilation that I missed the sounds of footsteps from soldiers. Camouflaged, they moved in stealth amongst trees.

On this day, when I heard their radios, I knew it was too late to alert Grandma. So I hid and watched soot-stained faces torment her and kick the thatch grass that had taken hours to cut. They forced her to raise her hands above her head, stand astride, and squat before lifting her dress with the tip of their guns to see if she was hiding any sweet potatoes or grenades for guerrillas. She was confused by their language and maddened by the failure of her words to convince them. She was alone, outgunned.

Afterwards, they marched her to the barbed wire, forced her under, and seized her sickle without which she could no longer work. I watched them throw it into the bushes from where I quickly retrieved it as soon as they disappeared under the foliage of trees.

I saw them follow the barbed wire, looking for holes and areas of penetration by guerrillas, but it would have been obvious to anyone that Grandma wasn't one of them.

And when I saw how they walked I realised that they treaded carefully lest the ground beneath them exploded. It was a heavy burden, this unbridled hatred. It slowed down their so-called progress.

When Grandma and I were tired, we sat on the grass and looked at tree stumps riddled with an acne of bullet holes, the waft of the phosphorous scent of the *ixhaphozi** and the dry elephant grass hanging in the air.

On the way home, we took a different route. The bypass on the other side of the mountain was shrouded under the foliage of trees. Here, in between pillars of rock, Grandma and I came upon a small group of guerrillas: solitary figures bathed in blasts of sunlight, their guns silent, for now. This was where they gathered before setting out to do whatever it was that they did at night. It was the first time that I'd caught a glimpse of them, these men and women who played hide-and-seek with Smith's soldiers: *Amalwecatsha!†* In those few seconds, my hair stood on end.

'Not a word!' she whispered.

I looked up and ahead.

---

* Swamp

† Derogatory term used by Smith's regime to refer to guerrillas as cowards who ambushed his soldiers and then melted into the forests. In the same way that American soldiers referred to North Vietnamese combatants as gooks. Again, the term was meant to dehumanise those engaged in the fight against racist oppression and to detract attention away from the true nature of Black struggle against racist White oppression and violent aggression.

The guerrillas didn't say anything or give the impression that they'd seen us.

And I could hear, right above the canopy of trees, the relentless *ko ko ko ko ko ko ko* sound of the woodpecker, and call of the bullfrog, sharply contrasted with the deeply sonorous cooing of the dove, booming out courtship calls. And the rock rabbit's chirrup.

And then there was the stock bird, reminiscent of an old man trying to look dignified, with its head and pendant pouch hanging from its neck.

The red-eyed turtle dove, with its dark priestly neck ring, cooed from within the foliage of trees, a deep nasal beat, a lament for a country drawn perilously close to a calamity.

Eagles and vultures glided higher up. From a distance, they looked the same. As we crept on our way, Grandma said that eagles killed their own prey, whilst vultures fed on carrion. She said that nobody liked or appreciated vultures, but they were a necessity. Unlike us, they didn't pretend to be something they were not.

She took me to a small stagnant pool right at the bottom of the mountain. A crop of water lilies floated, broad-leafed. Green velvet dragonflies hovered above the water, pensive, like military helicopters. Beneath their flight path, there were ripples on the surface of the water, reminiscent of the kind you saw on an animal's skin when it was frightened.

We sat quietly for a while on the granite rock overlooking the pool. The rock was impermeable; a red liquid oozed from underneath the carpet of wild lichens, straight into the pool. A long-legged ghost spider dashed across the tense surface of the water.

I took off my clothes and, as I dived deep into the boundless depth of the pool, sharp, sword-edged filaments of light revived something in the darkness. It was a tiny albino catfish, translucent like a newborn. It had spent too much time in the darkness and had lost its eyes, in the same way that Grandma said living in the reserve had dimmed our edginess.

But at the bottom of the pool the catfish looked weightless, free. On sensing my presence, it retreated under the rocks. I could feel my heartbeat. The water was cold, as if it had never been touched by the warmth of the sun. I opened my eyes and followed the spear of light to the bottom and grabbed the entanglement of the water lily's underwater stems, with its lateral roots. I broke a stem and brought it up to the surface.

Grandma said, 'Be careful with that. No one has seeds for these plants. Do you know that during a famine you can pound the stems into a soft flour and keep hunger at bay? Did you know that it takes these lilies years to grow to this size?' She took her dilapidated canvas shoes off, which were no match for the vicious thorns of the acacia tree.

'How many years?' I said, suddenly amazed at her mundane observation.

She ignored me and simply said, 'You too will grow, unless of course the war cuts you down in pieces. Just don't go around uprooting things for no good reason. It's not good for the soul,' she said, her voice low-pitched, loving, and endearing.

And then she told me that my own life had been implicated in Grandpa's death. She said that if he'd survived, I wouldn't be alive. As a child, I didn't know what she meant. Equally, I didn't dare to ask; she was oblivious to the power of her words, said things that stayed longest in your heart.

She took off her headscarf, revealing her crop of salt-and-pepper hair. Her big bright white teeth dazzled each side of her diastema. She was handsome in her own way. She washed her face slowly, with restraint, her age more pronounced in this stillness. Water dripped along her arms into her dusty apron as she pulled it above her knees, as though preparing to ride a bicycle, and then she immersed her cracked, mud-encrusted, worn-out feet underwater. I watched her grind her cracked heels against the rough grains of the granite rock. She tilted each foot this way and that way, to make sure that she covered all the angles. But the cracks were too wide; she had to grind harder, deeper. So, she grated layer after layer after layer of her callused heels away until she started to bleed. Something leapt out of her face. 'I can feel my feet now,' she said. Since Grandpa's death, I'd never seen her cry. She was cocooned inside a silent rage.

I dived back into the water again.

A red tinge spread from her feet as I rose into the calmness.

Afterwards, she engaged in her usual half-body wash routine: armpits, legs from the knee down, arms from the elbow downwards, and she sat on a rock and inhaled her snuff one nostril at a time, in obeisance to the departed. There was something about this place that made her sad, and I was not sure what it was. Perhaps it was love and the land. In our country it was always those two things.

Her distraught voice broke startlingly into the silence.

'When I was a little girl,' she mused, 'I used to herd cattle with boys. I could not bathe in the river; I could not allow them to see any of my weaknesses. I fought fiercely, with sticks, with my bare knuckles. I never lost a fight. To this day, I'll fight anyone who dares cross me!'

With that, she got up, lifted her burden of heavy thatch grass, and we continued on our way. The sun was about to go down and we were two hours from home. We met people along the very narrow footpaths, where new paths radiated from the old, and spread in different directions. She talked to them, the heavy bundle of grass still on her head, and firewood tied to her back like an infant. Each greeting became a question: but what can we do? Because there was no mechanism through which Black people could openly air their grievances. Each grievance attracted harsher laws, mass incarcerations, detention without trial, and sometimes executions. And the answer led even to more questions. What can we say? We are alive, what else can we do?

The sun went down more quickly than we'd anticipated. We'd breached the curfew, again. The dark amplified our fear; everything felt new. In the darkness, outlines blurred, people merged with trees. Each step was carefully placed for fear of stepping on something harmful, a black mamba or cobra out to feed, perhaps.

As we walked home, Grandma simply held my hand, her bundle of thatch balanced on her head, with her sharp sickle in the other hand, without a shred of certainty. There were flares ahead of us, spectral outlines, light that appeared haphazardly. In this darkness, only the flame from home fires burning led us to familiar places.

CHAPTER 7

As much as I enjoyed following Grandma around, I was getting bored. I needed a new adventure. My attention was drawn to my sisters; each morning they dressed up in their uniforms, grabbed their books, and disappeared along the small path towards the Growth Point. They treated their books like new clothes – wrapped them up in clean brown paper, repurposed from old cement bags, neatly tucked in at the corners with Sellotape, as if the books were the most precious things that they'd ever held in their hands.

The more I watched them, the more I felt cheated. I was just under five years old; Grandma said that the White man's law stipulated that I could not go to school for another two years, although White children my age were allowed to do so. They said that Black children were stupid. Our conditioning was such that we had to embrace our preordained social destiny – like the dust, dirty water, smoke, and violence of the reserve.

'But I am ready, Grandma!' I said indignantly.

'Are you sure?' Grandma asked, rather attentively, which was not like her. 'Because if I send you to school, I don't want you to

come back here crying, you hear me? I've better things to be getting on with rather than attend to your every whim about stupid
things. It's only yesterday that you wanted to be a mechanic and
learn to drive lorries, and now you want to go to school. Which
is it?'

'I want to learn to read and write things for you!' I pleaded.

Just then my sister Thoko entered the kitchen, ears pricked up,
eyes glowing with incredulity. She was six years older than me.

'Who wants to go to school? *You?*'

There were only the three of us, so I ignored her sarcasm
and retorted with a resounding confidence, 'Yes, I want to go to
school!'

'Mm-mm! she exclaimed sardonically. 'And what do you think
school is, huh? Child's play? You must be joking!'

'Well, if you can go, I can go too!'

'You think you can handle Mr Socks; he'll eat you alive!'

Grandma interjected, unexpectedly. 'You can talk, busy mouth.
If the boy wants to go to school, let him go. And who took you
to school the first time? You weren't so brave then, were you?
You were clinging to every tree, shrub, and blade of grass all the
way there. At least he's volunteering!'

And, turning to me, she said, 'You must tell your mother that
you want to go to school. Because you'll need a uniform, shoes,
pencils, and God knows what else. The list keeps getting bigger
and bigger by the day!'

Armed with Grandma's blessing, and as part of my preparation,
I observed my sisters getting ready for school. I concluded that
there were far too many unnecessary things they did. Top of the
list, full body wash, combing hair, and wearing clean underwear.

76

Besides, Grandma didn't always wash, and she didn't smell that bad. Unlike her, I didn't stuff snuff up my nostrils. And, unlike my sisters, I didn't have to wear big knickers that needed washing all the time. Once I'd dwindled that list to one or two things, I reckoned that school wasn't as complicated as they made it out to be.

So, for Christmas, Ma bought me a brand-new uniform with black shoes, grey knee-high socks, and a grey jersey, along with exercise books, pencil, and pencil sharpener. She made me try everything just to make sure. When I tried the shoes, they were a bit too tight, especially around the small toes. Afraid that I might never see them again, I curled my toes to hide the discomfort.

'They are fine!' I insisted, even though they were not.

Ma worked at Toppers; she knew all there was to know about shoe sizes. She could tell I was lying.

'Come here,' she said, clearly unconvinced.

When I got closer, she pressed hard on top of my toes. When I winced and pulled my foot away from her strong grip, her mind was made up.

'I'll take them back,' she said. 'You need a slightly bigger size that will leave room for your feet to breathe.'

She made me try the uniform. When I put it on, though still disappointed about the shoes, I felt bigger, puffed up. The shorts had no zip at the front and an elastic band that clung to my waist, leaving imprints on my skin.

Gift fell over laughing. 'How are you going to pee without a zip?'

'Like this,' I said, about to demonstrate.

Ma anticipated what I was about to do and slapped my hand. She yanked the waistband up towards my ribs and shouted: 'Stand still!'

And then she made me perform all manner of exercises just to be satisfied that the uniform was a perfect fit.

'Raise your hands above your head! Stay there and don't move unless I tell you to!' She circled me and pulled the shirt around my armpits and made all manner of observations.

'A bit loose, but it's okay. You'll grow into it.'

And back to me.

'To the side!'

'Bend over and touch your toes!'

She nodded her head with satisfaction.

When I stood up straight, she ran her hand inside the rubber band on my shorts and then pulled it sideways to see if there was sufficient room for expansion. And then she pulled the shirt from the front as if to loosen it from the tight grip of the waistband.

'Pull your elbows backwards!'

And then from the back, 'Push your arms forward!'

'Good,' she said, now expertly satisfied that everything fitted.

I was beginning to sweat. To make matters worse, the uniform was one hundred per cent polyester like Grandma's Terylene dress. It had a rough, starchy feel. It shouldn't have been allowed anywhere near human skin. One spark from the flame and it would melt.

'Stay away from the fire and make sure you change into your everyday clothes as soon as you get home. And never ride down the rocks on your *Isikhukhukhu** tree rides with your uniform on, you hear me?' she threatened me menacingly. 'Are you listening?'

'Yes, Ma.'

'You think it's funny, huh? You should be grateful. If it was down to your father, you'd be walking around with your buttocks exposed like an orphan. Really, I don't know why you're laughing. Now turn round so I can look at you one more time!'

I turned slowly.

Finally, sounding rather satisfied, she said, 'Good, that's perfect. Now take it off. I'll send your replacement shoes with Salani's mother next weekend. I brought her groceries – it's her turn next.'

Meanwhile, Grandma folded the uniform and locked it away in her trunk. I could hardly wait to wear it.

Uncle Sami had now been missing for weeks. Since he'd left with the policemen that fateful night, Grandma had continued the search. The situation was unsettling. As her schedule became more erratic, and with her eye off the ball, Salani and I were back on the main road, where we played our usual game: choosing cars based on our favourite colours; his was blue, mine red. It was an aspirational game.

One day, a lorry with a solitary red flag attached to its long antennae whizzed past as passengers in the rear guarded a coffin

---

* *Isikhukhukhu* (Ndebele) or Soap-nettle (English) is a small tree with a very slippery dark purple bark, which children in rural areas use to slide down rocks or as sledges. It also has medicinal purposes. It is found mainly in open woodland, particularly amongst boulders and on rocky *kopjes*.

under the cover of a red blanket. The red colour again. We had dived under the culverts when we saw a military truck approaching. As we dusted cobwebs from ourselves, we saw a luxurious double-decker bus a short distance behind it with the word WENELA emblazoned on its side. It was an acronym for the Witwatersrand Native Labour Association, an agency set up by big mining conglomerates to recruit cheap migrant labour for the mines of Johannesburg. It went twice weekly; when we saw it, we searched for familiar faces so we could inform their relatives. Many did not openly discuss their imminent departure. It was believed that doing so would bring bad luck. It was the same with those who'd gone to join the war. They left in the middle of the night; most never came back.

All we heard was the adults whisper: 'So-and-so has gone!'

As the bus got closer, a man forced his slim upper body through an open window, and frantically waved and whistled to gain our attention. It was Uncle Sami. We ran along the barbed wire and tried to keep up with the bus, but within seconds it had vanished over a hill and round the bend. We'd feared the worst. After nearly a year of trepidation and uncertainty, I still couldn't believe my eyes. I ran home to tell Grandma. She wailed as if he'd already died.

Weeks later, a blue self-contained letter, folded in on itself, emblazoned round the edges with red and white chevrons, arrived. This time, it was written in blue ink, so it wasn't a message of death. It simply confirmed to Grandma that I hadn't been mistaken. Uncle Sami was now working deep in the mines. Daily, we scanned the news of those who had perished. And it became a preoccupation. As the war intensified, Grandma's prayers intensified too. And she increased the frequency with which she visited Grandpa's grave, because our world and the world of the living-dead were intertwined.

Even through the stresses of the war, and Uncle Sami's departure for the mines, our herd of cattle had doubled in size, and the amount of work had too. There was the manure to be dug and spread in the fields, the *kraal* and fence to be mended, and various other things that Grandma could no longer do on her own. So, in Uncle Sami's absence, not that he'd ever done anything much, she hired a helper, a man called Enock, to work for us. Enock was a recluse and an unrepentant thief with a penchant for female donkeys.

Compared to most men his age, he was uncomplicated. He sought Grandma's approval and validation in ways that I could never understand. He fixed her fence, dug her manure, and repaired the damaged thatch on Grandma's huts. I never heard her castigate or shout at him. Instead, she said that all men should be like him: respectful, hard-working, diligent, and kind. So, I did not tell her about him having sex with donkeys and his threats to kill me when I caught him doing it.

When he stole a White man's bicycle, he brought it straight to Grandma, hoping to impress her. It was a black Raleigh, with a big light at the front, and had mudguards front and back, and a cushioned saddle. It was different from the scarecrow variety that we saw around us.

Grandma interrogated Enock as if she already knew what he'd done, because, in our world, very few people could afford the luxury of a brand-new bicycle. Bicycles and gold-plated watches were only ever given to old Black men when they finally retired from years of servitude, when they could no longer walk or see properly. To this day *Blacks Still Don't Crack.** And yet the very notion of Blacks' perceived agelessness suggests that Blacks do not deserve respite or respect. Whites could work them to the bone or till they dropped because in their eyes they were mere beasts.

'Enock, my son,' she said, 'where did you get the bicycle from?'

'I found it,' he said, his eyes cast to the ground as Grandma unflinchingly tried to hold his gaze.

'They'll kill you, my son!' she lamented. 'How many times have I told you not to steal? You have hands, no? All you must do is eat and rest to replenish your strength and you can work some more, my child. There is no shame in hard work. But stealing?'

'I'll take it back. I am sorry I lied to you.'

'Hold on,' she said. 'Wait till dark. Take it to the dam, throw it in the deepest spot where they'll never find it. If they do find it, they'll never know you left it there!'

Grandma brushed her hands against her hips in quick succession as we watched Enock's head bobbing away in the distance like a lone tractor driver ploughing a farm not his own. She sucked her teeth, registering a dissatisfaction with Enock's pilfering.

---

* Perhaps this is one of the most enduring and harmful racialised tropes. At surface level this can sound complimentary: the idea that Blacks generally don't age at the same speed as their White counterparts. But if we dig deeper, it refers to the embedded, 'historically and politically determined systems of exploitation and domination' that are intended to 'dehumanise, inferiorise, and marginalise racialised groups based on physical, cultural, and symbolic differences,' which often leads to a malevolent and terminal neglect of their needs.

Meanwhile, he swerved like a drunk. First this way, and that way, before he vanished over the hill.

The very next day, an unmistakable death shrill, *isililo**, disrupted the morning tranquillity. Grandma grabbed my hand. We walked up the hill towards Enock's house, where the scream was coming from. She briefly let go of my hand to tighten her headscarf as if gearing up for a fight. Her grip loosened as we entered Enock's compound.

Enock's house lay between two *kopjes*, behind which lay old, abandoned graves. Next to the graves stood dead lemon trees that had turned soot black. And, right in the middle of the yard, there was a grey police Land Rover, at the back of which lay a metallic coffin, with Enock's dry feet sticking out over the edge. He resembled a drunk, fast asleep: soiled and dishevelled, with grass and twigs in his hair. A brown liquid oozed from the corner of his mouth.

'Sorry I lied to you.'

Those were his last words to Grandma before he left our house. And now he was dead.

A Black policeman was trying to explain something to Enock's mother, while his partner, a White man, who rested in the shade, kept some distance.

Grandma harangued the Black policeman, who seemed rather ashamed to say anything. 'What did he do that he deserved to be killed? How did you kill him, huh? Why, my son, why?'

Although her language was cryptic, coded, the Black policeman understood that Enock was one of us. He knew that the ease

---

* Wailing

with which he'd been killed signalled our collective vulnera-
bility. As Grandma would say, if you wounded one of us, you
wounded all of us. Which is why when you seriously wounded
someone, especially when they were in the throes of death,
you washed your hands and drank the cloudy water. Then your
victim, followed by both families, drank the water too. The
washing of the hands symbolised forgiveness because no one
healed alone.

'They are killing us!' she said.

As if on cue, the White man came out of the shade. He was
wearing a brown T-shirt and a pair of green army shorts, the size
of a small boy's, and boots with thick socks, despite the heat. At
the front, the shorts disappeared under his rotund belly.

He didn't look like a policeman at all. Since he was a White
man, we assumed that there was a justifiable reason for Enock's
death, however mundane.

The Black policeman was labouring under his oversized khakhi
uniform, which made him look more like a prisoner than a man
of authority.

The White man gave him a nod. They dragged the coffin off
the vehicle and let it drop to the ground. Enock's body tumbled
out unceremoniously. His mother covered him with a blanket.

The White policeman gave Enock's mother a piece of paper.
Like Grandma, she could not read. She nervously folded it.

'What does it say? Does it say that you've killed him? Tell me!'
she asked the Black policeman.

And, pointing to the White policeman, she asked: 'And what's
he doing here?'

And then back again to the Black policeman, 'Don't let him stop you from telling me what you've done to my son!'

The Black policeman busied himself latching up the back of the jeep. *Clunk! Clunk! Doosh!*

He was trembling, despite the heat.

The old woman, now pointing at the White man, continued.

'*Hambanini!* Go!' she said. 'You kill us every day like flies!'

She spat on the ground right in front of him, before swivelling round to face the Black policeman.

'My son is dead, murdered by you. I want him back, intact, his dignity, *ubuntu bakhe**, restored, you hear me? And if you can't say precisely what it is you've done to him, then your word is so defiled it is not even worth knowing!'

'*Gogo*,'† he said, 'I did not see anything. I was merely instructed to bring him home!'

Grandma, who up until then had been looking at the White man with evil eyes, interjected.

'If you're a messenger, as you say you are, is this how you bring people home now? Dead?'

'Like I said, *Gogo*, I was only asked to bring him home! Sometimes accidents . . . He died in custody,' he finally managed to say.

---

* A person's humanness (as distinct from humanity). The essence of who we are as sentient beings, especially the inviolable dignity with which we are all born.

† Grandmother – a respectful way of referring to an older woman, the same age as one's own grandmother. Because in most Black African cultures, filial piety has historically been a traditional African virtue.

She pushed his gun away from Enock as if she was afraid he'd shoot him again. And then turned to Enock as if he could still hear her: 'Now look at you? Did I not say that they'll kill you? Why did you not listen to me?'

The Black policeman looked at Grandma as he jumped into the passenger side of the jeep, his antique rifle between his legs. The Land Rover vanished behind a cloud of dust.

Grandma sent me home as adults attended to Enock's body. The heat was beginning to subside, and the shade from the tall mahogany trees had already changed direction in anticipation of sunset.

Later, when Grandma came home, it was almost dark outside. She risked being shot by soldiers, but she'd forgotten that there was a curfew. She called out our names and asked us each to bring a cup full of water to the gate before she entered our homestead. She dipped her thumb into the water, touched the ground, and picked up soil. And then she rubbed each of us across the forehead. While she did this, she uttered not a word. She could not afford to bring bad spirits into our home.

For weeks after Enock's death, Grandma was engulfed by agitation and became increasingly intolerant of me. I simply resorted to being afraid of her because that was what I knew best. I became accustomed to the tight knot in my stomach, the crippling anxiety. Perhaps there was something else bothering her and all the adults around us.

Following Enock's death, many young men and women had disappeared too.

'So-and-so has crossed over!' people would whisper.

'Crossing over' meant joining guerrillas across the border in Mozambique, Botswana, or Zambia.

It was at the same time that we witnessed an increase in the number of mangled military vehicles deformed by landmines, cars riddled with bullet holes, buses burned out, and the upsurge of military ambulances – day and night – rushing towards Bulawayo, a clear indication that there was an escalation in the war.

Small white planes circled higher in the sky and cascaded thousands of pamphlets. The first batch denounced guerrillas as nothing more than cowardly communist dogs – *Amalwecatsha*: poorly trained, predatory opportunists who did nothing but rape women and girls and spread venereal disease. There might have been an element of truth in it, but the deliberate conflation of the Black liberation struggle with communism glossed over a hundred years of the most brutal and violent occupation of Black lands, the oppression of Blacks and the continuing gross human violations by Ian Smith's illegal regime. Above all, the moralist stance was a lie. When all else failed, Whites evoked the tired trope of Black men as insatiable predatory beasts.

But news filtered through *mujibhas*, young boys and girls who worked closely with the guerrillas and provided them with food and intelligence about troop movements. It was through *mujibhas* that collaboration between the masses and guerrillas was established. They came back with the latest news of the progress of the war, instructions for community leaders and the latest revolutionary songs, which contextualised each phase of the liberation war to ordinary people. The songs encapsulated the prevailing feeling, that we had to fight for our land.

In fact, it was through song and dance, or 'meaningless gyrations' as Whites called the secret meetings, that Blacks' collective consciousness about racist White injustice was slowly raised. Besides, Black people had concluded – through years of observation, shared communal experience, and some hard truths – that their oppressors saw in their every interaction an opportunity for their exploitation.

Months later, a second batch of leaflets carried a direct plea to the guerrillas themselves to lay down their arms and come home, 'because the people wanted peace'.

By then, most Black people had started to hate Whites as a matter of principle. With time, the hatred became fully entrenched. Instead of expecting Whites to throw things at them, people threw stones at their fast-moving cars, sabotaged phone lines, cut and destroyed the barbed wire that kept them and their animals hemmed in, and set fire to the grass on the farms. Blacks had finally understood that White tyranny could never be dismantled without bloodshed. And, from then on, it was always going to be about those two things: violence and land.

As Grandma would say, 'They'd much rather we worked as gravediggers in plush White cemeteries, or swept their streets daily, or suffocated down in asbestos and coal mines, and dwelt in persistent despair and disease, than recognise our humanity.'

But war wasn't the only thing in her mind.

★

We were in the fields. Grandma was weeding; I was busy fighting rhinoceros beetles, besides decapitating and pruning locusts.

88

Suddenly, she turned round and announced: 'You know you start school next week, don't you?'

'What?' I said, slightly confused because I'd thought that the new year was a long way away. At least, that's what Thoko had said. Had six months been and gone that quickly?

'Next week, just make sure you're prepared!' she gleefully remarked.

And so it was that my carefree world ended abruptly.

CHAPTER 8

It was the rainy season. Today was my first day at school.

I ran to Grandma's hut, changed into my new uniform, and paraded in front of Thoko.

'Got everything?'

'Yes!' I said, with glee.

'Sure?'

'Yes!'

'Pencil, books, brains?'

'Yes!' I said with a resounding confidence.

'Why are you lying? Think Mr Socks won't notice your unkempt hair?'

'Who is Mr Sokisi?' I enquired, rather annoyed by all these ominous threats.

'Oh, you'll know who he is, all right!'

When Thoko left, I ran after her as if my life depended on it. When we got to the main road, I was even more concerned to see so many terrified faces: books clutched under armpits, brown miniature suitcases dangling on reluctant arms, Red Seal mealie-meal plastic bags repurposed as book carriers, and snotty urchins being dragged everywhere. It was chaos; everyone was rushing in the same direction. I clocked Salani being reluctantly hauled along by his grandmother and Siza being tormented by his equally determined but also ferocious mother, who kept nudging him forward at intervals.

'This is what you wanted, huh? Now move along quickly because I have better things to be doing with my time!'

No one was happy. I had completely misunderstood everything about going to school!

Thoko slowed down, bent to the level of my ear and shouted: 'When we get to the assembly, I want you to go to the front. Whatever happens, don't even think about coming to me. Do you hear me?'

'Yes, but what is the *asembeli*?' I enquired yet again, to her consternation.

'Look, the assembly, not *asembeli*, is where we sing and pray first thing in the morning before school starts. But we must be there on time, and, before you ask me, again, you are in Grade One. The bottom of the pile! All Grade One pupils stand at the front!'

Every so often, she stopped and shouted in my ear as though I was deaf.

'At the front! Just follow the instructions given by the teacher!'

'How do I know which one is my teacher?'

'Right, I am done with you, totally done! Like I said, if you embarrass me, I swear to God, I'll kill you with my own bare hands. Do you understand?'

I nodded. 'Yes.'

'Good, cause right now you are on your own, my friend. Grandma won't be there to hold your hand!'

★

As soon as we arrived at the *asembeli*, I was on the lookout for a giant with one eye, dressed in nothing but socks, towering above children, searching for unkempt hair. My sister pushed me towards the front row, where children like me, who wore slightly oversized uniforms, were standing. As I scanned the area, my eyes landed on a frighteningly tall scarecrow, whose ill-fitting black suit slackened slightly over his right shoulder as though it had been hung on a tree to dry. His jacket pockets looked as though they were full of pebbles; he had an irreducible hump on his left shoulder. He animatedly bashed his bible against his left palm and all I could hear was his out-of-tune howling. Being a veteran of Grandma's church, I knew that God had a strange effect on people. I quickly surmised that he had an invisible human incubus or *tokoloshi* hidden under his jacket and was to be avoided at all costs.

The girl who stood to my right started crying. Another started yelling for her mother, and a little boy desperately clung to his sister's uniform. Confusion reigned and all around me was a sea of petrified faces. It was all too much. I turned round and started calling my sister: '*Sis'Thoko! Sis'Thoko!*'* I ploughed through row upon row of green and grey uniforms, like a cornfield, hoping to catch a glimpse of my sister. But she had simply vanished into thin air. By now everyone was laughing at me.

Desperate, I fled homeward.

---

* Because she was slightly older than me, I was not allowed to call her by her first name. The prefix 'sis' stands for sister and that's how I addressed her.

When I got home, I forgot to change into my daily clothes, the earlier trauma of the school assembly buried deep at the back of my mind. Whatever happened, I was not going back. Or so I told myself.

When Grandma got home later in the day, she was surprised to find me at home.

'Why aren't you at school?' she enquired with a puzzled look in her eyes.

'I don't like it. There was too much noise and far too many people,' I said, bending yet another piece of wire for the axle. I was busy working on my toy car.

'I see,' she acknowledged, rather casually.

And then she nonchalantly probed me as if school wasn't important at all. I had anticipated that she would be cross with me. So, I relaxed a little.

'But I thought you said you wanted to go to school, yes?'

'I don't like it,' I responded without a care in the world.

'That's new. Remind me again, what was it you said when I asked you if you were sure about school?'

'Yes, but I thought school would be nice. There were people everywhere, shouting, and a mad man running around with stones in his pockets, hiding something frightening under his jacket,' I added, trying to convince her of the justification for my dereliction of duty.

'I see!' she exclaimed, with an incongruity written all over her face. 'I told you in no uncertain terms that, once you start, there is no way out. I am afraid that tomorrow you must go back to school!'

'Maybe next year,' I suggested, trying to wiggle my way out of it.

93

'This year is as good as any,' Grandma responded firmly. 'You'll get used to it.'

Her words were final; my fate was sealed.

Just then Thoko arrived. She was all salty and puffed up like an angry cobra.

When Grandma saw her, she confronted her: 'Why wasn't the boy at school?'

'Grandma, he ran away from the assembly. I've been looking everywhere for him!'

With that she threw a sideways glance directed at me, laced with hostility.

'Mm-hmm,' said Grandma. 'From now onwards, the boy is your responsibility. If he ever goes missing again from school, you'll be answerable to me!'

Out of Grandma's hearing, Thoko threatened me: 'If you run away from school again, I'll kill you. I spent the best part of the day looking for you and missed half my lessons because of your stupidity. I'll tie you to a tree if I must!' And then she opened her eyes wide at me like a ruminating goat before she disappeared into the kitchen.

Our school sat at a crossroads of dusty tracks. The gate consisted of two triangular concrete structures, head high, filled to the brim with soil. On top of these grew Christ-thorn bushes, whose intricate branches displayed a crop of red flowers. Both concrete structures on either side of the gate were whitewashed, and the name of the school was emblazoned across them in big, bold black letters: **Mawabeni Primary School – Knowledge is Power.**

Our uniform was grey for the boys, and mulberry-leaf green, with a yellow trim on the short sleeves, for the girls.

A broad gravel path led to the school compound. A few metres in was the teachers' accommodation, a hasty assemblage of small apartments built from mud bricks, with corrugated zinc for roofs. Each one was no bigger than a monastic cell, with room for a single bed, a Primus stove, a chair, and a small table. It was in these confined spaces that, every morning, women transformed themselves into our teachers.

The headmaster's house, on the other hand, was big, white, and square. It was covered in beautiful bougainvillea and befitted the home of a big man mountain like Mr Socks.

The school itself consisted of six blocks corralled into a *laager**
formation. The assembly area, a slightly raised rectangular square surrounded by whitewashed stones, was outside the frame of the *laager*. Despite the vast amount of empty land round the perimeter of the school, there was not a single fruit tree, not even the ubiquitous sweet lemon tree.

Not too far from the assembly point, tall elephant grass obscured the remnants of an old ruin. The school bell chimed from an iron beam chained to the neck of an old tree.

The mornings were busy times. We were inspected for cleanliness and, if found to have infracted any of the hygiene laws – long, dirty fingernails, unkempt hair, yellow teeth, and slovenly dress – Mr A. R. Socks, of whom more later, was quick to discipline said miscreant in front of the whole assembly.

After inspection, the Lord's Prayer was recited in English. But,

---

* A defensive encampment encircled by wagons.

alas, not all of us knew the words to the prayer. So, when we prayed, we sounded like a beehive on the move, with a cunningly placed and timed rise-and-fall drone of voices, a choric verse of sorts, punctuated by *'give us this day our daily bread'*, grudgingly trudged over by *'forgiving those who trespassed against us'* followed by the rush to the finish: *'And for ever and ever, amen!'*

Sometimes, we sang religious hymns too. Everything was conducted in English; as soon as we walked through the gate, we were forbidden from using our language, isiNdebele. We had no idea what the hymns meant, let alone the correct wording or pronunciation. Mr A. R. Socks, however, seemed frenzied by the singing alone.

After assembly, following various announcements, we followed our respective teachers back to our classrooms.

With time, I fell into a routine of my own; I treated the journey to school like one of Grandma's mindless perambulations. I fell into the rhythm of things and navigated the whole world of books with enthusiasm. I liked the fresh smell of Parker pens; the humdrum of voices reciting the times table in the morning; the squeaky sound of the chalk; the rhythmic bounce of Ms Khumalo's backside as she wrote the alphabet on the blackboard, interspersing capital letters with small letters. There were animal pictures too, to go with each letter of the alphabet.

I immersed myself in the collage of memorable images and visual representations of sounds – mouths opened wide to pro-nounce vowels and consonants, hand to the ear for listening, and clapping hands for applause.

Daily, on our way to and from school, we had to cross the treacherous road. Drivers negotiated the curve at hair-raising

FRANK THABANI SAYI

speed, and it was hard to see cars fast approaching from both directions. Besides, Whites were not obliged to stop; there was a war going on. They feared an imminent ambush.

Adults called it the cursed curve. Often, children were struck by fast-moving cars, but there was no outrage about young Black lives needlessly cut short. Just a sombre resignation.

There was no safe crossing spot built for us – no footbridge, no road bumps, and no traffic lights – even though the headquarters of the Ministry of Roads and Transport were nearby.

The first casualty I knew was Dennis, a mild-mannered boy who appeared out of nowhere and stayed. He had no family; nobody knew where he came from. War did that to people. When their lives fell apart, they just drifted to find solace elsewhere. Dennis worked for a local businessman as an errand boy. Early one morning on our way to school, we found him stuck to the tarmacked road. His head had been split wide open, brain leaking, his face shimmering toothlessly and his limbs, and other body parts, in places where they shouldn't have been. Several haulage trucks, unable to stop on time, had already gone over his body. By the time the police arrived, they had to scrape him off the tarmac to place his remains into a metal coffin. Grandma said that at least he was resting in peace. But she also said that he was not dead, really, that the businessmen would continue to use his spirit to make their businesses flourish. Like us, he'd remain suspended between this world and the next in eternal servitude.

The next victim was a donkey struck and thrown into a ditch by a military truck. When Salani and I first saw him, he was alive. We agonised over what to do, whether we should finish him off with stones, or an axe, but we didn't have the courage for it. So we left him alone, in his agony. When we returned a week later, we found him fly-blown, bloated, his teeth exposed in a semi-frozen smile like a dead comrade. When we pierced his distended abdomen, a foul odour exuded.

Mr Thebe, the village postman, threw stones at us. 'Are you dogs?' he said. 'Are you going to eat that donkey? Why are you bothering dead things?'

As a cloud of carrion flies rose, we ran down the road and played bus conductors by swinging on the gates, which infuriated him even more.

Salani and I were best friends. We first met at Grandma's church. Whilst the adults were busy praying, we were high up on the branches of the mulberry tree, gorging on its dark, juicy berries. Together, we explored the landscape around us and took great risks to satisfy our curiosity. We ate wild fruit, drank water straight from the river and sometimes from stagnant pools. Unbeknown to us, the water was infested with bilharzia worms and other dangerous parasites. At some point our stomachs swelled and we started passing blood-stained urine. At first, it was a novelty, but the fun stopped when we started urinating small blood clots. I experienced an extreme light-headedness, loss of appetite, and profuse night sweats. Grandma fussed over me, and constantly wiped my forehead with a cloth immersed in cold water. She thought I'd been poisoned and took me to the traditional healer. But when my condition got worse, she took me to the District Hospital in Essex Vale. At the hospital, I was prodded and pricked, and my blood siphoned off with long stainless-steel needles into glass syringes for all manner of tests. I stayed under observation for a while.

When I got better, I moved out of the main hospital building into one of the small concrete houses with asbestos roofing, cold cement floors. I had cornmeal porridge in the morning, *pap* with overcooked cabbage for lunch, and in the evening beef stew, served on aluminium plates. But I was sick most of the time and couldn't keep anything down, because of the medication they were giving me.

I don't recall how long I stayed in hospital, however, one thing stayed at the back of my mind: Ma did not visit me. I missed school and the routine that Salani and I had established.

When I was discharged, Grandma and I walked along a small path with red soil, parallel to the rail track, which glistened in the sun. We crossed over the railway bridge that straddled a very deep gorge, then over the railway line, straight into the calm of Essex Vale, with tarmacked roads, paved streets, and beautiful white buildings that had red terracotta roofs and beautiful front gardens. Essex Vale was home to the district commissioner's office, administrative assistants or DAs, and a significant population of Whites, many involved in farming, mining, and commerce.

As we approached a small café, White women were sitting on chairs drinking soft drinks on the veranda. Grandma wanted to buy us a small bottle of Fanta and a bun so we could share. That was our ritual whenever we took little trips. But, because we were Black, we had to make our purchase from a side window. When we turned the corner, we found Black men and women patiently queuing in the hot sun to buy refreshments.

For some reason, Grandma just grabbed my hand and whispered to me, 'Let's go home, son. We'll drink water when we get home.'

There was no hurt or dejection in her voice. She calmly held my hand, and we walked away. We walked for nearly ten kilometres in the blistering heat. Sometimes she carried me on her back, just to give me a little respite. Cars, mostly driven by Whites, zoomed past us. None of them offered us a lift. It was just the way things were. But, in hindsight, Grandma had taught me one of life's most important lessons: that when you're no longer treated with dignity, you walk away.

When we got back home, Grandma's version of the treatment commenced. Above the wall, between the rafters, hung mysterious objects, all wrapped up in old newspapers: odd shoes smoked and curled inwards, curios wrapped up in smoke-tinged old newspapers, and *ugwini*, her dry tobacco leaves. Most of the mysterious objects wrapped up in newspapers were remedies for unsettled stomachs.

And Grandma, ever the wind-whisperer, responded to any whiff of flatulence, including her own, with a well-rehearsed repertoire. Such was her obsession with our digestive systems, it even compelled her to inspect our stools. Following any speculative diagnosis of gut-rot, or giardiasis, an ominous bundle was retrieved from the rafter, sending cockroaches scattering all over the place. When the *Bulawayo Chronicle* finally revealed its contents, elephant root, carapace of rhinoceros beetle, and small dehydrated and contorted roots visible only to the discerning eye were all mixed and left to stew in water.

The length of the soak was determined by Grandma's diagnosis. Certain cases of gut-rot required much stronger concoctions.

Extreme cases demanded consultation with Makhalima or any of the self-proclaimed specialists.

So it was back to the boiled guava leaves, wild mint, bitter herbs, and a tincture of wild honey to ameliorate the bitterness. Any sign of laboured breathing, raised temperature, a random cough or listlessness warranted yet another diagnosis. I must admit that I sometimes feigned illness to avoid work or numerous tasks on Grandma's never-ending list of things to do.

Sometimes, she administered enemas, and that wasn't even the worst of her special treatments, which came with no warning!

'Thabani!'

'Ma!'

'*Buya lapha** – come, take off your pants!'

She sat with her back against the rondavel, all set up, holding a bright orange enema dispenser, the size and shape of a small tennis ball, filled to the brim with her ominous concoction. She plugged in the four-inch tip, asked me to lie over her lap then lifted her knees so that my bottom was hanging in the air. She inserted the cold tip of the enema tube up my bottom and squeezed in the warm liquid. And to stop me from running away before the medication took effect, she held me upside down by my ankles and shook me – vigorously. When she was satisfied that the concoction had taken full effect, and that I could no longer hold it in, she let me go. As I disappeared behind the bushes, I could hear her calling my sister:

'Gifiti! Gifiti!'

'Ma!'

---

* Come closer.

'Come!'

When I was done, I came back and fetched Grandma for a further inspection. And I surmised from her lopsided look that this was only the beginning. To make matters worse, Thoko, now in her teenage years, had refused the enema.

It was not for the first time that there had been a stand-off between her and Grandma. Infuriated by her intransigence, Grandma decided that we all had congestion. What kind, she didn't say. She tossed white granite rocks in the fire until they glowed red-hot.

Meanwhile, she disappeared with her small axe and when she came back, she was holding a thick bush of wild mint and leaves with pods from the eucalyptus tree. I watched as she transferred the hot rocks from the fire into a large metal basin, and then added the wild mint, eucalyptus leaves, and drops of Vicks VapoRub on top. She then added hot water over the rocks, which generated a ferocious steam. She threw a thick blanket over the basin and forced all three of us to go under the blanket and instructed us to hover our heads above the steam and to breathe normally.

But inside the blanket the steam was dangerously hot. I tried to breathe through the nose first, but the heat was just too much. And when I tried to breathe through the mouth, hot air hit the back of my throat and I retreated backwards and hid my head behind the basin. But I couldn't stay too close as the metal still felt too hot to the touch. My head collided with my sisters' kneeling right next to me.

As soon as Grandma noticed bottoms sticking out in the air, under the blanket, there was a swooshing sound, followed by a sharp pain on my bottom through the thick blanket. Our heads rose simultaneously, and we bumped against each other in the steamy darkness, which gave rise to a commotion under the blanket.

'Stay on your side!'

'No, you stay on your side!'

'Stop hiding under my dress!'

Grandma patrolled the periphery of the blanket, dispensing punishment with her stick.

'Grandma, you're hitting the wrong bottom! It's him – he is hiding under my dress!'

'I want you all to breathe normally for this to work!'

Voooop!

'Grandma, you're hitting *me* again!'

When Grandma finally removed the blanket, a stream of cold air kissed my face. As soon as she opened the door, I bolted outside. But I was too weak and dehydrated from diarrhoea and Grandma's steam treatment to go very far.

I got back to school after three weeks and joined Salani. We defaulted to our usual routine and worked twice as hard to avoid Mr Socks. Mr A. R. Socks, or Mr Ncube to our parents, came by his nickname because his trousers always hovered fifteen centimetres above the top of his socks. His other nickname was 'Busy Body', or simply 'BB', because he seemed to be everywhere. He had been in the school for so long he knew individual pupils' names, their siblings' and parents' names, and a whole litany of familial antecedents.

The initials A. R., although indelibly printed in our minds, remain an enigma up there with Grandma's real name and date of birth, which are still a mystery to me. It was the combination of A. R. Socks's name and initials that gave it a flair of sophistication and distance. The same arresting formula was adopted amongst our teachers: R. Sender, V. Gola, T. K. Khumalo, M. M. Mlambo, and so on.

You could hear A. R. Socks shouting across the school compound throughout the day. Whether he was disagreeing with a teacher over a matter, caning a pupil over lateness or castigating a parent for the misdemeanours of their child – it really didn't matter.

'Speak up! Speak up!'

To make matters worse, there was a standing rule that stipulated we should always speak in English. Except it was hard to conjure up words for things that did not exist in our world. Mentally, it was exhausting. Many of us kept silent and only spoke when spoken to, or in response to a teacher's question.

To go to the toilet, first, you had to raise your hand to gain Ms Khumalo's attention. We had a girl in our class. Her name was Proof. She was a very quiet, timid, and harmless little girl, who never bothered anyone. She seemed petrified most of the time, maybe she was dyslexic. But there was no such thing as dyslexia in our school: woe unto you if you were labelled a dunderhead: there was only one cure – the cane!

And when it was Proof's turn to humiliate herself, she coaxed her thin voice to get the teacher's attention.

'Excuse, Ms Khumalo.'

'Yes, Proof, how may I help you?'

'Please go to the toilet.'

'No thank you. *You* need to go to the toilet!' She animatedly illustrated her point by vigorously pointing at Proof.

'Now repeat that in the same way that I've taught you.'

'Excuse, Ms Khumalo.'

'Yes, Proof, how may I help you?'

'I go to the toilet.'

'How many times must I teach you to say the simplest of things in English? Am I wasting my time, class?'

'No, Ms Khumalo,' we sang in unison.

At that, Proof lost her confidence. She started fiddling with the sash on her uniform.

'Ms Khumalo, please can I go to toilet?'

This went on for a while, with Ms Khumalo trying to coax the right words out of Proof, and her trying to put words in the right order, compounded by the urgency to relieve herself. Meanwhile, she desperately crossed her legs and squeezed her thighs together. The rest of us just stared in amusement.

As her tongue stalled, she urinated right where she stood. Relieved, but completely soaked through with urine, she sat down. During recess, we helped her dry her underwear on the Christ-thorn flowers beneath the classroom window.

In our lives, humiliation served a purpose. Being forced to speak in a foreign language made us feel insecure, because without our language we were not free to be ourselves, to be our best.

So, when it was my turn to go to the toilet, I impatiently waved my hand. When Ms Khumalo ignored me, I desperately shouted and made a nuisance of myself.

'*Ms! Ms! Ms!*' and clicked my fingers to get her attention.

From her chair, she craned her neck upwards like a sloth disturbed from its slumberous repose.

'Yes, what is it, Thabani?'

'Toilet, please!' I shouted, totally ignoring the required etiquette.

'Yes, what about the toilet?' She gently lowered her glasses until they started to kiss the tip of her nose.

'Toilet!' I repeated, unapologetically.

'Look, don't waste my time!'

I reverted to our language: 'Ngicela ukuya etoileti.'*

She ignored me.

'What did I say you should say when asking to go to the toilet?'

'I've forgotten!'

The whole class burst out laughing, but I was in excruciating distress.

'It's no skin off my nose should you choose not to listen to what I teach you.'

'I really need to go! I can't hold back any longer!'

All eyes were on me. I grabbed my shorts, squeezing hard whilst I performed a jittery dance.

'Please, Ms!'

'You can urinate in your shoe for all I care!'

With that, I pressed the tip of my right shoe against the heel of my left shoe and wiggled my foot out. I picked up the shoe and immediately started urinating in it. A commotion ensued. Girls sitting closest to me started pointing at my penis, others in the furthest corner of the room stood on the benches and craned

---

* Can I please go to the toilet.

their necks to see what was going on. And the boys pulled each other and pounded the desks with their fists.

Ms Khumalo was shouting too, her voice a mere squeak above the cacophony of boisterous voices.

'Quiet! I said *quiet!*'

Sometimes, no matter how hard one tried, it seemed that the universe had preordained that, eventually, all roads led to Mr A. R. Socks's office.

His bombastic voice entered the classroom first. As soon as he appeared, pupils planted their backsides on the benches.

'What in the Lord's name is going on here?'

The question was not directed at anyone.

Ms Khumalo was shaking, unsure how to respond. Sometimes head teachers beat up teachers too.

When he saw me still standing, he covered the short distance between the door and the back of the classroom, in less than half a dozen strides.

He looked me up and down.

'Are you an animal?'

'No, sir,' I answered, slightly confused and petrified at the same time.

'Then why in the Lord's name have you urinated in your shoe?'

'Ms Khumalo said I could,' I responded brazenly.

'She said what?'

'Yes, she did!' I said as I pointed at her with equal vigour and zealousness.

He looked at me, then at her, then back to me with absolute incredulity written all over his face.

'And do you urinate in your shoes at home?'

'No, at home we use *turu*. Also, we don't have to ask in English to go to the toilet. We just go when we feel like it!'

'I see! And what is this *turu* thing you mention?'

The whole class burst out laughing.

Annoyed, he turned to Ms Khumalo.

'What is this *turu* business?'

Despite her big frame, she seemed to shrivel in size and simply shrugged her shoulders.

'You come with me!' He beckoned with his finger for me to follow him.

Mr A. R. Socks was never one to miss opportune moments for redress. In fact, he was always on the lookout for pupils walking around with hands in pockets, unauthorised eating on school grounds and laughing out loud. These were distinct and separate from the more obvious infractions such as lateness, being found in possession of things other than your own, legitimate or otherwise, and basking in the winter sun during lessons. Malingering, or generally being what he called *marudu*. The term was his own creation. It meant, simply, someone rude, uncouth, unkempt, and rebellious. In his world, a cosmic harmony prevailed. It only took a mere child to unravel it.

You could walk past him and think nothing of it, only to feel the sting of his cane.

Thwack! Thwack! Thwack!

'*Go and comb your hair!*'

Or: '*Pull up your socks!*'

I emptied my shoe of urine by tipping it upside down. When I put it back on, my left foot squelched as though it had been immersed inside a warm swamp. I quickly ran after him towards his office. As I walked past Ms Khumalo, I gave her a defiant look. She gave me an equally threatening look as if to say, 'Wait and you will see!'

When I finally made it to Mr A. R. Socks's office, I stood still, arms folded to the back.

'Do you know what a toilet is?'

I nodded 'yes' and pointed in the direction of the pit latrines for added emphasis.

'And now this is very important: do you know how to use them?'

'Yes,' I said, thinking what a silly question to ask.

'Good, I want to make sure that you understand what toilets are for, so that in future you don't have to relieve yourself into your shoe!'

'But Ms Khumalo told me to, sir!' I pleaded and tried hard to convince him of my innocence.

'Civilised people don't do that now, do they? Grab that bucket over there and follow me,' he commanded, his voice imbued with a resounding malice.

I trotted behind him as surreptitious stares burned the back of my head from the classroom. We were heading in the direction of the pit latrines. In my mind, I thought that all he wanted to do was show me how to use the toilet, which I thought would be very amusing.

'See that?' He pointed at the latrines with a smirk, whilst he vigorously pulled his trousers towards his ribs, up to a few inches from his nipples, exposing two different socks on each leg and a big bulge at the front of his trousers. 'I want them spotlessly clean! When you finish, come and fetch me.'

With that, he swivelled round and walked off. I could hear him clinking away by the sounds of things in his pockets: metal ruler – substitute for a cane – keys for the entire school, chalk, blackboard duster, and a hymnal tune on his lips. Later, I heard screams coming from the direction of the assembly point from malingering pupils fleeing from the wrath of his cane.

CHAPTER 9

The long-drop latrines sat on a red mound of earth, two metres above the ground. They were two rectangular structures, built from concrete breeze blocks, with L-shaped entrances at opposite ends, but no doors. To reach them, you had to walk up rudimentary concrete steps. A cloud of flies greeted me. Inside, there were small trenches, ten centimetres deep, five wide, indented in the concrete floor at the bottom of the wall, and these served as urinals. They were covered in a crusty yellowish substance. They stank of rotten eggs and old manure. And at the far end, individual holes on the concrete floor separated by short walls for privacy.

I surmised that I needed a lot of water. The only source of water was the borehole just outside of the school perimeter. I grabbed the bucket and made my way there. But when I reached to pull its elongated arm down, I was left dangling in the air.

Just then a dishevelled, vicious-looking woman arrived.

'What are you doing here?' she asked, her eyes curiously searching me for any obvious signs of mischief. When you were a child, adults always thought you were up to no good. Many took the whole notion of a village raising a child to extremes. It was not unusual for random strangers to drag children to the nearest tree and swiftly administer punishment.

'Fetching water,' I said.

'I see. Aren't you supposed to be in class?'

'Yes, but today I am cleaning toilets.'

'What? On your own?'

'Mr Socks said I must do it as punishment for urinating in my shoe.'

And then she looked at me with an open incredulity. With her hands akimbo, she asked me: 'And, did you?'

'Yes, I did. Ms Khumalo made me do it!'

'Look, you don't make sense. First, your teacher forces you to urinate in your shoe, yes? And as punishment she makes you clean the toilets. Why urinate in your shoe in the first place? What kind of schooling madness is this?'

'English,' I said.

'English indeed! Look,' she said, 'I am going to help you with the pump, but please leave before your English madness or whatever else is on your mind infects me too!'

With that, she fixed her loose head-wrap and grabbed the pump.

The borehole mechanism was old and rusted. It squeaked and belched at first, but once it got going fresh water gushed out of its snout.

I filled the bucket to the brim, but it was too heavy. Water spilled over my legs and shoes. I had no gloves, no mask or protective clothing, and I was using tree branches as a brush. It took at least ten trips to dislodge the filth from the floor.

When I finished, I grabbed the empty bucket and made my way to Mr Socks's office, but he'd long gone. The rest of the school compound was like a ghost town. Exhausted and hungry, I abandoned the bucket outside his office, and made my way home.

As soon as Grandma saw me, she yelled at me, 'Where have you been? I've been worried sick thinking you've been run over by a car crossing the road!'

When I got closer, she screwed up her face and sniffed the air like a hunting dog.

'What is that smell? Turn round,' she said. 'Did you just shit yourself?'

'No, I have been cleaning toilets all day,' I announced dejectedly.

'What do you mean *cleaning toilets*? Why were you cleaning toilets?'

'Mr Socks made me do it!'

'I send you to school to learn to read and write and they make you clean toilets? This man, what's his name again?'

'Mr Socks.'

'What kind of name is that?'

I shrugged my shoulders.

'Is he right in the head? My own child cleaning toilets? Does this man know who I am? *Mina ngingumuvu!** Take off your uniform right now!'

I took my uniform off and handed it over to her.

She brought it closer to her nose just to be sure.

'*Iyanuka! Iyanuka phu!* You pong! You pong!' she lamented.

She threw my uniform into a bucket full of hot soapy water and left it to soak. Meanwhile, she vigorously scrubbed me like I

---

* I am Muvu!

113

had an incurable skin disease, whilst muttering obscenities under her breath.

'I'll teach that clown something he'll never forget! Nobody makes my child, my own blood, clean toilets like a convicted murderer and gets away with it! Mark my words!'

When I got up in the morning, my uniform was ironed and ready. Grandma was ready for war. She looked as though she hadn't slept all night.

'Nobody, and I mean nobody, touches my child without my say-so!'

She scrubbed me furiously again.

When she'd calmed down, I told her all the juicy bits that would make her even more enraged.

'I had to go more than ten times all the way to the pump to fetch water. The bucket was too heavy, and the sun was very hot!' I added emphatically.

That renewed her ire.

'But you are a child! You're there to learn and not spend time cleaning toilets! I thought that education was supposed to improve people's way of thinking. Quite clearly, your head teacher is the biggest fool of them all!'

And then, 'They'll never lay hands on you again as long as there is still blood coursing through my veins, you hear me?'

And she continued, unabated.

'I was worried sick. Children disappear all the time. And all along they had you cleaning toilets. The nerve!' She clenched her teeth and grimaced.

When I was ready, I said to her, 'We'll be late. Mr Socks will be waiting for us by the gate with a stick!'

'Don't you worry about that useless man!' she reassured me. 'Today I want to show him that you're not an orphan, that he cannot make you clean toilets like you're nothing. And if he thinks that because I am an old woman, I am incapable of defending my family, he's wrong. They don't call me Muvu for nothing.'

Grandma's nickname was Muvu, a type of hornet that built its nest in the rafters and brought all types of insects to feed its young. It was ferocious when disturbed, and it defended its nest with all its might. Grandma was renowned for both: raising orphans and her willingness to use violence to defend her home. Once, and for reasons best known to her, Grandma knocked Khulu, her brother, unconscious when he became reckless and underestimated her strength. She upended him using elements of both speed and surprise. And he survived, courtesy of a neighbour's timely intervention. When he left, he staggered away, covered in blood.

She was frothing at the side of the mouth. Her grip on my wrist tightened. We walked at lightning speed towards school.

'And Ms Khumalo made me urinate in my shoe. I asked her several times if I could go to the toilet, and she wouldn't let me,' I added, deliberately omitting the bit about my failure to speak English.

She stopped, turned round, and looked at me.

'What do you mean urinate in your shoe? What kind of monsters are these?'

'I asked Ms Khumalo if I could go to the toilet, and she refused. She said I should use my shoe. And, when I did, that's when they made me clean all the toilets!'

'*All* the toilets?' Grandma asked with a slight incredulity in her voice.

'Yes, all of them, including the teachers'!' I nodded my head vigorously to stoke Grandma's already inflamed rage.

When we got to the school assembly area, Grandma pushed me forward.

'Go on, show me your teacher!'

I walked with trepidation towards Ms Khumalo, who looked back at me with terrified eyes.

Grandma tightened her headscarf, clenched her fists, and yelled: 'Why am I spending money on shoes for my child, so you can force him to urinate in them? Is this what you do all day? Treat our children like your worst enemies? Come back here, you overfed, lazy swine, and explain this to me!'

Ms Khumalo was wearing the kind of shoes that Ma wore when she went out drinking, what Grandma called whores' shoes. They were unsteady because they had thin, pointy heels, which didn't help because of Ms Khumalo's size. As soon as she saw Grandma walking towards her, she wobbled in between rows of pupils in the opposite direction, Grandma right behind her.

'Tell me why my grandchild is cleaning lavatories? We hand over our children to you so you can teach them and all you do is prepare them to be toilet cleaners, you lazy swine!'

In her attempt to escape Grandma, Ms Khumalo tripped on the small bricks embedded into the ground demarcating the spaces between lines for students of different grades, and toppled over into the grassy area, a metre or so below the assembly-point elevation.

'You spend precious time terrorising people's children and you can't even fight. Get up and come here so I can show you what a real fight looks like, you fat cur!'

And she was determined to follow through with her threats.

Just then Mr Socks intervened.

'*Hayi bo gogo**, what seems to be the problem?'

'Don't you dare speak foreign to me! You think that because you've read books, and wear a smart suit, you can abuse my grand-child? Is that what you think? You think you can hide behind that foreign language of yours?'

By now the whole assembly area was in complete disarray. Teachers and pupils alike had turned into willing spectators. There was uproarious laughter, necks craned, short pupils standing on their toes, heads squeezed between bodies. For the first time, Mr Socks lost his composure, completely disarmed by Grandma's simple truths.

'You think because you speak White man's language you are better than us? Well, we were here long before you, White men and their books arrived. We'll still be here when they are gone. And you will never, ever enslave our children like they do, by turning whole generations into toilet cleaners!'

'*Hayi bo mama*, I was trying to teach him a lesson!' Mr Socks pleaded, trying to convince Grandma of his pure intentions.

'Teach him a lesson? By making him clean toilets? Are you listening to yourself? Is that what they pay you for? You think my grandson doesn't know the smell of shit, huh? Where do you think they've been shitting all their lives? In your toilets? Teach our children to smell shit? We can do that ourselves, thank you!'

---

* Please calm down, Grandma.

There was a further uproar of laughter. The more courageous boys started whistling the way we did when there was a big impending fight.

As Mr Socks started walking backwards, the whole assembly followed the unfolding spectacle. When he inadvertently stumbled on a rock, he turned round and made huge strides towards his office where he barricaded himself in behind his closed door.

'Come out, you coward!' Grandma shouted triumphantly. 'If I ever hear about any of my grandchildren cleaning toilets, you'll hear from me. And I'll kill you with my bare hands!'

When she'd calmed down, she started to walk away, and I followed her.

She turned round and gave me the sternest of looks. 'Where do you think you are going?'

'Coming home with you,' I said, feeling exonerated.

'Who said you can come?'

'Well, I thought . . .'

'Thought what? That you'll spend all day doing nothing, dangling your balls like a cur? Next time come straight to me, not after you've covered yourself in excrement, you buffoon. You hear me? I thought I'd raised you properly. Now, go back in there and you might learn something!'

CHAPTER 10

As my war with Mr A. R. Socks scaled down, there was a rumour that there were talks in Geneva to resolve the war situation in our country. Many people believed that our oppressors were trying to cunningly disarm guerrillas and then annihilate them when they least expected it. Grandma commented on the fact that the so-called talks were being held in a foreign country behind closed doors. The sticking point seemed to be concern, mainly by Whites, of what would happen to so-called White-owned land after independence. But in our daily lives nothing had changed; all we had to do was wait to see how things turned out.

At home, the issue of my stomach had not yet been resolved; I was periodically sick. In hindsight, I can say that the trouble wasn't so much physical as it was psychosomatic, caused mainly by fear and anxiety and trying hard to stay safe in an environment where adults, instead of protecting us, posed the most serious threats to our lives.

It didn't help that we still drank untreated water. Although Grandma took me to traditional healers, nothing seemed to work. Grandma had heard, through word of mouth, that there was a Dr

Desai, an Indian doctor, in Bulawayo, who was very accommodating towards Black people, who could provide a second opinion. Besides, I still had not seen Ma since my release from hospital. Nor had she responded to Grandma's letters. So the possibility of seeing Dr Desai provided the pretext under which Grandma and I could ambush Ma.

On a Friday evening, 'I want you to heat up some water for a proper bath. We are going to town tomorrow morning,' she announced unexpectedly.

'Please can I come too?' pleaded Thoko.

'No, you cannot. You two must stay behind and look after things whilst I am gone. Besides, I don't want to leave him behind. God knows what he might do in my absence, this little swine!'

I stoked the fire and diligently watched the water as it came to a boil. When it was ready, Grandma used a kitchen towel to hold both sides of the pail, before emptying it into a larger basin. She mixed the hot water with the right amount of cold water until it stabilised into a nice lukewarm temperature. I undressed and gently slid into the basin.

Grandma scooped water on my head with both hands, and when I was sufficiently wet, she rubbed a small bar of detergent on my hair in a circular motion until she generated sufficient soapsuds. The suds trickled into my eyes, and when I protested, she slapped me behind the head.

'If you washed properly on a regular basis, then I wouldn't have to do this. You smell like a wild animal! I've never known anyone to detest water the way you do. I don't know who you take after!'

'But I swim in the river,' I said, still furiously rubbing my partially blinded eyes.

'Soaking your feet in water for two minutes is not the same as taking a bath!'

But I slept behind her every night, and she had never complained. Besides, she very rarely took a bath herself.

And then she grabbed a rough pumice stone and viciously scrubbed me with it.

And she kept repeating herself.

'And if you washed properly, I wouldn't have to do this!'

Or: 'This is for your own good, you hear me?'

'Yes, Grandma,' I said reluctantly.

'Besides, we don't want your mother to think that I am neglecting you, do we now?'

She stuck her fingernails in my ears, yanked me forward as she scrubbed me, paying particular attention to the elbows, knees, neck, and all the hard-to-reach areas hoarding sediments of dirt. Finally, she let me out after a quick rinse with cold water from a jug.

'Now that's better!' she said, sounding rather content.

I didn't answer, but rushed to the hearth, where I spread myself, naked, in front of the fire to my sisters' amusement. Grandma gave them the evil look: 'What are you giggling about? Now do something useful and empty the water outside before I scrub you both.'

The next day, we got up at the crack of dawn. I wore my Sunday best. Grandma combed my hair with the dreaded steel comb. And, because we were going to the city, she tied her money inside a handkerchief, which she put in a small purse, then into a plastic bag, which she hid inside a secret compartment of her special handbag with a rusty, contorted zip.

And when it came to pay for the bus ticket, she opened the handbag, went into the secret compartment, then untied the plastic bag and got stuck trying to untie the knot on the hand-kerchief to the consternation of the bus conductor.

'Now, now, Grandma! We haven't got all day. We've got better things to do than watch you fumble with your dirty handkerchief!'

She ignored him.

When she'd finally unravelled the knot, she retorted: 'Can't be too careful these days, what with all the thieves!'

And then she tied it again after paying for the tickets. When I suggested that perhaps I should put the money in my pocket, she slapped my hand.

I sat by the window and watched people, goats, and trees go past and disappear in the opposite direction. I watched the hills and the beautiful landscape roll by on either side of the road, and marvelled at the depth of the ravine as we made a steady climb up a very steep hill. There was an eerie silence in the bus; I feared the bus might tilt backwards. My ears were blocked as Grandma shouted, 'This is *Danger* – many people have died here!' and pointed towards the deepest side of the gorge.

Just then, I caught a glimpse of White people sitting on the pre-fabricated concrete tables and seats right by the edge of the cliff, enjoying a picnic. I could also see guns right by their side. Even in this most serene of landscapes, they still feared an ambush. And yet we had no guns, they had.

★

We survived *Danger* unscathed. Grandma pointed out to me the Nite Star Drive-in cinema complex, where Whites watched films from the confines of their cars at night. It was a different world from the dusty and noisy affair that was the Native Bioscope; everything seemed so devastatingly serene. Much more beautiful than Essex Vale. As we drove past Ascot Racecourse, there was a certain calmness. White picket fences surrounded short green lawns, there were trees with purple flowers and as we glided by Bulawayo Centenary Park I feasted my eyes on a gushing water fountain, tall palm trees, and flowers the likes of which I'd never seen before. Small clusters of White people sat on the grass whilst their children played around the water fountain, watched over by a coterie of Black nannies.

We were heading towards the bus terminus, Renkini, where hundreds of buses from all over the country converged. And as soon as we exited the bus, chaos reigned. Grandma firmly grabbed my hand as we bulldozed our way through the crowds. We walked past Ross Camp where I observed policemen coming in and out through the turnstile gates. We trudged along the red dusty, stony pavement, all the way to Lobengula Street, where we were accosted by young women wearing tight-fitting clothes, trying to entice Grandma into buying something. Instead, she clutched her tattered handbag, gave them a vicious stare, and we marched on.

'*Come in! Come in, customers!*'

Music was blaring from loudspeakers, with people and merchandise sprawled out on the pavement. And I could smell the oil and vinegar from the fish-and-chip restaurants. Grandma could sense that I was hungry; every time we walked past a restaurant, she yanked me forward and I almost lost my balance.

As we entered the city on foot, we walked past White people exiting exclusive Whites-only shops like Meikles and OK Bazaar. Some were holding hands, walking at a leisurely pace. It was noon, the end of the working day, the city almost calm. There were Rixi and Skyline Taxis parked diagonally against the pavement as we walked past City Hall, under the shade of tall palm trees surrounded by beautiful exotic flowers and shrubs.

When we arrived at Toppers, Ma's last known place of employment, the Indian man told us that she no longer worked there, but refused to divulge information about her whereabouts, though Grandma and I had no idea what he was saying most of the time. Everyone expected us to understand English in its various mutations, as if we were born speaking it. None made any attempt to speak our language. Even though most were guests in our country – Coloureds, Indians, Lebanese, Chinese, Greeks, and Italians – they very rarely, if at all, interacted with us. Everyone accepted their allocated space within these hierarchies of humiliation, so long as they were not Black, because being Black was the most hideous thing anyone could be.

Frustrated, we headed straight to Mkambo Market, to establish Ma's whereabouts through Grandma's network of informants. She said that anyone who has a mouth will never get lost. In a world full of obstacles intended to frustrate her, intuition was all she had.

Mkambo market was a world of intrigue, with an amazing array of curios: python skins, dehydrated roots, reddish-brown concoctions, black substances in calabashes, dried animal parts, and snake oils. Murderers, thieves, housewives, and the wretched all converged there, searching for the perfect talisman. Despite being a Christian, Grandma lived in constant fear of a multiplicity of gods who played havoc with our lives, and against whom we had to be protected. Sangomas*, self-taught healers, con men and outright scammers plied for trade.

Many a white-feathered chicken – for cleansing bad luck – and black-feathered chicken – for casting spells – was decapitated and the credulous victims doused with their blood to cure their maladies. But it was agreed by a consortium of Grandma's confidants that superstition didn't work on White people. Yet somehow their pubic hair was deemed invaluable in the whole alchemy of manufacturing luck. Quite how one acquired it, without breaking the law, remained a mystery. Within the same stalls amongst okra, pumpkin leaves, umfushwa†, idelele‡, guavas, catapults, amanyathela,§ and love potions, one could also find preserved human hearts. But they were not on display. Some things were best kept secret.

Grandma's enquiries led us to Thokozani Flats in Mzilikazi township. It was a short walking distance from the market across the bridge over the Mazai River¶. After knocking on several doors,

---

* Traditional healers.
† Sun-dried green vegetables.
‡ A type of green leafy vegetable (abundant during the rainy season) which is slimy when cooked and whose consistency is like okra, but it is a different plant. Only its leaves are edible, and it does not have pods like the okra plant.
§ Sandals with soles made from disused tyres, worn mainly by poor people.
¶ The river runs past Belmont, Steeldale industrial sites, and Thorngrove Sewage Treatment Works. And because it is heavily polluted with industrial effluent and sewage, it smells like a rotten egg which is where the name Mazai (eggs) derives from.

we identified Ma's flat on the first floor. When she opened the door, her taciturn, sour look announced that she was not pleased to see us. It was a frosty reception. I hid behind Grandma just in case things took a nasty turn.

I understand now that our mother had us when she was very young. She was a single mother trying hard to make ends meet, still grieving the loss of her parents, whilst trying to live the life of a young woman in her prime in the city. It was as if we were a constant reminder of her mistakes, and yet I never heard her expressing any regrets about having us.

'We just thought we'd come and visit, seeing as you haven't bothered responding to any of our letters!'

When Grandma mentioned 'our letters' Ma looked at me as though silently accusing me of something more ominous than simply drafting polite ransom notes.

'Mama, I was busy working. And, as you can see, I've recently moved address,' declared Ma with the hostility of someone unnecessarily disturbed from an afternoon snooze.

'What? So you think hiding from your responsibilities is going to make them disappear? Children just don't vanish. Once they're out, they're out. You can't push them back. You should have thought about that before giving birth to them!'

'No, I am not hiding from my responsibilities, Mama. I just moved address and I didn't think it urgent to inform you. Besides, I wasn't expecting you to just turn up at my doorstep. But, quite clearly, I was wrong!'

'Ah, well, life goes on,' responded Grandma, unabashed. 'And your children need feeding, which is why I am here.'

She totally neglected to mention my stomach problem or Dr Desai.

Whilst they argued, I stood by the window and observed other children on the swings across the road. I asked Ma if I could go outside and join them.

'Don't go too far, and don't get your clothes dirty. You are going back home tonight!'

I thought her announcement was more for Grandma's benefit than it was mine.

I ran across the road towards the swings, located an unoccupied one, and secured it. I removed my shoes and stood on the metal seat, with my toes wedged into the corners where the vertical chains met the seat. I held the chains to steady myself, bent my knees slightly and jerked the swing backwards and forwards to gain momentum. As the swing carried me higher and higher, I could see the city from above. I watched girls jump over hopscotch grids, dresses pinned to the side, bent toes corralling smooth pebbles into small squares drawn in the sand with small sticks. They hopped, jumped, skipped, and twisted in the air. Their faces hardened with concentration, lost between squares, dust, and township dreams.

I watched the Lyons Maid ice-cream man in his starched red-and-white finery. At the sound of his bell, small black dots appeared from behind the hedges, and swarmed him. They walked away, tongues tinged red, blue-green, and yellow by ice lollies.

Out of the corner of my eye, I caught sight of the silver-grey Lobels van, ferrying bread and confectionery as it took corners at speed. Tower lights and electricity pylons pointed towards a blue sky.

Close by, I watched the sluggish, oily flow of the Mazai River, its water tinged black-green by the mixture of algae and raw sewage.

It was just before sunset, and the earlier heat had given way to a nice cool breeze. The township was coming alive with people taking a stroll after a hard day's work. From the height of the swing, I could see a man creeping like a cautious hunter behind a couple holding hands, taking a lovers' stroll. At first, I thought that it was a game that adults played, until I saw a blinding light from a metallic object rise above the heads of the couple. Then I heard two sounds in quick succession. The first was that of something breaking, like an old tree branch snapping. The shiny object rose again and fell swiftly. The second was a violent scream as the man's legs buckled underneath his body weight. The rest of his body, seemingly uncoordinated, swayed until he fell right where he'd been struck. The girl, who earlier had been holding his hand, took off, and disappeared through the maze of milk-tree hedges.

I inadvertently let go of the swing and hit the ground at full speed, grazing my knees, elbows, and forehead. I grabbed my shoes and ran towards the commotion, bulldozing my way through the dense crowd until I could see with an indisputable certainty that the man had died. The blade had cut all the way to the beginning of the neck, splicing his head wide open, like two partially ripe half-melons. When, finally, his lifeless body came to rest on the tarmac, the blade dislodged itself. It had been crafted from a big piece of heavy metal, the shape of a scalene triangle, with the broad end sharpened into a deadly weapon. The man had stood no chance.

As more and more people gathered, the dead man's assailant

retreated as the crowd turned on him. In his haste to flee, he tripped and fell backwards, with stones, bricks, and bottles bouncing off every part of his body. There was no longer any panic in his eyes; he smiled the way a dying man was not supposed to smile.

When the baying mob had finished with him, someone had left a knife sticking out of his temple. A man, barefoot, stamped on his head, pulled the knife out and, without a care in the world, wiped it on the grass, folded it, and placed it in his back pocket. Then he left.

Shaken, I ran home to tell Ma and Grandma. They jointly berated me for watching men die. I said that I'd had no choice because when I first saw the whole thing, I thought they were playing.

Ma gave me a glass of fizzy Fanta and a sweet bun, but I could not erase the dying man's desperate look from my head. Suddenly, I lost all appetite.

And then Grandma simply said, 'Go and wash your hands and face. We have a bus to catch!'

We left. There was no embrace, just a hard, cold goodbye. Grandma and I caught our bus home as dusk fell and as the towers came alive with fluorescent light.

It was the first time that I saw two men die, up close. I was eight years old.

So, no Dr Desai.

CHAPTER 11

The following week, I went back to school. It was still hard for me to process what I'd witnessed in the city. I was in a dream-like haze. It was Grandma who shook me awake from the grip of night terrors.

And, since the toilet scandal, I tried to keep away from Mr A. R. Socks. My ears had become attuned to his movements: the jingling of the keys, heavy footsteps. But, in haste to get to school on time, and with everything else happening around me, I recklessly washed the front of my legs and missed the back, leaving behind a patchwork of dry skin. When I combed my hair, I neglected an area of undisturbed shrub land on my crown. But my uniform was pristine and ironed, courtesy of Grandma, who used the same technique she'd employed whilst ironing Grandpa's chef's uniform. With my shoes polished, I was beaming with pride. When I arrived at the assembly, Mr A. R. Socks was his usual energetic self.

His daily inspections began once we settled down. And when I felt his footsteps behind me, I straightened up, pushed out my chest and fronted the countenance of a soldier on parade. As he circulated me, my heart started pounding. Right there and then, he hauled me to the front of the assembly.

'Look how smart this boy is!'

Feeling slightly relieved, I relaxed my shoulders a little.

'And what does he do, I ask myself?'

And then he answered his own question.

'He doesn't wash properly. What's worse, he doesn't even bother combing his hair!'

Just then Thoko's voice entered my head. 'It won't be me he'll come looking for if you don't comb your hair!'

I really should have taken her advice. But it was too late.

'*Foolishness is bound in the heart of a child; but the rod of correction shall drive it far from it!*'

Without further ado, he walloped the back of my head twice with his monstrous bible. I stumbled forward, and nearly fell over. Humiliated, I scuttled back to my position in line. I became the butt of jokes for the rest of the week.

But, despite the vicissitudes of war, at school I was making good progress. I came top of my class. My favourite subjects were English and Ndebele Composition. I liked the freedom of creating stories. Grandma's fables, the plays we listened to on Mr Likwa's wireless radio and the everyday happenings in our lives, which at times felt surreal, were my inspiration.

We took school trips too and visited the tomb of Cecil John Rhodes. We were taught that Cecil Rhodes was the founder of our nation, that before he arrived there was no country, except wildlife, rivers, and trees. But Grandma would say that without the back-breaking work, sweat, tears, and generosity of Black people, Rhodesia could never have been what it was.

We visited Chipangali Wildlife Orphanage, where we saw elephants and lions feed, venomous snakes too. Whilst there, I surreptitiously strayed from the main group, and visited a monkey cage. The monkeys were engaged, curious, almost human-like. I gave them sweets, but then I started teasing them with the last one. Eventually, one of them lost its temper. It scratched me across the face. I was standing too close, despite being given specific instructions not to do so. That was the highlight of the trip. I was teased all the way home on the school bus.

But the event of the school calendar was the annual visit by Whites from the Department of Native Affairs. The White inspectors were there to make sure that we were receiving the *right* education. There was a reason why we were not being taught our own history: the Rhodesian education system was designed to stifle the ambition of Black children, who could only legally start school at the age of seven, while White children began at five. Black children were deemed to be educationally subnormal, less intelligent. Ours was an identity that carried preconceptions – always, everywhere.

After leaving school, many Blacks couldn't read or write or articulate themselves well enough, *in English*, to get meaningful jobs. The education system in Rhodesia was only ever meant to produce a certain type of Black person: docile, compliant, unquestioning. And when Whites spoke to their employees or Blacks in general, they used a special language called Chilaphalapha, or kitchen *kaffir*, which was no language at all but a set of instructions – *bisa lo!** *Hamba lo!*† – in much the same way that one might encourage a dog to fetch a stick. Overall, it stifled conversation and negated meaningful interaction between the races.

On the days preceding the visit, Mr A. R. Socks had not been himself. He seemed consumed by something bigger than this world.

I shared my concern with Salani who looked at me. 'We have *spekshin* soon.‡ The White people are coming – that's why!' he said jubilantly. That to me sounded rather ominous, like an imminent invasion. Because to us Whites were the overseers of a harsh, cruel system. They were ghosts who came into our homes in the middle of the night, and at dawn we heard the shrill cry of devastation.

Even at school, we couldn't avoid their cold, calculated White gaze.

'And when is this happening?'

'Today after assembly. Oh, and Mr Socks said that we should all be on our best behaviour. He doesn't want us to embarrass our school in front of special guests!'

I wasn't sure about that. These visits didn't always go as planned.

The classroom door opened, and a cloud of perfume wafted into the room, followed by our class teacher, Ms Khumalo.

---

* Bring that here!
† Go away!
‡ We have an inspection soon.

She put her bundle of books, her small cane, and a bottle of Fanta on the desk before leaning on it.

'Good morning, class. How are you today?'

She had a way with the English language. She was free to move in this other world with ease, as if she spoke English all day and night at home.

'Good morning, Ms Khumalo. How are you today?' we answered in unison.

'I am fine, thank you.' And then she signalled for us to sit.

'Today we have White visitors!'

A wave of excitement erupted across the room. Even club-foot Alfred had a glint of excitement in his dull eyes.

'Calm down! calm down!' she said. 'Now, I want you to be on your best behaviour. If you need to use the toilet, please do so now!'

There were no takers.

'Our guests won't be here for a while. So, before they arrive, I want us to rehearse "Little Jack Horner", just so we're comfortable reciting it. Also, I want you to start reciting it as soon as our guests enter the room, but not until I raise my hand!'

This was highly unusual. When White people visited us, we just sang and danced for them. Conversely, they pretended to enjoy our dreadful singing even though they had no idea what we were singing about. Mostly, they seemed bored, but then we never knew what they were thinking.

We nodded our little heads in agreement and cleared our throats.

Little Jack Horner,
Sat in a corner,
Eating a Christmas pie.
He pushed in his thumb,
And pulled out a plum,
And said, 'What a good boy am I!'

'And again!' shouted Ms Khumalo.

We didn't know who Jack Horner was. Or what a Christmas pie was. The only plum we knew was *umqokolo* or *kaffir* plum. The *kaffir* plum was small, slightly bigger than the wild grape. The tree was hardy and replete with thorns. Years later, I can see that even the size and quality of fruit validated who we were inside. And it seemed that we could never overcome the curse of our Blackness. We were tethered to this past, which sought always to magnify our limitations, never our talents. From very early on in our childhood, we were being programmed to recognise the inviolability and sacredness of White lives, but never our own. We were encouraged to willingly accept what diminished our dignity, and to embrace our own subjugation, forever hidebound by a convention to devalue ourselves.

As soon as we heard the car engine, we knew that the Whites had arrived. To Ms Khumalo's dismay, we dropped the chorus and kept our eyes glued to the windows overlooking the visitors' parking bay.

'*Bona amakhiwa, bona amakhiwa!* Look at the White people!' Chubby fingers pointed at the ghostly figures as they exited their cars, heading towards Mr A. R. Socks's office.

Soon after, a White woman entered the room. We stood up and

burst into chorus. As she motioned for us to sit down, we looked at our teacher for confirmation, but she surreptitiously flicked her hand up, which indicated that we should remain standing. Confusion reigned; our eyes darted between the White woman and our teacher.

On close inspection, the White woman looked like an aberration: pale, translucent skin, replete with moles and a paper-thin nose. I wondered how she managed to breathe. She was holding a small handbag in the hook of her elbow. Her form was rigid, and unwelcoming. She smiled, the way White people smiled, when there was no reason for it. We avoided her gaze because it was considered a mark of disrespect for Blacks to look at a White person in the eye. There were other things that adults had to do too: men had to cross to the other side of the road at the approach of a White woman or take off their hats in obeisance to White men. We used different toilets, restaurants, buses, and shops, all because Whites feared contamination.

The White woman was not close enough for me to confirm that White people smelled too. There was a rumour that they didn't scrub properly, and that they smelled like sugar ants, in the same way that Whites claimed we exuded a distinct *kaffir* smell.

But the visit had ruffled our teacher disconcertingly. She spoke as though she was tossing around hot food in her mouth, whilst she tried to regain her composure under the stern gaze of the White woman.

Behind her stern gaze, the White woman tried to engage with us.

'Good morning, children,' she said.

Chorus: 'Good morning!'

But we didn't know what to call her. Perhaps madam would suffice. The same way we were required to refer to every White woman, including little White girls. In our world, they had no names, but they were all as equally important. Conversely, they called us *kaffirs,* because in their world we all looked the same. We had no intrinsic human value except as servants. Grown men were boys, grown women, girls. Black children of all ages were *piccaninnies*.*

'How are you today?'

Chorus: 'Fine, thank you,' we sang, amused that we were finally speaking English to a White person.

And then she asked, 'What is it you like best about school?'

We did not understand the question. Everything we did was by rote. Open questions were off script. After several futile attempts to engage with us, she knew it was pointless. We were worlds apart, manifest in the separate languages that we spoke and the ways in which we lived.

As soon as the White inspector left the room, Ms Khumalo unleashed her rage on us for failure to understand what she

---

* The picaninny was the dominant racial caricature of Black children: bulging eyes, unkempt hair, red lips, with mouths wide enough to stuff slices of watermelon – hence the racist expression, melon smiles. It also justified the systemic neglect of their needs as they were seen as 'wild', shrewd, cunning, impervious to pain, and wise beyond their young age. This persists and has evolved into what sociologists call the 'adultification of Black children', a form of racial bias where Black children are treated as adults; are subjected to harsh discipline regimes from authority; with their needs neglected both in education and healthcare settings. And are more likely to be arrested, imprisoned or both.

deemed a simple enough question. She made us stand for the rest of the lesson until break time.

But speaking in English was hard for us, because, first, we had to formulate the questions in our own language, in our heads, and then convert the answer into English. A bit like mental arithmetic under duress. That took time and ingenuity, and it made us come across as less intelligent. And yet the same demand was not placed on White children to speak indigenous languages.

Days later, I conjured up a plan to avenge our humiliation on the day of the visit. Ms Khumalo had the habit of sending me on numerous errands, which I detested. As expected, she sent me to the shops to buy her Stone's Ginger Beer and scones for her elevenses. On leaving the store, I decided to take a bite of one of the scones. And, using my teeth, opened the drink and took a swig before replacing the bottle top. On the way back I concocted a watertight story as a riposte to any accusations of theft.

And before Ms T. K. Khumalo could say anything, I ambushed her.

'The shopkeeper sends her sincerest apologies,' I said unashamedly. 'They've recently had a terrible infestation of rats!'

This might have gone some way in explaining the half-eaten scone, but not the drink. This wasn't helped by the other pupils on similar errands who'd brought back their merchandise still intact.

Ms Khumalo gave me an inscrutable look and said, with a flat voice devoid of anger whatsoever, 'Not to worry. These things happen. I'll just throw away the drink and bun. Surely, we cannot be expected to share drinks with rats!'

I desperately hoped that she would hand them over to me for disposal, but she didn't.

Instead, she scribbled something on a piece of paper and handed it over to me.

'Go and give this to Mr Socks. Tell him it's urgent.'

Just as I walked out of the room, she cut a soft, knowing smile.

I immediately went to Mr A. R. Socks's office and gave him the note.

When he read it, he threw a throaty chuckle, and bubbled uncontrollably with a worrying self-satisfaction.

'Such cunning rats indeed,' he said, 'with teeth as strong as humans', hands as equally strong and dexterous, and minds as cunning as those of seasoned thieves! Tell me, did you say rats opened the bottles with their teeth?'

He then asked me to explain what happened one more time. Which I did, with all the necessary embellishments, including the pregnant nun crossing the road, the apologetic shopkeeper, poor storage facilities, and more. But, no matter how fantastical, the tall tale wasn't convincing, and Mr A. R. Socks was never one to entertain any impudent rigmarole. He instructed me to bend over, and for my troubles I received ten lashes across the buttocks. And, contrary to my original intention, which was to avoid running errands in the first place, I was summoned to his office daily to do just that.

CHAPTER 12

After school, I enjoyed hobbies of my own – that is, if Grandma didn't catch me first. Behind our house, there was a small hill with a mouth-shaped cave. One afternoon, I crawled to the top of it, from where I could see the whole village sprawled out in front of me: rugged terrain, outcrops of rock and a sprinkling of mud huts. From up there I could also see Phani's house, built with real bricks, on uneven ground. His father, Mr Likwa, was a rich, educated man. He wore expensive safari suits, the kind we saw White men wearing. When he was around, his boisterous voice boomed with a sprinkling of big English words, even when he talked to Grandma, who, most of the time, had no idea what he meant. It was at his house where I'd first heard the voice.

As Grandma would say, no one can fully express their pain in another's language. There were things far too complex in our world for which there were no words in our own language, let alone in another's – in the same way that there were trees that had been brought from foreign lands by White men, for which we had no indigenous names. In our eyes, they were just weeds that blemished our landscape.

But, despite his education, Mr Likwa brutalised his first wife till she fled. He had remarried a much younger woman straight from the city. She was the stepmother from hell, who terrorised his children from the first marriage, hoping that they too would leave and follow in their mother's footsteps.

When it rained, I watched his young wife as she tiptoed around in her stilettos, arms spread out to the sides as if she was afraid she'd step on something very delicate: snail, millipede or the silver two-headed snake*. I watched her as she fastidiously groomed herself like a fly before she slowly sauntered to the Growth Point. She came back with half a loaf of bread and a family-sized bottle of Fanta and sat in the shade to enjoy the feast alone.

Afterwards, she harangued Phani relentlessly.

'Phani!'

'Ma!'

'Don't insult me – I am not your mother! What are you doing in the kitchen? Stealing food?'

'No.'

'No what?'

'I am not stealing food; I am filling up the water container like you asked me to.'

'Are you telling me that that's all you've done all morning? Because if you are, you need to get a move on, and fetch firewood

---

* Brahminy blind snake (*Indotyphlops braminus*). A fossorial snake commonly found in Africa and Asia. They are non-poisonous and their colour ranges from silver-grey to a light-yellow beige. Their head and tail look similar; which is why it is generally believed that they have two heads. In isiNdebele mythology their appearance augurs calamity.

so I can start preparing the evening meal. I am not feeding you until all work's done. Nobody eats for free in this world, that includes you!'

'Yes, Ma.'

Once, Phani ran away from home. I guess he couldn't take it anymore. When he came back, she bound his feet with the inner tube of a bicycle tyre which disrupted the flow of blood. I told Grandma when I hadn't seen him move for days. And it was Grandma who finally forced his stepmother to untie him. But by then he had monstrous blisters covering his feet as if he had been exposed to the most searing heat.

And when I watched him, he was all alone, his world confined to his feet. And yet he was surrounded by grown-ups. Grandma, too, saw him slaving away in the blistering heat. She could hear him too, while he choked, coughed, and sneezed from starting early morning fires. Daily, she saw him run endless errands: gathering firewood, fetching water, going to the shops. Now that he shuffled like an old man, it took him all day just to fill the repurposed oil drum with water, while his stepmother sat in the shade and complained about the heat.

'How are you, my child?' Grandma would say.

'I am all right, Grandma,' he'd reply obediently, but he never stopped.

Grandma sometimes spoke to Phani's stepmother over the fence. They shared news of the war: who had been killed where and details of those who'd been kidnapped. But she neither asked, nor pleaded with her to stop abusing Phani.

And now that he no longer wailed, no matter how bad the beating, all I could hear was his stepmother's incessant, waspish voice, the doors banging and the tinny clatter of pots and pans. But, strangely enough, it felt as though I was with him, and I went up there just to hold his hand, if only from a distance, because Grandma had said that if you wounded one of us, you wounded all of us. And that it took a village to raise a child.

Occasionally, Grandma lamented the plight of the boy whilst she shared snuff with Masuku, our neighbour. I could hear them say that God was watching. But Phani's house was a stone's throw away, and yet neither of them crossed the footpath that led to his house to save him. They found it difficult to look beyond their own scars.

And the violence wasn't just confined to Phani's house. Adults everywhere treated violence as if it was an inescapable part of who we were.

Elsewhere, Whites became more aggressive, crueller. I guess what infuriated them the most was our audacity to hope, our failure to turn the other cheek as we'd been beaten into doing: Blacks had decided to take a stand and fight back. The purge started from within our communities. A new word entered our shared lexicon – *sell-outs**: the soldiers, policemen, administrators, teachers, and those who propped up the racist White regime and wrought terror in our communities were burned alive inside their homes. For many Whites, the retaliation of Blacks and the

---

* There were different types of sell-outs, collaborators, or snitches depending on context. At times ordinary people were deemed sell-outs if they provided information or assistance to the soldiers, worked directly or indirectly for the Rhodesian government or did anything arbitrary to impede the revolutionary goal of freeing Blacks from racist White oppression.

extreme violence were a form of moral whiplash, and the tremors from the explosions of landmines sent shock waves that they could not ignore. It was the eruption of the repressed violence that Whites had nurtured, curated, for so long.

I was in fourth grade when Grandma and I started writing letters to Ma. I had a penchant for language, for second-guessing what Grandma wanted to say; I had spent so much time with her that I had inherited her idioms. As soon as I could read, I instantly recognised Ma's handwriting because everything seemed joined together as if she was struggling to breathe as she tried, unsuccessfully, to convince Grandma how tough things really were, that sometimes she needed to be subsidised. Grandma openly castigated Ma through her excoriating soliloquys, for my benefit. I carried the letters in my head for days since they took time to compose in Grandma's language.

'What kind of a woman abandons her children, tell me? Even the worst kind of whore knows when she must feed her children. Men and alcohol, that's all they ever think about, which is why they have fatherless children in the first place. This would never have happened in my day. Never! Women keeping their legs wide open like taxi ranks! Pass me that hoe and go and get my snuff pouch from my apron, will you? I've only got a week's worth left if that. God knows how I'll survive this. Only God knows!'

With an unshakeable fervour, Grandma disliked women who drank. Her own disposition towards tea, sugar, tobacco, and violence aside, she was adamant that drinking alcohol was the worst thing that could ever happen to a woman.

And then she would turn to me.

'You know what the problem is with that mother of yours? She can't just say no to men. Next time she comes here with another child, she can keep it. Oh, yes, she can keep it! As for the men, they are worthless dogs. They go from woman to woman. Lord knows what they're looking for. Your grandfather slept right next to me every night. When he wasn't here, he was chopping firewood or mending the fence or fishing. Oh, he was a real man, all right! And, as for you, when you grow up, no smoking or drinking or womanising like your father, that useless cur! And stay away from whores. You hear me?'

'How will I know if a girl is a whore?'

And then she would turn against me. 'Who asked you to join in my conversation? And what kind of stupid question is that? Have I not taught you anything? Sometimes I wonder why I waste my time trying to teach you how to be a man. In any case, who asked you? Answer me before—'

'But, Grandma, you said—'

'When are you going to learn that when I am talking all I want is for you to listen? Go and find other boys to play with so they can teach you how to be a real man. Now go before I do something I'll later regret!'

'But, Grandma, I am helping you with digging!'

'Who said I can't dig on my own? Tell me, am I a cripple? What do you think I was doing all those years before you were born?'

Despite her barrage of insults, I did not leave. I stayed till she calmed down. And when she ran out of insults, she called me as if she'd forgotten that I was standing right next to her.

'Thabani!'

'Ma!'

'Go and fetch paper and a pen. We need to write a letter to that mother of yours!'

As I detached the double page right at the centre of my school exercise book, knowing full well that I'd pay for it, Grandma sat down cross-legged on bare ground, and fetched her tobacco pouch from the big pocket on her apron that somehow managed to hold everything. She took a pinch of snuff, placed it inside the palm of her hand and sifted it between her forefinger and thumb. She stared into space as if she was reading someone's fortune.

'I want you to write exactly as I say. No lies, you hear me?'

'Yes, Grandma.'

But, as soon as I started to write, she'd stop me. 'Repeat that to me!'

So I read back to her: 'My beloved daughter!'

'*Ahaaa*, good boy! Don't forget to mention sugar and mealie-meal. This war is going to kill us all, what with the rising cost of living!'

She scooped the remnants of old tobacco from the inside of her mouth and cast them viciously towards the wooden fence behind us as chickens dashed towards the brown sludge, thinking it was food, only to turn away in disappointment.

'Stop, what does that say? I want you to make clear that things are getting tougher, what with the war sanctions! You hear me?'

Grandma had an amazing propensity for exaggeration and detail. I knew that when she kept asking me to read out loud to her, she was trying to catch me out. As I wrote, she pondered every sentence until she was satisfied with our joint fabrication. Sometimes it was hard to make an accurate inventory of

Grandma's foibles and caprices. One minute she could be kind and, the next, unbearably cruel. She could bring a room full of laughter to a standstill if she chose. And those who lacked confidence shrank involuntarily just from her stern look. Even so-called strong men approached Grandma with trepidation. She could reduce them to a tiny speck without so much as a word.

But being able to read opened my eyes to a whole new world beyond Grandma's fables.

CHAPTER 13

Swathes of time passed in this greyness of war. As war intensified, guerrillas started closing schools, clinics, and hospitals.
They kidnapped pupils and teachers and herded them across the
border into neighbouring countries where they trained them as
combatants. But many of the children didn't make it; Rhodesian
soldiers ambushed and killed them. Whites' desire to win the
war at all costs meant that they were willing to sacrifice innocent
Black civilian lives.

Every war has its own myths. Black nationalists had long
convinced the Black masses that guerrillas were impermeable to
bullets. As Whites vied to control the narrative of the war, they
sought to prove, once and for all, that guerrillas were not immune
to bullets. A ramped-up body count was the only way they could
convince themselves that they were winning the war.

It was then that government soldiers started to bring dead
bodies straight to the Business Growth Point. Black children were
being exposed to trauma daily.

War left behind holes that were impossible to fill. Grandma
would say we do not relinquish our dignity in death. War had a

mind of its own, and its purpose was to rip us apart, and to disrupt. She said that the White soldiers were far too young to be meddling in death. It was hard to fathom, she said, whether they truly understood the consequences of their actions. Death was far too big for any one of us to carry by ourselves. Instead, we should always seek to understand why things happened, because we were all responsible for the lives that were taken.

However, there was no obvious sadness in the eyes of the White soldiers. We were confounded as to why they'd want to display mutilated bodies in front of us children. We watched as they stood with triumphant glee over dead bodies. Their victims were child soldiers and civilians who had been ambushed. After all, soldiers got paid extra money per body.

Thousands of soldiers on foot descended upon us, their faces daubed in warpaint. Daily, we saw hundreds of trucks heading to the eastern highlands where fighting was at its most intense. The smell of diesel permeated the air; time slowed down. Wind ruffled the sails on the water tanks trailing behind the trucks. The mood was sombre; guns were at the ready.

Sometimes it was animals, not soldiers, who were destined for slaughter, their skins tightly compressed at the back of the trucks, terrified eyes bulging, pink nostrils pressed against the iron railings. They'd come back as frozen carcasses, destined for the Cold Storage Commission to feed the war.

In the not-too-distant past, trucks heading to the eastern highlands would have been empty, but laden with hope. And when they came back they would've been laden with papaya, wild guavas, mangoes, and overripe tomatoes. Now the same trucks brought nothing but death.

The trucks had mammoth engines, and V-shaped underbelly hulls for deflecting shrapnel from landmines. Some were designed to traverse rugged terrain like spiders on wheels. Even their thick bottle-green windscreens were bullet- and blast-proof. They were all named after dangerous wild animals and serpents: cheetahs, pumas, mambas, crocodiles, and honey badgers. Occasionally, they had disarmingly innocuous names such as eland, a type of antelope, or *pookie*, a night-time ape.

White soldiers remained inside these vehicles, but their camouflage was just an illusion. We knew fear; we could see it in their eyes. When we waved at them, they wouldn't wave back. The trucks picked up speed, and the last of the White faces, daubed in shoe polish, vanished in the distance. We would wait for them to come back; when they did, the trucks would be damaged beyond recognition. Their hollow, charred remains were carried on the backs of recovery lorries. The damage was irreparable; no one would speak of the spectre of the missing. Yet we never saw the dead bodies of White soldiers on display.

To survive meant negotiating obstacles just to get through the day. If it wasn't soldiers looking for guerrillas in our homes, then it was the various groups of armed men out to terrorise just about anybody they could find: reservists, district assistants, police officers.

Despite the curfew, my sisters still had to fetch water from the river, gather firewood, and write their homework in semi-darkness. They prepared supper as soon as they got home from school, cleaned the dishes, and by sunset the fire was out and we were huddled in Grandma's tiny hut, with the shaky wooden door all that stood between us and the warring factions outside.

Every bark of the dog, every cough, smell of cigarettes, sound of boots, filled us with trepidation. The war was getting perilously close every day. It was as if the walls and trees had suddenly developed ears. A distrust ran so deep that it was hard to discern who the real enemy was.

At night, Grandma removed her headdress; exposing her grey hair was a defence mechanism – her camouflage. Because as soon as soldiers or guerrillas saw her hair, they usually left us alone. We lived on the edge of our nerves.

To pass time and to counteract the fear of war, my sisters and I took turns to read chapters from a book that Thoko brought from the mobile library for Blacks: Ukuthunjwa kukaSukuzukuduma*. It was the story of a boy who had been kidnapped and how he never forgot his home, his language, his culture, his people.

We embraced the book because it was written in our own language. As one of us read, the kerosene lamp dimmed just so, Grandma was attentive, quiet, engrossed.

We read a chapter a night. In between, I conjured up what would happen next, as characters came alive in my head while I headed home after school. Sometimes, my sisters and I crawled under the barbed wire and listened to the news on Mr Likwa's radio next door. To get there was a quick dash across no man's land. And we risked being shot every time we ventured out in the dark. We gathered around the small wireless radio in total silence. And then the voice broke into the airwaves, a slow, deliberate monotone:

---

* Geshom M. P. Khiyaza, *Ukuthunjwa kukaSukuzukuduma* (Bulawayo: Mambo Press, 1978)

Pambeeri ne Hondo!
Forward with the people's war!
The gallantry of our soldiers!
Down with imperialism!
Zimbabwe *ichauwa!*
Our victory is certain!

If the aim of racism was to make us feel incomplete, insecure, unsure, then the war of liberation was our ultimate sacrifice to free ourselves from tyranny. There were big words, such as imperialism, and complex ideas expressed in that monotone voice, but it made it clear that we were a people with land but no shelter, and no rights.

The voice, although it brought sad news, contextualised the war, and put everything into perspective, better than Grandma or rumours ever could. Even as a child, inside I felt that we were vindicated, that all the killings and the maimings were justified if they meant that in the end we would be free from the tyranny of Whites.

Because we were exposed to extreme violence daily, at night I experienced night terrors so real that I had difficulty going back to sleep. And it was Grandma who comforted and soothed me. To this day, those night terrors haven't ceased – they come and go at will – only she's no longer there.

The violence became more intense, brutal, and sporadic.

Selous Scouts, a Rhodesian special-forces unit, whilst pretending to be guerrillas, infiltrated Black civilian populations to gather intelligence and to kill insurgents. They slaughtered Black soldiers on leave, only to come back and avenge their deaths, as part of the so-called 'grey propaganda', in which the Rhodesian state used violence to sow discord within the insurgency, to deprive it of support from the civilian population.

They developed a reputation for brutality. At the end of the war, they were the only unit to be dismissed in ignominy, as 'vainglorious killers and psychopaths'. In the eyes of the Black nationalists, the extreme violence that they had inflicted on the Black civilian population was unforgivable even in the context of war.*

Rhodesian soldiers contaminated supply chains with food laced with poison and clothing contaminated with parathion, an organophosphate insecticide. And ordinary civilians unknowingly passed on the poisoned food and contaminated clothing to the guerrillas, who unwittingly ate the food and wore the clothes. Organic compounds slowly dissolved into their skin. Many died desperate deaths, alone in the forests. As revenge for the deaths of their comrades, guerrillas, too, unleashed extreme violence against civilians. As each side blamed the other, ordinary people were caught up in the wrath between warring factions. By the end of the war nearly thirty thousand had been killed.

But by far the biggest weapon in the guerrillas' arsenal was fear. Like us, Whites felt death's ever-present menace. In response, Ian Smith's regime treated Blacks as the infrastructure that underpinned the insurgency. They could not destroy one, without

---

* According to Ken Flower, head of the Rhodesian Secret Service and founder of Selous Scouts, the unit attracted 'vainglorious extroverts and psychopathic killers'. Many of whom operated without authority or beyond recall. See Flower, Ken, *Serving Secretly* (Alberton: Galago Publishing Ltd, 1987), p. 125.

destroying the other. So curfews, collective punishments, forced removals, and starvation were all part of the strategy to weaken Blacks' resistance, our resolve to free ourselves.

White violence was like dust. It penetrated the most intimate part of our lives. Since there were no welfare programmes, which would allow Blacks to live dignified lives, many had no choice but to break the curfew to attend to their fields and their animals; many were killed just a few metres from their doorstep.

Daily, we woke up to the sound of aeroplanes, and strange parcels drifting across the sky. We ran across the open veld, picked up the government propaganda leaflets, only to be confronted by the news of yet another tragedy, a massacre.

'*Remember Manama!*' read the leaflets.

Manama High School was a boarding school for Black children. Four hundred pupils and teachers had been kidnapped from there by the guerrillas. As the war intensified, and as many guerrillas were killed in the battlefield, they resorted to kidnapping school-children to boost their numbers. Up until then, most schools had remained open. Would we be next? But Manama encapsulated the true cost of war, everywhere: the violation of children.

At times, it was the pictures of children's mutilated bodies splayed across pamphlets. Or it was the helicopters, flying slightly above treetops, dragging nets bursting at the seams, with the previous contact's crop of corpses. There was no light inside this darkness; everything happened without warning. We remained silenced, caged.

There were rumours that, to expedite the war, Ian Smith's army had built what they euphemistically called Protected Villages, where the military arbitrarily detained innocent civilians to starve the guerrillas of support. To prevent people from leaving the so-called Protected Villages, the army randomly planted landmines, which detonated, killing and maiming people and wild animals alike.

As gunfire became our lullaby, Grandma was our superhero. Although conflicted at times, she never doubted our own capacity as human beings. She had her own double-braided wisdom: she adhered to her own convictions and she was unwaveringly self-sufficient. In a world full of constraints, her fearlessness didn't have any limitations. Since she could not change big things, she rearranged small things daily to make sure that we survived.

'Suffering is like morning dew,' she'd say. 'With the full blast of the sun's rays, it'll pass.'

In her world, all things came to pass. The biggest miracle was the smallest thing we could do to survive.

'When you grow up, tell the world what White people did here,' she'd say. 'Speak truth so that someday the world may understand how we came to be as a people. That because of all the gruesome things that they did to us, none of us walked away unscathed.'

We called Whites *amakhiwa*. In our collective imagination they were like ripe figs: perfect on the outside yet filled with worms and rot on the inside. But White power remained formidable, distant, and inaccessible.

Grandma said that our oppressors wanted fear to rule, so they could drive us mad by telling us that our grievances were groundless.

She said to us, 'Listen, when you talk to people, look them straight in the eye, you hear me? And never let them know that you are afraid – never! Stand your ground because everybody bleeds. And everybody is afraid. And I mean *everybody*!'

To fortify our courage, she regaled us with the biblical tale of David and Goliath. She said that if you struck someone with precision, even the biggest men fall. But if we integrated our capacity for violence with strength of character, we could create something wonderful.

Her gnomic utterances were a kind of prophecy.

An elephant was killed by an ant.

A small flame burns down big logs.

'Look at the trees,' she said. 'Do they not nurture us, but also provide shade for murderers?'

CHAPTER 14

As the war raged, in the cold winter nights, Grandma regaled us with tales of adventure, magic and intrigue. We grilled sweetcorn on the edge of the fire and sat around the hearth. Storytelling was a collective activity. We were expected to participate as the tale unfolded, because Grandma said no one sang alone unless it was a sad love song. We listened to fairy tales, myths, stories of cannibalism, betrayal, survival, and ingenuity. We leaned far out on the edge of our real world and imagined the impossible. In times of famine, women fought, overpowered, and ate men. Inside this dystopia, animals had a language. As we entered Grandma's tales, we hopped, skipped, and sang along with the hare, and shrivelled at the roar of the lion. She ululated, spat, and growled like an angry dog. She entered a trance, shaman-like, and stalked her prey like the lion.

Her songs were so uplifting that even a funeral dirge sounded like a beautiful love song. Small shadows danced on the wall as if the departed were watching over us. With each telling, a story assumed a life of its own. New stories emerged out of the old, each determining its own path and intrigue.

Whilst she regaled us with these tales, she weaved baskets, with the tenderest branches, around which she rolled dry river reeds or *ilala*, soaked in hot water to make them more malleable. Each design was determined by her mercurial mood. When she wove, she was calm, as if her temperament was harnessed into her design.

Each production was a reworking of something niggling at the back of her mind, however mundane. She used the threads from the Saharan aloe vera cactus, *iskusha*. Its heavy succulent leaf was about a metre long and about fifteen centimetres wide. It flowered once before it died. Its flower, a wound of a flower, used its nectar to trap insects. It was abundant on the periphery of our home. Grandma's chickens and their chicks embedded themselves under its thorn leaves until the shadow of the hawk from the sky above disappeared, just the same way we had dived deep into the caves at the sound of fighter bombers.

But, first, she disarmed its razor-sharp serrated hooks with a sharp knife. And with the back of the knife she tenderised the succulent leaf, displacing the soft green cushion of its exterior to expose the white fibre buried underneath. If you dug deep, she said, there was always good to be found in all of us.

Once she'd harvested the fibres, she twisted them into shiny cords, like byssus, by rolling them on the inside of her thigh with her palm, her dress pulled all the way back.

Then she wove the dyed fibres into a flat tripartite rope which she turned into spirals the size of small plates.

When she delved deep into her pain, she came up with rare patterns – little red triangles, purple and green squares, small circles – all juxtaposed on the surface of the winnowing basket.

She embroidered a new joy out of these colours. To her that was the language of love, of compassion. In her designs she wanted to disrupt time, tear it into shreds, weaving again and again the threads of a new time.

Once, she let it slip that, as kind as he was, Grandpa sometimes violated her too. It was expected of him as a man, she said. Because, she said, a man who didn't beat up his wife didn't love her enough. But then she said that if she'd really wanted to, she could've fought back and won. But men were at their most dangerous when they felt disempowered and weak, she said. So, she let it be.

All her life, she belittled men. They were dogs, she said. Conversely, she derided any men who showed any signs of femininity, which she likened to weakness.

She pushed and pulled the needle through as she wove the tales, the vigorousness of each motion determined by the improvisation of the characters in her tale. In the near darkness, she missed, hissed, and pierced the needle straight through her fingers. All she did was wince, then continue as if nothing had happened.

We sang in unison. We knew the songs by heart, but we did not always understand what they meant or where they'd take us. And that was the joy of singing. A song could tell you the story of a lifetime. And that was Grandma's gift.

She absent-mindedly threw to the floor the unfinished basket as she clapped and moved to the rhythm of the song.

In this waking dream, she turned fabulist. She amended and then portrayed the future as something gloriously good, where Whites didn't exist, and our world was as it was before their arrival.

159

We encountered ghostly hauntings, *imikhobo*. Grandma said that the ghost flame was a repository of our collective grief, a symbol of rebirth.

Then she'd suddenly stop.

'Did you know that the termites are the hardest-working creatures in the world? Just look at termite mounds. These tiny creatures, as light and transparent as hungry lice, build cathedrals of mud and consecrated them with their saliva!'

But, to save a piece of wood from the torment of termites, she threw it into the middle of the fire. And then she watched the termites scatter through the tiny holes straight into the fire, their short lives and ours momentarily juxtaposed.

In this other world, we experienced an unbounded optimism. Everything was permissible, flight even. We were like those termites inside an anthill, building our own city of joy, with its own night and day. We huddled around the fire, life's little decoy. Grandma's stories created illusions that worked against reality.

We turned the sweetcorn one section at a time as it obtained a golden glow and popped open, releasing the fragrance of its nourishing oils. Sometimes it burned ever so slightly, but we didn't mind. When it was ready, we passed it to Grandma so she could open a path along the length of the cob, because her callused hands were resistant to heat. This way we could push the loose kernels into the newly created pathways. And in Grandma's meandering she created small mazes, puzzles; it was a game she played with us whenever she was content, if only for a moment. Because in our world not everything had an answer. Sometimes there was no reason why or how – our world just was.

Grandma's stories and the warmth of the fire made the pain in the remotest parts of our being fade away; we were cleansed from the ill wind of violence. The night ended and, as gunfire subsided, we ate green caramelised cucumbers drenched in hot creamy milk. When the glow of the flame died down, Grandma lit the kerosene lamp, cupping its flame to protect it from the wind, and her fingers glowed into a reddish pink in the dark. We walked, single file, in the throes of sleep. Tired but satisfied. Things would be different tomorrow. As Grandma would say, no day ever followed another's footsteps.

In the morning, nearby, we would come across clusters of bullet casings, small nests of shiny yellowish brass, next to furrows on the ground, from military boots right where soldiers had taken cover, risen, aimed, fired – boots new, some never to been worn again.

As the war intensified, refugees arrived in numbers from the eastern highlands, where there had been a massive incursion and infiltration by guerrillas, and where war was at its most intense. Some had open bullet wounds, lacerations, scars, and open sores from chemical weapons. Mentally, they seemed lost, depleted. It was as if they'd encountered something too big to grasp, everything they said about the war seemed like an exaggeration: the horrible deaths they'd seen, revenge killings by guerrillas, people being burned alive in their huts and people being forced to kill their neighbours after they'd been accused of being sell-outs.

Sell-outs were individuals who had allegedly betrayed guerrillas by providing information to Smith's soldiers. * But, with time, guerrillas recognised that they were being used to settle scores over land disputes, business transactions, and pure jealousy. So, when a person pointed a finger of accusation at anyone, first they had to do it publicly, by openly stating what evidence they had, and then afterwards do their own dirty work. Which meant beating someone to death using the crudest of methods: wooden poles, thick sticks, and hatchets. When the witnesses failed to provide the evidence, they themselves got killed. Guerrillas wanted people to understand that the war of liberation was a people's war. That everyone had to put in the hard work to liberate themselves, even if it meant killing or being killed. Because when you fight for it, sacrifice for it, freedom has a different resonance.

The war had finally arrived on our doorstep. A new girl moved in next door. She was covered in big yellow pustules, behind her ears, between her buttocks, and around her elbows and groin. She scratched until she bled. And there didn't seem to be a remedy for her ailment. Besides, the nearest clinic had been raided and then closed by the guerrillas. She sat in the dust and rotted away whilst people gossiped about her. Sometimes she came closer to the wooden fence and stood there, as if she'd been silenced by the war. Her pustules were because of the biological and chemical weapons used by the Rhodesian military in the war zones.

---

* Sell-out or collaborator was a catch-all phrase that was used to describe any one whose actions were judged as counter-revolutionary. This included soldiers, policemen, civilians, and those whose work supported the Rhodesian regime.

Grandma said we could talk to her but warned us not to touch her.

'You hear me?' she said. 'Never touch her! Besides, we don't know who these people are. They arrive here like a cloud of locusts, expecting us to warm up to them, speaking in that funny and incomprehensible language of theirs!'

She stopped weaving her basket and pointed at me: 'You especially, you little swine. Don't go foraging for pestilence. If you ever come back here with lumps and bumps, I'll throttle you myself! Do you hear me?'

'Yes, Grandma!'

'We must be thankful for God's grace. That poor child's mother has been killed, and she sits there not knowing what to do. And they've done unspeakable things to her!'

And then she stopped. This time she warned all of us, with an excessive agitation.

'And I don't want you calling her names!'

She pointed at each one of us, separately, with her sharp needle. A certain rebuke was implied in her words, carried by her countenance.

'But she never speaks, Grandma, even when we try to talk to her,' my sister Gift pleaded.

'Everyone has a name. Go and find out what her name is!'

'But you said . . .'

A glint of malice shone in Grandma's eyes – a frozen lake, dimly lit by a fading moonlight. And her very dark complexion was set off by the red dye in the bucket. Suddenly, she withdrew all kindness, and a thin veneer of saliva flashed over her teeth. We knew we had to leave her alone for a while.

★

Bongani was nine years old, a year younger than Gift. When we first approached her, she squeezed her tiny face between the poles on the wooden fence, but never spoke. We talked to her, but she just stared at us. There was something odd about her mannerisms. It was as if her mind had gone quiet. We just didn't know what to do.

Since the little girl's arrival, Grandma seemed indignant about something.

Gift suddenly said, 'Comrades do terrible things to girls, you know?'

'And how would you know?'

'Grandma said so.'

'When did you hear her say that? Go on telling lies and you'll eat the cane tonight from Grandma!'

'She was talking to Aunt MaNcube yesterday. She said that they cut girls and use Vaseline to have sex with them. That's why that little girl can't walk properly!'

'Guerrillas won't know you're a girl anyways. Besides, you're too thin, and have a bald patch on the back of your head, and you cough too much!'

Gift punched me so hard in the chest, and I punched her harder in the face. Grandma came round the corner like a whirlwind. Before I got up, she caught me right on top of the right ear. For a moment, I felt dizzy. I could not hear what she was saying to me. Whatever she was saying couldn't have been good. When she picked up a brick, that was enough for me. I took off running, and she threw the brick at me with such force that on hitting the ground it smashed into small fragments.

And she shouted after me, 'What did I tell you about hitting girls? Why don't you come back here and fight me if you're so strong, you lousy cur?'

I decided enough was enough; there was only so much I could take. Grandma's threats to kill me had taken a serious turn. I was convinced they'd soon become a reality. After sunset, I stole out of the kitchen and disappeared to the *kopje* behind our house. The very spot that I was looking for consisted of four rocks in a rectangular formation under a big mahogany tree. The crypt was deep and wide enough to contain a small body. The bottom was covered in leaves, making it a perfect refuge for a fugitive. I hastily lowered myself inside the crypt only to plunge into cold water and slimy rotten leaves and branches.

Ponging, drenched and soaking wet, I lifted myself out of the crypt. While I contemplated what to do next, the voices of my two sisters rang out in the night. I had underestimated the level of panic my absence would generate.

'*Thabani! Come home!*'

But my escape plan had been flawed right from the outset. For a start, I had no food or water and I'd forgotten to bring blankets and warm clothes, but I stayed, out of sheer stubbornness, to show Grandma that I meant it this time. And when it got darker, all forms of life emerged from the undergrowth: giant snails, armoured crickets, millepedes, and bullfrogs. The frogs croaked and competed with the crickets, engaged in a choir of their own. And I started to see moving shadows everywhere. Every time I squatted, they squatted too. And then there were the strange noises made by all sorts of wild animals. That was enough to contend with for one night! My career as a fugitive had come to a very abrupt end. I quickly ran home and sneaked back into the kitchen. Grandma's fermenting millet beer was a welcome treat. It had the consistency of warm porridge; I took a gourd and scooped some of it into a cup. Like the men at Kiki's shebeen, I drank it in huge gulps and refilled the gourd. Finally, the warmth of the fire lulled me into a deep sleep. In the morning, I woke up right next to Grandma. She said nothing.

CHAPTER 15

Up until the raid at Manama, our school had remained open, unlike others in the areas where the war was at its most intense. Our proximity to the colonial administrative offices, and the presence of the military barracks nearby, came to our aid. The final push for the guerrillas was to ensure that nothing worked, and that Ian Smith's government collapsed. So guerrillas instructed head teachers to close schools and for teachers to return to their homes. The guerrillas argued that there could be no education when Blacks were not free. Besides, they said, the education system, as it was, taught nothing but indoctrination. It was only ever intended to prepare Blacks for a life of servitude. They'd fight, they said, till the last drop of blood to free us all.

As nocturnal raids by guerrillas became more and more daring and frequent, teachers fled in droves. Only Mr A. R. Socks stayed behind, but after the daring raid at Manama High School he, too, seemed shaken. He was quieter, his voice subdued, the glow in his eyes gone.

In our teachers' absence, chaos reigned. We upended benches, piled them on top of each other and pushed them across the slippery concrete floor at breakneck speed. Fights broke out between us and the new boys from the war zones, resulting in broken benches, upturned tables, torn uniforms, and bleeding noses.

For the first time, Mr A. R. Socks didn't make an appearance to stop the fights. However, he did say that if ever there was a gunfight or a raid on our school, we should lie flat on the floor, cover our ears, and remain quiet. We had small pieces of paper stuffed in our pockets with our names and details of our next of kin. The earliest sign that there was a raid would be a random ring of the bell, five times, and not our usual recess bell, which he rang promptly at 10.30 a.m. We practised diving under the tables, and we identified escape routes between buildings, which led to a gulley nearby. Finally, he paired us up, so we could help each other out. Things had changed for the worse; school felt more like a prison.

It was inevitable that our school, too, should close.

One early morning, on our way to school, we saw a cloud of thick black smoke hovering above Bambazonke's Store. The strangest thing was that there was a group of White soldiers standing right next to two Land Rovers, a short distance from the smouldering building. It seemed they'd maliciously set the building on fire. Word had it that Mr Bambazonke had been arrested on suspicion of collaborating with the guerrillas. Like many of our leaders, he had been taken away to a discreet location, probably for torture, then execution.

And when we got to school the gates were closed. There were no teachers around. Mr A. R. Socks's office was locked and there was no singing from Mr R. Sender's class. It was as if something had sucked the life out of our school. Salani and I walked over to the teachers' accommodation and knocked on each door, but there was no answer. Then a sudden panic hit me. I wished that the guerrillas had left our school alone and continued their war without us. Neither Mr A. R. Socks nor any of our teachers had ever uttered a word about the war. All they ever did was teach. That was all. Their departure marked the dearth of any hope we might have had of a brighter future. All day, we wandered around in a daze, hoping that perhaps our eyes had deceived us. But by noon we were more than convinced that the school was closed.

Since we now had time on our hands, Salani and I invaded Mr Chuma's yard. His homestead was surrounded by a graveyard full of old cars, stripped bare, with missing headlights like the empty sockets on the skeletons of dead people. We slid into the cars, all frame no flesh, with rusty springs for seats, and turned the rigid steering wheels whilst we pretended to be sophisticated drivers offering lifts to beautiful girls. I blew the imaginary horn, as Salani played the conductor by animatedly hurling the imaginary heavy suitcases on to the roof of the car.

Boom! Boom! Boom!

'Let's go, let's go!'

'*Vrrrm! Vrrrm! Vrrrm!*'

I revved the engine, peeped my head out of the window and shouted, 'The engine is refusing to start!'

And Salani yelled, 'Open the bonnet!'

And then we pretended to be mechanics purposefully looking at the yawning gap where the engine was supposed to be.

'We've run out fuel!' exclaimed Salani despondently.

With that, we abandoned play and stole mangoes, before leaving Mr Chuma's sprawling homestead.

Afterwards, we raced up the back of the hillock behind Grandma's house. On the way up, we turned the unfortunate speckled tortoises upside down to see if they could save themselves. And, armed with our home-made hatchets, we hacked through aloe vera, exposing its translucent flesh, its flowers small sprouts of flame, to the dismay of the hummingbird who depended on its nectar. When it rained, we sought shelter inside the caves and rode he-goats like donkeys until we stank.

Sometimes, we climbed the slippery sycamore fig trees and swung from branch to branch as we pummelled each other with unripe figs. We chose the biggest figs, hard as rock, and aimed for the tenderest spots with precision.

In between, we hitched rides on the backs of recalcitrant donkeys. When they got fed up, they suddenly dived into thickets of thorn trees. We caught double kicks to the stomach and ribs and survived till the next ride.

We slid down rough granite inclines by riding slippery logs from the *isikhukhukhu* tree. When dislodged mid-flight, the only braking mechanism we had was our bare heels. Inevitably, we ended up with ripped shorts and bruised buttocks.

At night, we slept fully clothed with our shoes by the door just in case someone torched the thatch whilst we were asleep.

Sometimes, we visited our school out of curiosity, in the hope that it might be open. But it was sad to see the school grounds covered in weeds, and termites' mounds creeping up the walls and rafters.

Yet things were about to change.

CHAPTER 16

It was June 1979. But for the war, I should have been midway through fourth grade at school. One day our country woke up to a new name: Zimbabwe-Rhodesia. Some called it Rhobabwe, like an orphan with two fathers, neither of whom wanted it. But nothing had changed, except we had a new Black prime minister, Abel Muzorewa, who also happened to be a bishop. Grandma said that he was a clown, and that, like all Black men, he was going to ruin the country. She wondered how he'd pray, run a country, and organise massacres – only Whites could do that, she said. If in the past there had been a promise of freedom, now there was no guarantee of freedom. Blacks did not understand freedom. But Blacks had never known freedom, so how could they possibly know what it felt like to be free?

The election of a Black prime minister offered a brief hiatus in the war. Those who had fled the country started to come back. Nobody asked where they'd been or what they'd done – it was enough that they had returned.

One day, Edwin, a boy who lived even closer to the Growth

Point, came running towards our homestead. Breathlessly, he announced, 'Sami is back. I am telling you he is back!'

'Are you sure?' Grandma asked, tightening her headdress.

'It's him,' said Edwin, still trying to catch his breath. 'Come and see for yourself if you think that I am lying!'

Thinking that it was too good to be true, I took off in the direction of the Growth Point. Gift followed. Uncle Sami had been gone for almost two years. The news that he was back was something to celebrate.

When we arrived, we found Uncle Sami standing right next to a lorryload of furniture: a brand-new mahogany wardrobe with a body-length mirror in the middle; a matching bed with a headboard and plump mattress, unlike the emaciated steel-springs-and-bolts affair that was Grandma's recent acquisition; a mahogany table; six wooden chairs with cushions; and, to our delight, a Supersonic record player with speakers hidden inside a wooden cabinet with glass at the front.

Grandma was thrilled; it was as if Uncle Sami had just risen from the dead. He brought her a beautiful pink dress and black shoes but no socks. She was so excited, she tried the new dress over an old dress, and the new shoes barefoot. She twisted her ashen and swollen ankles this way, and that way, before rejoicing: 'I never thought I'd live to see this day! My son, my only son. He protected you! God works in wonderful ways; he has answered my prayers!'

She gently rubbed his arm, before placing both her hands on her chest as if praying to a higher power.

To our dismay, Uncle Sami said that he'd lost our presents. Apparently, he'd accidentally swapped suitcases with a stranger on the plane. He went into a detailed description of the clothes, the shoes, the wonderful colours.

'You should have seen them,' he said, trying to convince us that the lost suitcase existed. I quietly observed that he didn't have the stranger's suitcase.

'But I'll find him. I know I'll find him!' he said, flicking ashes from his Kingsgate cigarette.

I knew he was lying.

He had new scars on his face, lacerations on his scalp, and a gap where his top incisors should have been.

He now spoke the language of the mines: *isilaphalapha*. A conglomeration of Bantu languages across sub-Saharan Africa, necessitated by the demands of the mines. Grandma said that it was a language that spoke of the agony of those crushed by falling rocks, those who died chasing the White man's gold. When the Black miners died, Boers left them where they fell and mined a different vein. And the men's loved ones received a simple letter, notifying them that they were gone. There was always trepidation in Grandma's eyes when we received the letter with the picture of an aeroplane. In her eyes, the airmail letter was nothing but a harbinger of bad news.

Uncle Sami wore *iBostoni*, a wide-brimmed grey hat with a peacock's feather attached to a red band that ran round its circumference; two-tone shoes, red and brown; a pair of turn-up trousers with pleats at the top; a shirt with breast pockets; and a double-breasted trench coat with a belt in the middle and cuff straps with buttons that also buckled like the belt on his waist.

Come rain or shine, that was how he dressed every day. He was an iNgoli now. And to be called an iNgoli was an accolade, it distinguished him from the rest of the men, as someone who took chances deep down the mines and survived. It was also an attitude: the extra bounce in his step, and the reckless, carefree spending. INgolis were better off and more revered than guerrillas who went to war and came back with nothing. In our world, freedom wasn't just a feeling, it was also tangible, like shoes.

Sometimes he wore his Bata canvas tennis shoes, washed, polished with white nugget polish, and left out to dry in the sun. His blue polyester trousers hung just so, exposing the small crack on his bottom. When he moved, he dropped and dragged his left leg. That was how *tsotsis* or gangsters moved. I watched him practise his *knife-wallet-knife* routine. He never left the house without the Okapi knife in his back pocket, and a pack of Peter Stuyvesant cigarettes and a box of Lion matches.

When we were alone, he showed me his knife, a ratchet-lock, three-star Okapi, with a brown mahogany handle, a stainless-steel blade, and a small ring where it folded. It was his *Saturday Night Special*, he said. Every gangster worth their salt had one. When he ratcheted it, he menacingly widened his eyes, demonstrating to me that he could change according to his circumstances. Because, in our country, everyone was a chameleon. You either pretended or you died.

'*Ngiyakubula!*' was his favourite phrase: 'I'll kill you if I must!' And I knew that he meant it. When I came of age, I should get one too, because killing was a big part of who we were.

And with a wardrobe full of clothes, and so much time on his hands, Uncle Sami found himself a wife. I say wife, loosely, because there was no wedding or celebration. We woke up one day and Bonani was there: beautiful, plump, childish, shy. But he still frequented Kiki's shebeen. Grandma, fearful that he would spend all his money on alcohol, cigarettes, and women, used some of his money to buy two female calves. She called one of them WENELA, a reminder of what he'd gone through in the mines. Despite the war, the future looked promising. And Grandma looked forward to her own grandchildren. Those who'd inherit Uncle Sami's land and carry the family name.

That's what everybody had hoped for, that the brief hiatus in the war would soon be followed by an everlasting peace so people could raise their families, and watch their children grow into decent human beings.

But that was not to be, because the negotiations between warring factions had failed. Abel Muzorewa had struck out on his own, without the blessing of either Joshua Nkomo or Robert Mugabe, key figures within the Black nationalist movement. Despite there being an interim election, which Muzorewa had won, exiled nationalists felt that the election was not representative of the people of Zimbabwe, that it was designed to further entrench White rule. War-hardened Black nationalists wanted an outright victory on the battlefield. Ian Smith vowed that there would be no Black rule for another thousand years.

So both sides went back to war.

What was the true value of the land, Grandma asked, when people were starving?

She said that in our culture nobody owned land. We were nothing but its custodians. We had no more right to the land than the animals and the birds that used to roam freely on the landscape before Whites started slaughtering them and hanging them as trophies on the wall. In our folklore and totemic system, there were animals so sacred we would never have dreamed of killing them, let alone eaten their meat. For all the talk about bringing civilisation to us, we were the only ones to have conducted ourselves with dignity.

To our exasperation, aeroplanes continually circled the sky above us. There was a rumour that the government was poisoning our animals from the air. Strange meat started appearing in the bush. Soon after, we began to come across dead animals too. Whites thought that the little that we had would feed the guerrillas. In turn, the guerrillas thought that it was we who were poisoning them. Apart from people, dogs, too, began to disappear. They'd wander off deep into the hills and die in isolation.

Grandma started burning anything given to us by soldiers. Sometimes they would give us sweets or biscuits as part of their psychological warfare to win hearts and minds. But Grandma said that if the guerrillas were to die the trail would soon lead to us.

It seemed that the war, however distant, made inroads into our lives. What we witnessed was far more powerful than what we were told.

Out of the blue, our dog, Sport, went rabid. She was frothing excessively, and she viciously attacked our neighbour's goats. I hit her hard with a stick, but she just ripped into the animals. When I pulled her hind legs, she snarled. It was as if she didn't recognise me anymore. I ran home to fetch Grandma, but she wasn't there. Although Uncle Sami was at home, I decided not to tell him. I'd seen so many times men hurt each other badly for the most trivial of things. Instead, I ran to Mr Jenkins, whose goats were being mauled. I pleaded with him to wait for Grandma, but he grabbed a sharp axe, and headed down the footpath that led towards our growling dog and his bleating goats. Petrified, I sprinted all the way to the fields to fetch Grandma. When I got there, I babbled about the dog and the goats and the axe and Mr Jenkins. She dropped her hoe, tightened her headdress. With her feet still caked in mud, she took off like a hurricane. By the time we got back, it was getting dark.

Grandma simply said, 'It's too late, son!'

The next day, I continued the search. I found Sport deep in a gorge. She had axe wounds to her head and body.

I ran home to tell Grandma, but she just snarled, 'What else are we willing to do now that we have no mercy even for defenceless animals?'

I did not know how to answer. Instead, I asked her if we should bury the dog.

She looked at me and said, 'I am just tired of burying young people and animals. I am just too tired for any of this!'

She decided we should leave Sport where I'd found her.

Let us see, first-hand, war's bitter harvest.

CHAPTER 17

Although Grandma continually warned Gift and me not to wander too far, one afternoon we took off running after leaflets falling from the sky. Between us, we scooped a few and started reading them. Gift suggested that we take them home and show them to Grandma because there were pictures of dead people on some of them that she might like to see. Because Grandma liked to gossip with her friends about the brutality of the war.

Grandma emerged from inside the rondavel, and before we'd even managed to say anything she shouted at us: 'What did I tell you about running? If the soldiers see you running and they start shooting, what will you do?'

When my sister finally got her breath back, she answered Grandma.

'It says here, Grandma, that the new army has arrived. They are called "the Spear of the Nation", and they are here to protect us from the guerrillas.'

I quickly interjected.

'It says "the Spear of the People"!'

Grandma cut in: 'Spear of the People, Spear of the Nation.

Rapists. All of them! They'll spend more time hunting for girls than they will fighting the war. Oh, yes, we've heard about them already and what they do to girls. These useless men who can't even fight. This war has gone on for far too long – it should be over by now. What kind of men are these? Tell me, hm-mm? Look at that poor child Bongani! And they say they are fighting a war? She can't even walk because of what these animals have done to her. And now they come here, change uniforms, and tell us more lies, lies, lies, and I am sick of it! And you two bring those lies here! *Umkhonto we Sizwe, Pfumo reVanhu, Madzakudzaku.* Get out and find something better to do than going around peddling lies!'

The next day, we woke up to the sound of soldiers singing. The noise came from the valley below, towards the river. Gift and I ran and climbed the nearest hilltop. We could see, right below us, in the distance, figures in brown uniforms, the colour of the earth. Everything was brown, like anthills on the move. Curiosity got the better of us. We ran down the hill towards the valley. And when we reached the fence of what had, up until then, been the Ministry of Transport compound, we were stopped in our tracks. There were soldiers lying under the cover of trees, wearing brown T-shirts. Inside the perimeter of the fence, there were others digging trenches. The compound had been converted into a military camp. There was a brown flag with the symbol of a black spear, with the words '*Pfumo reVanhu*' emblazoned across it. The pamphlets were not lying. The people's army was here.

★

In the weeks that followed, we watched soldiers as they carried out drills, marched and sang songs, mainly about dying. For some reason, a few were selected for special treatment and forced to turn round the same spot with their forefinger inserted into the sand.

'*Tenderera! Tenderera! Tenderera mpfana iwe!*'*

The soldiers rotating around their finger could barely stand up straight, as the rotation seemed to throw their bodies into a free spin. Rifle butts connected with their backs, and military boots raised dust as they kicked bodies off the ground. They rose and fell in the sun-baked dust, their T-shirts soaked wet with sweat. Others were made to run while holding their guns right above their heads with the instructors yelling obscenities at them.

We saw recruits, their heads shaven, being brutalised daily while they were frogmarched in the punishing heat. Soon, we would learn all their marching songs by heart.

Nobody explained why it was necessary to build a military camp in the vicinity of our homes, or what these soldiers were training to do, but it was inevitable that they'd soon end up on our doorstep, making demands of their own. Word had it that these were Bishop Abel Muzorewa's own mercenaries.

Before the soldiers arrived, we were free to go anywhere. Now we could no longer use huge swathes of the river, because they had erected their targets for practice on the other side of the riverbank. Their targets were caricatures of guerrillas, carved out of human-sized cardboard. Gunfire filled the air from dawn till dusk. So what if bullets strayed? Our cattle were now decimated

---

* Spin around, spin around!

in this way – why shoot at cardboard when they could practise on moving targets? Guerrillas, after all, were known to vanish into thin air: men with invisible faces.

As soon as the soldiers arrived, women from all over the country started to converge on the area. As a result, we could no longer play hide-and-seek amongst the small caves on the hills behind our house. It was for the first time that we saw women wearing trousers in our village. They painted their faces with all kinds of wild colours, and they adopted a very slow, deliberate walk.

Even my Uncle Sami's wife, Bonani, and her two best friends were in on it. Our diet changed too. We developed a relationship with the soldiers; most boys spent time with them and developed an affinity with their weapons and equipment. They let us forage through their rubbish dumps, where we found all sorts of intriguing things: folding aluminium frying pans and cups, small military-issue Swiss army pocketknives, and used military radio batteries. Uncle Sami let the green batteries bask in the sun and, once fully charged again, he played his favourite records on his Supersonic turntable.

Salani and I and a few other boys ran errands to buy cigarettes and alcohol for the soldiers in exchange for money: Madison Toasted, Kingsgate De Luxe, Everest Menthol and Peter Stuyvesant.

We followed the trail of prostitutes into the secluded area of the bush, where we collected empty bottles of beer, Black Label and Castle, along with Smirnoff and exchanged them for money at Ngenisa's. As soon as we got the money, we ran to MaMampofu's store where we bought pink marshmallow fish, cherry pies and Fanta. Life felt good, if only for a while.

In time, Grandma's resistance melted away when she was short of money, but she never asked directly – she was far too proud for that. She would start a long-winded conversation before she got to the point.

'My snuff is all but gone. I don't even have a *penny* with a hole in it. What with things as they are!'

Knowing full well what she was up to, I tried to run away before she trapped me. But, once she started, it was already too late.

'Are you still selling your bottles?'

'Yes, Grandma.'

'Then *we* mustn't waste all the money on sweets. How much do you have on you?'

'Three bob, Grandma.'

'Now let me see if I can keep it safe for you. And then, when there is enough of it, you can buy yourself something nice!'

I had no option but to hand the money over to her. And I knew that this would be the last I'd see of it.

'*Awww*, thank you, my child. What would I do without you?'

And then her tone quickly changed.

'Now quickly, before the sun goes down, go and get me tobacco from Thebe. And tell him not to give me dust. I know what he is doing – he thinks I was born yesterday!'

So I'd take off to buy Grandma's snuff with my own money.

Grandma, who from the very beginning, had always been adamant that we should stay away from the soldiers, was now compromised up to her neck. The camp economy, like the soldiers themselves, had stealthily invaded our lives. Bonani bought Uncle Sami cigarettes and gave him money for beer. He took it, and he never asked his wife where she got it from. I knew it was best not to say. Even when she disappeared to fetch firewood dressed in tight-fitting clothes, Grandma said nothing.

Although she had decreed that I should always accompany Bonani whenever she ventured into the hills, as soon as we got closer to the perimeter of the camp, Bonani told me to wait for her nearby till she returned. But whatever she brought back kept us alive.

But Grandma would burst out in anger, especially when Mrs Chuma visited. They shared news of the war and, inevitably, the latest gossip surrounding women of ill repute.

'Bang in the middle of the afternoon!' Grandma said as she thumped the floor with a fist.

'Such an omen!' Mrs Chuma responded, equally disturbed. 'When do these women do their chores, one wonders? And how can a woman expose her shame underneath trees, and, come to think of it, in broad daylight, MaMoyo?'

'And to think that these are married women! What is this war doing to us? And they spread their legs wide open for money! But God is not blind – he is watching!'

If I sat still long enough, they'd continue to talk as if I wasn't there.

But it was hard for me to keep still, keep my mouth shut. In the end I just blurted it out, uninvited, risking an instant backlash.

'Yeah, we saw Langa and a soldier behind the bushes!'

Langa was Mrs Chuma's daughter-in-law. And I knew that Grandma and Mrs Chuma did not know about her activities with the soldiers.

'And who asked you, mm? Why do you insist on telling lies? And who asked you to join in adult talk? Mm-hm? And now that you've started you might as well finish!'

Mrs Chuma leaned forward. 'Well, what were they doing? Tell me, and she'll see when I get home!'

'They were—'

Grandma cut in. 'Go outside and stop hanging around like an abandoned orphan!'

Interruptions, particularly of that kind, did not bode well with her. I swiftly exited the room till she calmed down.

The war continued unabated. We saw mangled military vehicles every day and the ambulances carrying dead bodies went past so regularly that nobody stopped and bowed their heads or removed their hats anymore.

And at home a new war began between Grandma and Bonani. Grandma felt she was too lazy, that she spent too much time in bed with Uncle Sami.

She complained incessantly that Bonani's skirts were too short, leaving very little to the imagination.

With that, the battle lines were drawn. Grandma instructed my sisters to stay away from the kitchen or any physical work unless she said otherwise. Daily, she knocked on Uncle Sami's bedroom door at the crack of dawn and, as soon as the sun came up, which signalled the end of the curfew, she hauled Bonani along to the fields to gather firewood, fetch water and, when they got back, watched her as she made the fire, prepared lunch, and heated water for Uncle Sami's bath.

But, despite Grandma's strict instructions to my sisters not to help Bonani, a solidarity developed between them. As soon as Grandma left to trade war stories, they helped her.

School was now a distant memory; but the torment of Phani, the boy next door, by his stepmother continued. Phani was getting weaker and weaker; it was only a matter of time before something serious happened to him. The only person who could save him was his Uncle Lavi, who was still in the bush fighting for our freedom.

And still no one intervened.

Salani and I devoted some of our time to the continuation of the struggle, however limited and immature. Our hatred of Whites, inflamed by the war, graduated from mere observation to active participation. We still frequented the main road, but instead of playing our usual game we now counted the number of mangled military vehicles, recorded new types, and made any necessary observations, which confirmed naturally that we were winning the war. And whenever we saw Whites' cars on the move, we pelted them with small rocks before we dived under the culverts, crossed over to the other side of the road, and disappeared behind the small *kopjes*.

At other times, we undertook excursions deep into forests to locate guerrillas, but they never materialised. And, despite Grandma's severe warnings not to venture into the area behind the military camp, we took no notice and watched soldiers flat on their stomachs shooting at targets. Afterwards, we collected unexploded bullets, which we intended to use once we had guns of our own. But, to see how they worked, we made a fire and threw the live bullets into the flames. Once hot, they hissed, spun round, and exploded like fireworks. A single bullet grazed my knee; I was lucky I wasn't killed.

And it was whilst trespassing on the other side of the river that we came across the decomposing body of a young woman. It was in the secluded area of the riverbank frequented mainly by soldiers and prostitutes. Although her body was crushed under the weight of rocks, her blue and white floral dress remained visible underneath the pile of rocks. We recognised her instantly from the dress and ran all the way home to tell Grandma. Grandma said that she deserved to die like a dog, much like the rest of them were. With that, she gave Bonani a scalding look. Even as Grandma swallowed the food Bonani had brought from the camp, she was adamant that the women who frequented the compound should be stoned to death. As for us, she said she didn't want to hear one more word about dung whores.

'And what were you doing in the bushes? You dirty little swine! Always snooping around people engaged in private business. Did I not tell you not to go there? Tell me, did I not say to you, loud and clear, that you should not cross the river? What are you trying to do to me? Tell me – I am listening!'

In the haste to tell her about the deceased woman, I inadvertently revealed to her that we had been playing on the other side of the river, an area from which she had already barred us. As I left the room, I could still hear her making her usual threats to kill me. This had become so routine that it had no effect on me anymore. Besides, I'd already survived several attempts on my life at Grandma's hands.

★

The next morning, she called me.

'Thabani!'

'Yes, Grandma.'

It was too early in the morning, and I was still half asleep. I shuffled towards her, completely oblivious to what was about to happen to me. With school now closed, I had woken up with no plan in my mind. But Grandma, as always, had a plan for me. She was not one for idleness.

'Today I want you to help me plant some mango seeds. Do you hear me?'

'Yes, Grandma.'

'Then grab that hoe over there and bring it here.'

'Yes, Grandma.'

'Now, like a big, strong boy, I want you to dig five holes. Here, here, here, here and there. Not too deep, otherwise the seeds will just rot. You hear?'

'Is here okay?'

'Yeah, good boy. Mind your toes with that hoe! Now tell me, what is the river like these days? I haven't been for a while. I need to go there to wash your clothes.'

'What do you mean, Grandma?'

'What kind of question is that to ask a grown-up? Am I your playmate?'

'No, Grandma.'

'Good, as I was saying before you interrupted me, I was talking to Salani and he told me that you went swimming last Saturday. And, of course, yesterday you were by the river again as we both know.'

Then a pause, followed by a quick reflection, and then silence.

'And, as I recall, you brought home fresh fish, yes?'

She'd devoured the fish and even chewed the bones. There was certainly no mention of the river then. If anything, she couldn't thank me enough. But this was Grandma's world. It was vengeful and it was ruled by an ill wind.

'Good, keep the holes tight. Don't widen the gap too much. You are a clever boy. Now where did you get the fishing line and hook from?'

'Salani lent it to me.'

'I see, he is a very kind boy. Now, the day you went fishing, I couldn't find the money I hid behind the pots in the kitchen?'

'I didn't see any money!'

'Two *shillings* exactly. I intended to use it to buy my snuff. It will probably show up. I know you don't steal for sure. There are no thieves in this family!'

I had stolen many times before and she knew it. In fact, apart from laziness and malingering, theft was one of many things on her list from which she was determined to wean me.

'And did I not say to you not to go to the river?'

'You did, Grandma.'

'And what did you do?'

There was silence, followed by invigorated digging.

'What did you do? Is your brain frozen or are you deaf? I said, what did you do, besides stealing my money? You've forgotten now, have you? Let me remind you! By your own admission, you went fishing and then swimming. Not so? And you come back here dangling nothing but your balls like a cur. Are you a dog?'

And then . . . *pounce.*

'You know what your problem is? You don't listen. I will die and they will bury me! But, before that, I'll reinstate your hearing, cut your fingers to stop you stealing, and teach you how to listen. Oh, yes, you will listen!'

CHAPTER 18

Although Bishop Abel Muzorewa had been elected, Joshua Nkomo and Robert Mugabe, the leaders of the two guerrilla factions, ZIPRA* and ZANLA†, respectively, did not recognise the legitimacy of Muzorewa's premiership. He had no war credentials, no guerrilla army; they saw him as Ian Smith's puppet and traitor. According to the news on Uncle Sami's Supersonic radio, we were now entering the final phase of the war. The Whites were on the run, and our leaders were determined to uproot them once and for all. However, the propaganda leaflets continued to fall from the sky pleading with guerrillas to lay down their weapons and go home. But by then the hatred for White people and their oppressive ways was such that not many Black people doubted that supporting the guerrillas was the only reasonable thing to do. No amount of pleading by the leaflets or Rhodesian propaganda was ever going to erode that resolve.

Whites had carried war in their heads for so long that it had

---

* Zimbabwe People's Revolutionary Army.
† Zimbabwe African National Liberation Army.

become a mindset. Every step Whites took, every preparation they made, was to fulfil the ambition of war. Whilst we were starving, the White Rhodesian army had money for new guns, the latest dirty bombs, heavily fortified trucks, and a weapon for every White person. In fact, Whites couldn't swim in a river, have a picnic, or go for a stroll without their weapons. There was no such thing as White civilians: from nurses to doctors to housewives, many were involved in the collective brutalisation of Black people in one way or another. In the eyes of the Whites, Blacks' skin was a weapon against which they had to defend themselves.

As the nearby Shaw Barracks churned out new soldiers every six weeks, we watched them run up and down the main road in straight columns, singing with their beautiful voices.

Many Whites, despite evidence to the contrary, supported Ian Smith's idea of a thousand years of White rule in Rhodesia, however preposterous that sounded. There was anger in the air. Whilst they felt robbed of their future, we felt we'd carried Whites for so long that we were exhausted; we had nothing else to give. White mercenaries from all over the world descended upon our country to show solidarity with the White Rhodesians. Gunfire was a lullaby to sleeping children. And we crawled instead of walking for fear of being massacred.

Encouraged by shoot-to-kill policies, and with a growing sense of entitlement, Whites justified the violence thus: only they could save the land and prevent the reckless plunder of resources by natives; only they could save the natives from self-destruction. But Blacks' poverty wasn't accidental; it was carefully orchestrated. The wages that Whites paid to Blacks were little more than slave wages. Even if Blacks had worked hard seven days a week, from dawn till dusk, which they did, many could never have escaped poverty. It was how the racist system was designed. It was rigged in favour of Whites.

For the first time, apart from that one encounter when Grandma and I were trespassing on Mr Coulson's farm, we saw guerrillas in broad daylight. Two of them wandered straight into Grandma's yard as if there was no war. They walked with their guns slung over their shoulders like regular hunters on an outing. They told Grandma that they were hungry and would like something to eat. Grandma explained that there was a military camp nearby, that perhaps it was in their best interest for them to leave. They smelled like unwashed dogs, their unkempt hair and beards colonised by grass and twigs. Their clothes were in tatters. As for their shoes, they were just pieces of leather held in place by string. I went inside to fetch water, but by the time I returned they were gone. I didn't know what else Grandma had said to them.

When I looked across the landscape, I saw there were quite a few guerrillas at Mr Jenkins's. Although I couldn't hear what he was saying, like Grandma, he pointed in the direction of the military camp. But instead of leaving they sat under the shade of the big rondavel in Mr Jenkins's yard. Meanwhile, Grandma made us catch one of her biggest cockerels.

To our dismay, once the cockerel was cooked, Grandma sent me with a potful of meat to Mr Jenkins's house. When I arrived, there were eight guerrillas sharing mounds of *pap* and chicken meat that other neighbours had provided. Mr Jenkins grabbed Grandma's cauldron filled with chicken and sent me away.

When I got back, Grandma made us collect all the cockerel's

feathers and bury them in the garden. My sisters swept the yard; Grandma instructed me to drag a big branch over the guerrillas' boot prints. When it was all done, we gathered in Grandma's kitchen, and she said to us: 'Not a word about the guerrillas. You hear me? Not to our neighbours, not to the soldiers, and not even to your friends. You haven't seen or heard anything today!'

Even without her prompting, we understood that loose talk cost lives.

Not long after the guerrillas left, Smith's soldiers arrived. They had dogs with them. They let them loose and the dogs ran around for a while. First, they got to Mr Jenkins's house, and from there, they followed the trail back to Grandma's. And they didn't stop there, they proceeded towards the hills beyond our house, and the soldiers followed closely behind. The rest flattened Grandma's fence as they walked through our yard. In the evening there was an intense and sustained gunfire exchange, interrupted by intermittent explosions. Gunfire felt so close, the ground shook violently. We knew there would be more bodies to view, and the inevitable wrath of White soldiers to contend with.

That night Grandma asked Uncle Sami and Bonani to come and sleep with us. Since he'd returned from the mines, whenever there were soldiers or guerrillas around, he hid in his room till they were gone. If they found him, the soldiers would accuse him of being one of the guerrillas and the guerrillas would ask why he wasn't fighting for the liberation of our people. And he had no satisfactory answer for both.

Throughout the night, we huddled inside Grandma's little rondavel. We slept with our ears to the floor to listen out for the sound of approaching soldiers. But no one went to sleep because all the dogs had gone mad with barking. Throughout the night we listened to the sound of sporadic gunfire, and we heard soldiers walking across Grandma's yard.

Early morning found us wide awake. Heavy footsteps stopped right outside Grandma's hut. We waited for whatever was irritating the neighbour's dogs to smash through the door. A voice shouted from the other side of the door.

Grandma asked, calmly, 'Who is it?'

'Open the door!'

'I am just an old woman, my sons!'

'I said open the door!' the voice bellowed.

'I said I am old. I have nothing to give you, my sons.'

Whoever was outside kicked the door with such ferocity that it completely dislodged from the frame. Uncle Sami quickly put on his shoes and Grandma hastily threw a jacket over his shoulders.

'It's not that cold, Ma,' he whispered.

'We don't know when we'll see you again,' Grandma replied. The last time they took him, he'd been gone for months, and there was no guarantee that he'd make it out alive.

But there was no need to whisper. By now we were completely exposed because there was no longer a door. A group of soldiers stood outside.

For some reason, Uncle Sami said, 'Ma, it's me they are looking for.'

As soon as he stepped outside, they handcuffed him and pounced on him like a pack of wild dogs.

'Where are your friends?'

'I don't know who you're talking about,' Uncle Sami replied.

'But we know you are feeding them.'

'I haven't fed anyone, and that's the truth.'

'Just tell us where they are and we'll let you go.'

'I haven't seen anyone. If I did, I'd tell you.'

It could be true that these soldiers were decent human beings, but on that day they were out to terrorise. One of them leaned his gun against the wall, and quickly rolled up his sleeves, as if he was about to begin hard work. This was just a game. Even if Uncle Sami knew the truth, he had to deny everything until the violence became unbearable, in which case he had to tell them what they already knew, or slowly drift into unconsciousness, whichever came first.

I thought of Enock. So that was how it'd end for Uncle Sami too.

'We know you'll talk. Everyone has a breaking point!'

Uncle Sami played with the handcuffs and looked at the young soldier asking him questions, straight in the eye. It was as if he was about to say something, but he held back. His silence frustrated the soldier. He grabbed Uncle Sami and marched him to the area behind Grandma's rondavel. Afterwards, the other soldiers ordered all of us to follow them. We clutched on to Grandma's nightdress as we walked to where Uncle Sami was. Immediately, they kicked him, and he hit the ground before he managed to break the fall. They pulled his trousers down to his ankles, and he was completely exposed to the waist. One of them pressed his right boot hard on his ankles. And he inhaled as if he was about to start chopping wood. Another pressed his boot on Uncle Sami's neck and calmly said, 'I know you will tell us. All you must do is tell us where the *terrs** are!'

Grandma retorted, 'If you don't know where they are, what have you been shooting at all night?'

They didn't answer, but their actions made it clear that they'd kill Uncle Sami if not permanently maim him. They took turns beating him up with sticks. Uncle Sami wailed, and his voice pierced right through the morning air. He contorted his whole body, as if he was trying to lift himself off the ground. That was just the beginning. The soldier with the boot on his neck pushed it hard and pinned him to the ground. Uncle Sami sobbed as if he was a hiccupping child. He tried to lift his head from side to side, but he could not move. As the beating intensified, his screaming muffled. Soon he went limp, and when they asked him to sit up he couldn't, which infuriated the soldiers even more.

Grandma pleaded with them. 'Can't you see you'll kill him? My son has done nothing. And why are you killing us? My son does not deserve to die like this!'

Grandma's gamble was to seek for human kindness.

The soldier didn't listen to Grandma. He simply wiped off the sweat from his brow, grabbed Uncle Sami by the handcuffs, lifted his upper body off the ground and dropped him. There was a popping sound. Uncle Sami's breathing accelerated and waned. He was shaking like a wounded dog.

He whispered, 'Ma, don't let them take me. I know they'll kill me.'

Everything felt so close as Grandma pleaded with the soldiers.

---

* Rhodesian slang for terrorists.

'My sons, please have mercy!'

We were inside a storm. Even Grandma's war-worn wisdom could not reason with their savagery.

'Who will look after them?' she said, pointing at us.

Before she finished, there was a loud cracking sound. A small stream of urine drained into the sand and there was a smell like no other. Grandma's face suddenly became unfamiliar. It was as if she had a burning sensation inside and she could only alleviate the intensity of the heat by undressing. She stripped, and stood there, stark naked, her salt-and-pepper pubic hair untamed in front of the young White soldiers. She had just given up the only thing she had tried to preserve all her life. And, calmly, she said to the soldiers, 'Before you take my son away, you'll have to kill me first!'

And then she pointed at us.

'These are my grandchildren. They have done nothing to deserve this, and they have no one in the world except me. No one else. Now kill me!'

She was shaking violently, and her stutter became overly exaggerated. She picked up her clothes, threw them on to Uncle Sami, and she stood between him and the soldiers.

A different soldier pushed Grandma to the ground and struck Uncle Sami on the head with the butt of his rifle. Before the soldiers left, one of them warned Grandma not to take him to the hospital. He threw a packet of red pills at her and quipped: 'Don't go telling lies now!'

With that, they vanished.

I could see Grandma's indignation as she turned her attention to Uncle Sami, who had soiled himself. His back, his buttocks, and his thighs were completely swollen, with deep cuts and lacerations exposing the reddish-pink flesh below. Grandma poured cold water on him, and he burst into a cough. She gently lifted his head and poured more water over his face, and she started cleaning his face while Bonani fetched him fresh clothes. He continuously retched until dark bile dripped out of the corner of his mouth. He could not sit unaided.

We watched as Grandma tried to bring her only son back to life. Uncle Sami had beaten Bonani, his wife, close to death before, and Grandma had always maintained an aloof coldness and never intervened. But the terror wrought on Uncle Sami was too close even for Grandma to bear. And, for the first time, Grandma, never one to run out of words, was silenced.

The next day we heard wailing coming from the direction of the waterfall. I followed Grandma. We followed the dry brook as it meandered under the canopy of tall trees casting their shadows on to the rocks. Grandma nearly fell over; it was as if she was pushed by something I could not see. By the time we arrived, the whole village had descended into the waterfall like a herd of wildebeest. And right at the bottom of the waterfall lay the bodies of two men. As we got closer, I could see that they were the two guerrillas who had come to our home the previous afternoon asking for food. One of them had a big hole through his left shoulder, and the other an opening at the back of his head.

Grandma sat on a rock nearby, her headdress tilted to the side, exposing the grey hair alongside her temples. She placed her hands on her lap as if she didn't know what to do or say anymore. Although she'd previously said to us that children shouldn't see dead bodies, she now said it was my responsibility as a man to bear witness. She had forgotten that she'd taken me with her when Enock died. And when I asked what would happen to the dead men she said that all that needed to happen had already happened. That whoever killed them would come back and collect them.

'Do guerrillas themselves not cut people's tongues so they cannot tell lies? Or their mouths so they cannot eat? Or amputate people's hands so they cannot sustain life?' she asked. Besides, she said it was too dangerous to bury people we didn't know. And so we left the dead men's bodies where we'd found them and walked away in silence.

When Grandma attended to Uncle Sami's wounds, she dipped a small towel into warm water, wrung it, and gently dabbed his purplish skin. To get to his bedroom, he crawled on all fours, and he could only sleep on his stomach. When he tried to drink water, he vomited. In the end, Grandma encouraged him to take the pills that the soldiers had left behind, even if she didn't know what they were for.

With time, the vomiting stopped, and Uncle Sami gradually started to produce small quantities of urine. When he relieved himself, he leaned against the fence, and a stream of blood-stained urine came out with much effort, as had happened to me when I'd had bilharzia.

As Uncle Sami lay in bed, recovering from his wounds, the rumour that the government had poisoned our animals became a reality. Rumour had it that the small white aeroplanes, seen months before, had been spreading anthrax spores. How true that was, was anyone's guess. We believed what we saw. Our animals were dying in their thousands. It was the same with the dogs and rabies. We left them where they collapsed and covered them with branches as if they were already dead. It was far better for us not to see the terror in their eyes. We knew that this was the worst form of betrayal because our animals had always looked after us.

Inevitably, one of our prized calves, too, succumbed to anthrax and fell into a deep ravine. It was the animal Grandma had bought with Uncle Sami's money from the gold mines, the one we called WENELA after the Witwatersrand Native Labour Association, the agency that had recruited him to the perilous mines of Johannesburg.

Gift and I decided to salvage whatever was left of WENELA. Gift was wearing my oversized T-shirt and shorts. Grandma had cut her hair so close to the skin that she almost passed for a boy. She'd instructed my sister not to walk like a girl, but then she threw things at her when she sat like a boy. Lately, Gift had been constantly on edge, worried about being a boy and not a girl.

We walked through thickets of thorn brush, and finally made it to the small dry stream. From the edge of the ravine, we could see our calf right at the bottom. Mounds of soil had collapsed where she'd fallen in, exposing brown sinewy roots. They remained suspended in the air, unable to reach sustenance.

We entered the ravine from the shallow end, where it met the dry riverbed. Right above the entrance to the ravine, industrious weaver birds' nests hung precariously at the very end of thin branches of the acacia trees. These little birds had built the strongest fortifications out of straw, over thorns, right under the watchful gaze of poisonous snakes.

We negotiated our way over the rocks, where wild lichens spread out, over roots dangling at the bottom of the tall trees. Roots, in turn, climbed perilously over rock, penetrating the tiniest of crevices to reach water in the ravine below. But, for now, there was nothing but dry sand.

We continued upstream, and we found the calf in a deeper corner of the ravine. She was alive and groaning. A shiver rippled across her hide. Her once shiny coat had withered, its white spots collapsed between segments of ribs. Her bulging eyes were the only signal that she was desperate to get up. The only other discernible gesture of her desperation was a very weak movement of her hind leg – a gentle sweep of the sand. But we were not there to help.

I took two pieces of rope and tied her hind and front legs together, forcing her back into a slight arch. Once trussed up, she was ready for slaughter. Up until then, Gift and I had not spoken about killing. I asked Gift if she was okay. She never answered but gestured for the knife. When I handed it over, our hands touched. She didn't even look at me. She prodded behind the calf's neck with the knife, as if looking for a tenderness there. The calf followed the knife with its eyes. But then Gift changed her mind. She hyper-extended the calf's neck and cut through the soft cartilage. Blood gushed into the sand. The calf was too weak to fight. Everything quietened down. The smell of slaughter thickened the air.

This was not the first time that Gift had killed. Once, whilst out gathering firewood, a young impala had sought shelter at her feet whilst being chased by a pack of hunting dogs. Tired and desperate, it collapsed by her feet. She chased the dogs away and, without hesitation, dispatched the impala with the small axe she was carrying. She had more guts than I ever had.

With her hands bloodied, she looked on whilst I opened the chest cavity with the small hatchet. There was a slight resistance, followed by the sound of bone breaking. As I worked my way around the cavity, I was careful not to impale my fingers on sharp bone. Anthrax entered the body through cuts in the skin.

We harvested what could be retrieved and when we got home Grandma did not ask how the calf had died. Although we were forbidden from eating the infected meat, Grandma said that eating infected meat was just another addition to the list of things we had to worry about. Besides, we were too poor; our animals were our most treasured resource, we could let them go to waste.

Bonani came up with an ingenious way of preparing the meat. First, she sliced it into thin strips, doused it in salt and hung it outside to dry. Once dry, she let it bask next to the fire, and gently turned it till all the sliminess was gone and the fat was brown and the meat grilled tender. She cooked a special dish with it: *biltong** with ground peanut butter. She cooked the meat until it achieved a soft, delicate consistency. We ate the dish, *idobi*[†], with pumpkin leaf and *pap*. At first Grandma, Uncle Sami, and Thoko were apprehensive, but when nothing happened to us, they, too, enjoyed the new delicacy.

---

* Salted, spiced, and air-dried meat common in Southern Africa. Once ready, it is sliced and eaten as a snack or an accompaniment to a cold beer.
† Peanut butter stew

Although the meat brought a brief joy, Uncle Sami remained ensconced in his bedroom most of the time. And Bonani was homesick. She sang sad songs all day whilst she swept the yard, washed the dishes, and ironed his clothes. She was crying too. I guess she was still trying to process what had happened to Uncle Sami. We all were. But so many terrible things had happened in quick succession that we barely had time to get over one horrendous event after another.

When Grandma was not around, Bonani played Double-Dutch with my sisters as if she, too, were a child. She jumped over the rope, twisted, and turned in the air, still wearing the same short skirt of which Grandma disapproved. Because she was so young, she sometimes forgot to do what a wife was supposed to do, and that fuelled Grandma's litany of grievances.

'Even though my son is now married, I still must get up at dawn to make my own fire, sweep the yard and make my own tea as if I am the one who's recently married. One wonders, who teaches these women how to be women? I mean, how to look after themselves, their homes, their husbands?'

And, no matter what Bonani did, it was never enough: the *pap* was undercooked, the vegetables overcooked, the meat too tough, her dresses too short. And so the list went on.

It was as if Grandma was goading Uncle Sami to do something, but he had not yet fully recovered from the brutal beating. He was terrified that it might happen again.

When we were alone, he regaled me with the tales of an illicit love in the mining compounds of Johannesburg – young men who provided wifely comforts for the older, more established miners, because women were not allowed into the compounds lest they brought venereal disease. The young men were called *inkotshane* – a metaphor derived from the qualities of the milk bush, a green and tender perennial that has no spine. It is flexible, fragile, its finger-like stems easy to bend. He spoke candidly about the violence of the mines, of having to sleep with a *panga* and sharpened hatchets in anticipation of the raids by marauding gangs of Zulus.

I listened with wonderment as he told me about the beautiful boy-girls in prison. 'They paint their faces,' he said. 'And they are beautiful too,' he said, exposing his passion gap, *itsako*, another sign of his many stunts in prison. I imagined a big cage, iron bars and shapeshifting images of boys temporarily turning into beautiful girls.

But, with time, he regained his strength. Each morning, he'd crack an egg and pour its contents directly into his mouth, and Bonani made him delicious meals from the dried *biltong*. As his physical wounds started to heal, he got his bounce back. Inevitably, he started to frequent Kiki's shebeen. He spent a lot of time there with Kiki's daughter who was much older than his wife. He frequented the place so much that Grandma made him a concoction from various herbs kept in a calabash under his bed, which she insisted he must drink before going to Kiki's. The concoction was meant to prevent venereal disease, but inevitably he fell sick because he didn't take it as recommended by Grandma. That would have implications for Bonani too.

When I opened the calabash out of curiosity, its stench nearly made me pass out. When I asked Grandma what was in there, she castigated me.

'You little swine, always snooping around, looking under people's beds!'

'But, Grandma . . .'

'Don't you *but, Grandma* me! If you paid enough attention to the things that I ask you to do the way you pay attention to other people's business, the fence would be mended, and all the animals would be accounted for. And I certainly wouldn't be drinking tea without milk!'

I felt that the rage had been directed at Uncle Sami. Grandma was very skilled at projecting on to you what she really wanted to say to someone else.

CHAPTER 19

The combination of money, free time, and alcohol was not good for Uncle Sami. Every Friday, he would vanish. Grandma said that he was a man – he could do whatever he liked.

His wife, Bonani, spent all day sweeping the yard, cleaning, and ironing his clothes and cooking his favourite chicken casserole, before sprucing herself up to look good for when he came home. She changed into an even tighter, shorter dress, and her skin glistened from lashings of Ambi, the latest skin-lightening cream. He came back on a Sunday afternoon.

When he arrived back one weekend, Bonani was all smiles and she started teasing him.

'Tell me where you've been,' she said, 'and I'll let you have the food!'

She playfully brushed the fried chicken right under his nose, and gently tugged on his belt. He didn't respond; she'd inadvertently crossed the line. A storm of agitation was slowly building up, but she was so deeply immersed in her lovers' game she did not realise that she was in danger.

After she finally gave him the food, he grabbed the plate and threw it up in the air. My sisters and I chased after it and tried to catch the meat, but it was too late. The plate landed on the other side of the fence. The neighbour's dogs got to it first. And when we turned round Bonani was on the ground. Uncle Sami had her in a chokehold; he was dragging her backwards, towards their bedroom, her beautiful white dress caressing dust, and her heels drawing lines on the sand. There was nothing but muffled sounds of desperation as he slammed the door shut and locked it from the inside.

I grabbed a small wooden stool and watched the drama unfold through the small aperture of a window. He removed his belt from his waist, folded it in half, and used the buckled end to attack her. He worked her with such an intensity that I could hear the belt slicing the air like a cattle whip.

When she fought back, he was doubly enraged.

'Oh, you think you can fight me now, do you? Let's see what you've got!'

'Sami, I was just playing with you. I meant nothing by it. Please stop! It won't happen again!'

He completely ignored her plea for mercy. And he didn't say exactly what it was she'd done wrong. When he wrapped the belt round his hand, and boxed her like a man, she had nowhere to hide. He attacked her with such ferocity, and when I heard something break, I jumped off the stool and ran round the corner to get Grandma, but my excitement was short-lived when I found her sitting under the shade on the other side of Uncle Sami's bedroom wall, because she could hear everything. She was singing a religious hymn, as if to block out all the noise, and she was weaving her basket, using a beautiful tapestry of colours – yellow, red, green, and white.

On seeing me, Grandma inserted her forefinger into the corner of her mouth and removed a chunk of stale tobacco, which she threw into the nearby rockery. She spat out the rest, leaving a brown stain against the wall. Wiping her finger against her apron, she continued weaving her basket. I could still hear the heavy sounds of Uncle Sami's punches landing on Bonani, but she had stopped screaming or pleading with him.

All Grandma said was, 'She is very stubborn. She'll learn the hard way!'

But I wasn't sure what there was to learn. I was confused by the idea that one could claim to love but then terrorise those closest to them. And Grandma was a woman, and yet she was doing and saying all the things that made me wonder if she had a heart at all. Because, if she had, she would have defended Bonani with all her might.

In her reminiscences of Grandpa, she'd said that he used to beat her with an oxbow, made from real cowhide, twisted, flexible, and stronger than wood, so that when he struck her across the back it wrapped itself round her body, tearing her skin as it went. Perhaps she wanted Bonani to experience what she'd gone through.

'I let him win,' she said, 'because I wanted him to believe in the illusion that he was strong. Throughout our marriage, till the day he died, I let him believe that same lie. And that's life, son.'

She also said something that confused me even more: that if a man loved a woman, from time to time he'd have to beat her up just to prove his love for her. Grandma's world was suffocating. I could not breathe.

When I heard something heavy fall to the ground, I ran to the front of Uncle Sami's bedroom and tried to open the door from the outside. Suddenly, the door opened, and Uncle Sami came outside. He was barefoot and sweating profusely. He had a cigarette in the corner of his mouth. Still shaking, he struck a match and shielded the flame from the gentle breeze with both hands. He inhaled deeply, tilted his head backwards, and exhaled. He was still pacing up and down, agitated with post-bout fury.

Grandma asked me to bring him a chair. And she asked him if he was hungry. Although he never answered, she gave him the rest of the chicken destined for our plates. He ate quietly, like a labourer after a day's hard work. Soon after, he freshened up, changed clothes – and he was gone.

After he was gone, Bonani crawled out of the bedroom. Her face was swollen; she could only see through one eye. The other eye was completely closed. Grandma asked me to fetch warm water from the kitchen. When she mixed it with Dettol, the water turned cloudy, and a clean, sterile smell suffused the air. She grabbed a small towel and gently wiped the blood off Bonani's face. She spent more time around the deeper cuts. To each visible wound, she applied Vaseline, as if attending to a boxer by the side of the ring. There was a remarkable tenderness between them.

'You know you shouldn't argue with him; he'll kill you. A man is a man, and he can do what he likes in his own home!'

She tried to speak but squeaked. Her throat was too dry.

Eventually, she said, 'But all I did was give him food, Mama. I don't understand. He is the one who hasn't been home for nearly three days. All I did was welcome him home, Mama. That's all I did. What else did I do wrong? Tell me, please, just in case I am missing something!'

'But you undermined his authority in front of me, his mother. You should never ask a man his business in front of other people!' said Grandma unrepentantly.

'But he is the one who is in the wrong, Mama. He hasn't been home for three days and I am his wife. Surely, I deserve to know where he's been?'

Grandma didn't respond.

Afterwards, Bonani gathered what was left of her dress and retreated to her bedroom.

My head was spinning, and my stomach was churning in knots. I could not hold the world inside still and I felt a spell of dizziness coming on. I walked to the edge of Grandma's Garden, and I watched a rainbow lizard basking in the sun, just content to be alive amongst the rocks and the cactus in full bloom, its flowers a tinge of pink, red, and yellow. I could see why the lizard found it peaceful there, far from the madness in Grandma's house. I prayed for Bonani to pull through; I could not live with something as heavy as this. Whatever happened, I did not want her death on my conscience, because I had done nothing when she'd screamed for help. We'd all done nothing, including Grandma.

CHAPTER 20

Bonani stayed in her room for the best part of the week. Uncle Sami still hadn't come home. My sisters and I alternately brought her food. At first, she was too ill to eat; I thought her jaw was broken. But, gradually, she started to take some of Grandma's herbal porridge. When neighbours enquired after her, Grandma said she was unwell, but she never mentioned what had been done to her by Uncle Sami. Young as I was, I thought that love was the strangest thing of all, if indeed it existed.

Outside our home, violence continued. Muzorewa's soldiers in brown uniforms left at dawn on patrol and came back at dusk. They had such regular contact with the guerrillas that many of the soldiers deserted. We were no longer excited by the bodies of dead guerrillas; there was a general war weariness.

Whites, too, were tired of the war. Key factors finally forced them to concede to Black majority rule: the negative impact of the international trade embargo on the Rhodesian economy, and the reticence of front-line states such as Mozambique, Zambia, and Botswana to continue to host the guerrillas, because they, too, were being bombed by the Rhodesian air force as the war spilled across the borders. Besides, many had just come out of terrible wars of their own to free themselves from the tyranny of White rule. From Ghana to Kenya to Mozambique, the White terror that had long gripped sub-Saharan Africa was slowly loosening its grip.

As part of the negotiation process, Black nationalist leaders were released from prison to attend the Lancaster House Conference in London in December 1979. Since Rhodesia was an illegal state, it defaulted to being a British colony again for the purposes of the negotiations. Abel Muzorewa led the interim Zimbabwe-Rhodesia government delegation, Robert Mugabe and Joshua Nkomo led the Nationalists' Patriotic Front, and Lord Carrington, British foreign secretary, chaired the conference.

But the sticking point, as always, seemed to be the overriding concern for the welfare of Whites, and what would happen to so-called White-owned land after independence, not the welfare of Blacks, or reparations after nearly a century of disenfranchisement, exploitation, and wanton murder. After all, the war so far had cost more than thirty thousand lives – those that could be accounted for – plus those executed extrajudicially by marauding death squads or used as part of human experiments to test weapons. Nearly two million people were displaced, thousands more permanently disabled and exiled as refugees.

But, at every opportunity, Whites emphasised their collective concern about the lowering of so-called 'standards' under Black rule. The euphemism 'standards' was a racist trope of what Whites have historically perceived to be a universal and incorrigible Black incompetence, to justify the colonial project. In their eyes, Whites were the true custodians, notwithstanding the fact that they were the real murderers and occupiers of stolen lands. Many had never even had meaningful interaction with Blacks, except as servants.

And so the war came to a standstill.

Thousands of guerrillas emerged from the forests into the assembly points or APs. Apart from the occasional skirmishes between the guerrillas and security forces, the guns were silent, if only for a while.

Grandma said she had no idea why our leaders should go to foreign countries to engage in meaningless talks with the very thieves who had usurped our land right from under our noses. She said that when people met secretly behind closed doors to discuss distributing what didn't belong to them, that was theft.

'Why can't they meet here in the open since we are the main victims of past injustices? We know which bit of land belongs to whom. See what they are doing? Planning to thieve all over again. They are the same greedy swine who wine and dine with our enemies whilst we starve!'

For the first time in the history of our country, Blacks were permitted to vote and campaign for political office under the slogan: *One man, one vote!* With that, everyone joined a new political party called ZAPU – the Zimbabwe African People's Union. Besides, there was no other choice. Everyone had to join ZAPU or suffer the consequences.

Cde Brown or Bra Brown was the self-appointed leader of the local faction of the party. Every night, we went to political rallies organised by him after drinking all day. There was a lot of sloganeering, and not much else. We were all *children of the soil* now.

The country was ours even though Whites still owned the land and all the mineral resources – and guns.

'*Viva children of the soil!*' Cde Brown shouted at the top of his voice.

'*Viva!*' we responded.

'*Forward with Freedom!*'

'*Down with the Boers!*'

Afterwards, we took to the dusty roads. We sang provocative political songs and shouted political slogans, many contrived on the spot. We said rude things about the other political party. And, to demonstrate that we meant business, we exposed our buttocks to Bishop Muzorewa himself. There was much excitement as people performed cartwheel spins, punched the air with clenched fists, and thrust the bayonets of our wooden guns at our imaginary enemies. Indeed, we meant business!

Even refugees now claimed to have been real freedom fighters who'd brought down planes from the sky with Soviet Katyusha rocket launchers barely six months after they'd left home. Many left under the cloud of ignominy: theft, attempted murders, rape, and various other crimes that no one cared to remember in the fever of an imminent independence. Because we were all Zimbabweans now.

Bra Brown insisted that from then on we should call him Comrade Brown. Like many, he wanted to cement his war credentials even though he had never been to war, never fired a weapon in his life.

Salani and I carved wooden AK-47s using Grandma's *adze**.

---

* A carving tool similar to a small axe but the cutting edge perpendicular to the handle.

Every son of the soil worth his salt had one. We couldn't wait
to be given real ones, so we could kill all our enemies, not just
White people. Top of the list was Mr V. Gola, Mr R. Sender, and
Sakhile – of whom more later!

So we attended these rallies, armed with make-believe weapons,
just like some of the guerrillas during the war. And when Cde
Brown said *shoot the Boers* we spread out on the sides of the dusty
roads, dived for cover under thorn bushes, our wooden AKs at
the ready, and fired randomly at imaginary enemies.

We enthusiastically rode the wave of empty political protest
as we followed Joshua Nkomo in song right round the world,
as far as Zambia, Mozambique, Namibia, and Azania. Azania
was our name for South Africa. And Blacks there had yet to be
freed.

Cde Brown, in his drunken political meanderings, like
Grandma's mindless perambulations, spearheaded our movements. As such, directions changed on a whim. We picked up
people along the way, some carried pieces of burning rubber as
torches as we trudged along the gravel road, and suddenly scattered when haulage trucks approached at speed.

Drunks, too scared to walk home on their own, started singing
political songs only for their voices to trail off as soon as they got
closer to their destinations.

We got home late at night, only to provoke Grandma's ire.

'We went as far as Nsezi, Mlomoliwoto, then Gongo, and
then . . .'

And she cut us off before we even finished regaling her with
the tall tales of our escapades.

'And what were you doing?'

'Singing, *toyi-toying**, and dancing!' we shouted enthusiastically in unison.

'And what did they give you?'

'Nothing,' we said, feeling slightly deflated.

'You mean to tell me that you spent all night running up and down like clowns for nothing, doing God knows what, and come back covered in dust like ghosts and expect me to embrace you? Have you no sense? At least the other party, what is it called again?'

'UANC, the United African National Congress!'

'That's right, the *Nsee* gives away free T-shirts and whatnot to people singing their songs!'

And then she turned to me. 'And what's that thing in your hand?'

'A gun,' I said.

'I see. You carry guns now, do you?'

'It's not a real gun,' I replied. 'It's a make-believe gun.'

'I am not blind; I can see that's not a real gun. My question is, what are you doing with it?'

'Because we are preparing for the final showdown with the Boers!'

'Party of clowns! You wait until you've chased all the Boers away and see what happens to you, imbeciles. Have you not heard about Zambia? Or Malawi? Or Mozambique? They push wheelbarrows filled with cash just to buy a loaf of bread – that is if they can get it! As soon as they put a Black man's face on

---

* A high-kneed, stomping dance, rhythmically punctuated by exhaled political chants and call and response. In Zimbabwe and South Africa it is used as a method of political protest.

money, its value depreciates, like everything that they touch. Mark my words!' Grandma retorted as she brushed her hands against her thighs unnecessarily. 'Nkomo this! Nkomo that! Get your-selves cleaned up. You are not going anywhere near my blankets covered in dust!'

CHAPTER 21

But, despite Grandma's pessimism, the euphoria of independence engulfed the nation.

We felt it – we were going to be free at last.

We watched buses, lorries, military trucks, tractors with trailers, all filled to the brim with comrades returning from war zones. They pushed clenched fists through bus windows and shouted:

'*Amandla!* All power to the people!'

And thousands who stood along the road responded in unison:

'*Ngawethu!*'

For the first time in our lives, we felt like real human beings with voices, that from then on, after everything that had happened, our humanity would never be doubted.

But daily, as people lined the main road, many were looking for the familiar faces of their loved ones, with the faintest hope that they may still be alive. They watched with serious eyes as bus after bus, tractor after tractor, and lorry after lorry whizzed past without any sign of them. For them, the war had not ended. It had only just begun. And, for many, the war would never end.

It was forward with this, *viva* this, down with that. We were now called the *povo* which my sister Thoko claimed meant *people of various opinions*. But which in reality was slang for very poor people – which we were.

Grandma remarked, 'See, ultimately, this means that from now onwards we'll never agree on anything, which is why those greedy fools are now in a stalemate over negotiations, because they all want different things. But all we want is our land back, and that's not too much to ask. Somehow, I have the feeling this freedom they talk about will take a long, long time to come. Perhaps not even in my or your lifetime!'

And when Thoko explained to Grandma that at school they'd learned that democracy was a 'government of the people, for the people, and by the people' Grandma simply said, 'All being well, things may change if this democracy of theirs works for everyone. See, the problem with *your* leaders is that they're too greedy, and you the people are very forgetful. And, knowing what I know, we'll be back to where we started even before we get a sniff of our land. *So much blood wasted for nothing!'*

But we'd survived the war, whether through ingenuity or sheer luck. Here at last was what all those songs of freedom were about: the hunger for peace, the end of suffering and violence. The overriding message, above the cacophony of sloganeering, was that it was time to put aside our differences and rebuild. The AK rifle and the bazooka vanished, as the image of a soldier with a baby in one hand and a hoe in the other prevailed. It was time for *Freedom and Work*.

Small things began to change too. People seemed to walk a bit more upright. But Grandma, as always, remained sceptical about our brand of freedom.

She asked, 'Now that the war was over, what are the guerrillas going to do?'

And the answer to her question would come very soon.

In the valley below, we watched the soldiers in brown uniforms as they tore down their tents, lowered the lone brown flag. They left behind empty trenches, bullet casings, red mounds of earth. It was a sombre retreat.

At home, there was a ceasefire of sorts too. Things had settled somewhat between Uncle Sami and his wife, Bonani. Despite the sporadic bouts of violence, she seemed to be taking things in her own stride. Grandma left her alone. I watched Bonani wash Uncle Sami's clothes, sweep the yard and in the evening engage in embroidery or knitting. And, because of that, Grandma thought she was pregnant. She warned Uncle Sami against hitting her for now. Grandma gave Bonani so much food that her cheeks started to fill up and she started to swell in all the right places. She was even quieter; she didn't argue as much.

Next door, things took a dramatic turn too. Although feared dead, Lavi, Phani's maternal uncle, finally came back from the war only to find his sister, Phani's mother, gone, and his little nephew crippled. Before the war, Lavi used to be good friends with Uncle Sami. Each morning, they'd mime a war dance in which they'd raise and wave their knives in the air, whilst they shouted *Zhi! Zhi! Zhi!* And then kicked back like dying animals. Lavi was renowned for his unrestrained viciousness. His bulging eyes alone instilled terror in most people.

And, as soon as he arrived, we were interrupted by a scream

that came from Phani's house. 'Please help me! Please don't kill me!' a female voice pleaded.

'I don't care about your screaming. Come here, let me finish you off, you vicious whore!'

We stood outside Grandma's rondavel, and saw Phani's stepmother, barefoot, running towards our house. She was naked, save for a bloodstained white petticoat. There was terror in her eyes. Grandma quickly opened the door to the rondavel and let her in.

Grandma turned to face Lavi who, by the looks of it, was determined to kill Phani's stepmother. His white shirt was drenched in blood too. His eyes dilated as he circled Grandma, blade in hand, like a hunting dog deprived of its prey. He was tall, big, and he had the hugest hands I'd ever seen. With both hands crossed over her chest, Grandma pleaded with him.

'Please have mercy, my son!'

Lavi pointed his knife menacingly at Grandma.

'You were all there when she crippled that little boy. What kind of cowards are you?'

The veins on his neck bulged as he brought the knife back up again as if to cut Grandma.

Grandma ignored the knife as if it was getting in the way of something more important.

'Any more, you'll kill her. And what good will that do?'

Lavi turned round and walked away. A blood trail led from the whimper behind the door to our wooden gate and beyond. Grandma went into the kitchen to console her. I got a small shovel and a bucket and scooped up the blood-soaked sand into the bucket before the dogs started licking it. There was just no meaning to the things that adults did. Uncle Sami hid in his room for the duration of the commotion. He was too embarrassed to come out and face his old friend.

I asked Grandma what would happen to Phani's stepmother; she ignored me. I thought she needed help too. Everyone did; it seemed we'd lost everything, except this terminal neglect. Phani had suffered so much abuse at the hands of his stepmother, and yet, although visible for all to see, his plight had been ignored by everybody. If it took a village to raise a child, it also took a village to neglect a child, and to create monsters too. As Grandma herself would say, we were all responsible for what happened in our communities, and yet it seemed we had yet to free ourselves from the violence that had gripped us for so long.

Phani's stepmother fled later that night – we had no idea where she went. The very next day, his Uncle Lavi took him to the hospital for the much-needed surgery to straighten his toe and reconnect the severed nerves in his foot. But there were much deeper wounds, the psychological wounds that no one else could see or feel except him.

CHAPTER 22

When school reopened, we had a new national anthem: *Nkosi Sikelela iAfrica*, which means *God Bless Africa*.* As the flag for our new country unfurled, we sang the anthem in our own language for the first time. Until then, we'd had no flag of our own, no place we could call home. The anthem resonated with our struggle for freedom and independence. We could sing it straight from our hearts.

School resembled shift work. There were morning and afternoon classes; sometimes we took lessons under the trees. We were the first generation born on the cusp of freedom and a new dawn. We had so much to live for, so much to look forward to.

And Mr A. R. Socks was back with a vengeance! There would be no malingering, no insolence or rigmarole. First, we had to

---

* Interestingly the national anthem that was shared by both South Africa and Zimbabwe started its life as a Christian hymn composed in 1897 by Enoch Sontonga, a Xhosa clergyman with the Methodist Church. But in 1994, fourteen years after its independence, Zimbabwe changed its national anthem to *Simudzai mureza wedu weZimbabwe* Lift High the Banner, the Flag of Zimbabwe.

clean and tidy up the school. We cut the grass, did all the weeding, removed termites' mounds from the walls and erased all the crude drawings of Mr Sender and Ms Khumalo from the chalkboard. We dusted all the textbooks and replenished the supplies of chalk, courtesy of the new Ministry of Education.

Peace in my world was short-lived, however. I entered the storm that was fifth grade unprepared: Mr V. Gola's class. Things took a sudden turn from Ms Khumalo's casual, motherly style of teaching to a dictatorship. I had crossed the threshold into another realm. I could barely cope with the intricate demands of mathematics, let alone being taught by one of the most vicious teachers on the planet. And, as I walked into class, a knot of pupils was huddled towards the far end of the room. As I got closer to the blackboard, I could see, written in the most eloquent cursive script, Mr Gola's *Ten Golden Rules*. But, before I'd even finished reading the first line, he ambled into the room with a cigarette in the corner of his mouth. And, in his hand, a cane.

Mr Gola was a very heavy, thickset man. His ugliness complemented his violent temperament.

'*Class, stand up!*'

'*Sit down!*'

'*Up, down!*'

'*Up, down!*'

And then finally, '*Up!*'

We started the morning with the times table. He chose pupils at random; the sound of the cane was only interrupted by early morning recitations of the Lord's Prayer. The echo of the voices sounded distant: *Our father who art in heaven, hallowed be thy name!* And Mr Gola sauntered along the aisles, viciously jabbing us with the end of his yellow Bic pen in the middle of our heads. Afterwards, when I touched mine, it was soft, delicate, and moist. Pupils who failed to give correct answers remained standing. Torture would only end with the correct answer, however long that took.

'Fifteen times fifteen!' he bellowed.

Judging by the furious gaze directed at me, it became clear that he was pointing at me.

I had an inherent fear of numbers. My brain felt too dense to calculate at Mr Gola's behest. By the time he got closer, my throat was completely dry. As I stared up at the ceiling, all I could hear was the squeaky sound of the borehole pump, which registered a time lapse.

The failure to provide the correct answer carried the punishment of ten full slaps across the face. And Mr Gola would not stop until he achieved this.

When he tried to slap me across the face, I moved sideways like a boxer.

And then he started to count.

'One!'

And I moved again, only this time the tips of his fingers grazed my face.

'One!'

And I ducked again.

Every time he missed; he went right back to the beginning.

'One!'

'Two!'

'Three!'

Three turned to four, and there was six more to go. And that was if he didn't miss, and I didn't flinch.

'Four!'

'Five!'

'Six!'

After six, I raised my hand and his open palm landed on the outer part of my hand. It was an instant reaction; Mr Gola's eyes widened as I closed mine. My ears were throbbing. I had a sudden pounding headache.

'Remove your hands!'

But every time his hand twitched, I instinctively moved my hands to protect my face from any further onslaught. Somehow, it felt as though I had no control over this.

'Stop wasting my time! What did I say to you?'

'Remove my hands, sir.'

'What?'

'Remove my hands, sir,' I said, shoulders raised, neck retracted into the cavity between shoulders like a tortoise.

'If you can't follow simple instructions, we'll start right from the beginning, because you're wasting my time!'

I stayed glued to the floor and disappeared into an imaginary deep hole. All I could hear was the echo of his count as if from a long distance away. I stayed buried in this hole until I heard the magic number – *ten* – and then the brushing of hands. I knew the torment was over, at least for that moment.

There was a belief, strongly held by our teachers, actively encouraged by our parents, that you could teach a child any subject using the most extreme violence. There was always a sense of foreboding. It began early in the morning, stopped briefly after school, only for it to reinstate itself again when we approached school. We spent a huge amount of time trying to figure out the mood and intentions of adults around us, who, at the best of times, treated us like their worst enemies.

To add salt to our wounds, our party, PF ZAPU, led by Joshua Nkomo, lost the elections but won all the twenty seats in the Matabeleland region. Whites voted for the White Party, led by Ian Smith, and the people of Mashonaland voted for ZANU PF, led by Robert Mugabe. ZANU PF won the elections with a resounding victory. Even at independence we were still as divided as before. Many in our region had expressed disappointment that Joshua Nkomo had not won. But it was a numbers game. Nepotism was rife; people voted for individuals from their own ethnic backgrounds, and put their own interests first, before those of the nation. And this would have grave consequences, especially for the Ndebele people and White farmers.

Independence celebrations took place on 18 April 1980, almost one hundred years to the moment when Whites first invaded our country. Celebrations were held in football stadia, bald patches of land and school grounds across the country. The nearest venue to us was Essex Vale. I hitched a ride and squeezed myself between comrades drinking opaque beer straight from cartons. Our dear leader, Nkomo, was expected to drop in, but he never did.

Unfortunate beasts were slaughtered to aid the celebrations. We ate meat served with *samp**, but the organisers forgot to tell

---

* Dish made from dried corn kernels that have been crushed, dehusked, then cooked, and mixed with beans. In isiNdebele or Zulu, it is called *umngqusho* or *umgqushu*.

revellers that they should bring their own plates. I ate mine from a beer carton cut in half.

Later in the day, I watched the twenty-one-gun salute in memory of our fallen heroes. At dusk, a fly-by drenched the sky above with the colours of our new flag – green, yellow, gold, black, and white – which had earlier been raised by a lone soldier, who solemnly saluted as the flag unfurled. Unified voices sang the new national anthem, '*Nkosi sekelela iAfrica*', with such conviction, because many believed in the new nation. But one thing was noticeable: there were no Whites at the Independence Day celebrations. Perhaps they were elsewhere celebrating Founders' Day. It was a small but nonetheless significant sign of the fragility of our peace. Afterwards, I joined thousands of revellers as we headed home – on foot. We sang songs with revolutionary zeal all the way because we had been told we were free at last.

CHAPTER 23

Back at school, to contain some of the energy and exuberance from the independence celebrations, Mr A. R. Socks decreed that sports should now be part of the school curriculum. Once the grass was cut, and the football pitch and sports track prepared, the dreaded inter-class competitions began. The best athletes were selected from each class and the winners vied for the top position within the whole school. Good athletes had the opportunity to spend weekends away at inter-school and regional sports tournaments. As such, I was as determined as ever to win. Before the race, we took off our shirts and placed them in a pile. There were major competitors, of course. Top of the list, Tondo, who just took off even before the whistle blew, and Sakhile, my nemesis on and off the pitch. I quickly jumped on the inside lane, with Tondo to my right. He immediately started dispersing soil with his feet like a bull gearing up for a fight. In the third lane, Sakhile started breathing heavily. And Alfred with a harelip, in the fourth lane, was just focused on his lane. I deliberately pounded my chest to intimidate Tondo.

The first three quarters of the track were the most difficult. If I survived this, then I could count myself in. Conveniently, towards the finishing line, there was an area of dense bush that blocked the spectators' view. It was there I intended to trip whoever was leading the pack; I was prepared to do whatever it took to win. When the whistle blew, I took off at speed. When I started to feel fire in my chest, I glanced back only to see Alfred and Tondo trailing behind me. Surprised, I added more vigour to my stride; I had the feeling that I was going to win the race without the need for chicanery after all. The crowd was going crazy: '*Thabani! Thabani! Zhi! Zhi! Zhi!*'

In fact, I felt so energised by the promise of victory, I forgot to watch the track. Warthogs ventured out at night and dug holes right on the edge of it. As I blindly took the corner, I suddenly slipped into a deep hole, crashing to the ground, which completely stunned me. Whilst I gathered my thoughts, and removed dust from my ears, I could hear voices shouting, '*Tondo! Tondo!*' And then, '*Sakhile! Sakhile!*' as my arch-rival zoomed past.

I remained hidden in the hole until everyone had gone home. When I went to retrieve my shirt, I found instead a rag that had been trampled upon, held together by worn-out threads and stitches. Someone had stolen my new shirt. Slightly dejected, I took the rag home and showed it to Grandma. She reminded me that I should bring home my own shirt or come back bearing battle scars.

It took me a while to figure out who the pilferer of my shirt was. After a lengthy investigation, through a network of informants, I established that the culprit was Sakhile, who was in a different class to me. Sakhile and his belligerent group of bullies would torment just about anyone who displayed any sign of weakness. I was one of only a handful who was prepared to fight for what was mine.

I sought Sakhile out and caught him wearing my shirt. When I asked him to hand it over, he refused. I clobbered him with a blackboard duster, and left him covered in chalk dust, to the ire of the teacher who, frustratingly, decided that I could not prove that the shirt was mine, after all. Still infuriated, I waited till after school. After a further vicious fight, I ripped the shirt from Sakhile: torn and bloodstained. But, as I walked away, I had an ominous feeling that this was unfinished business.

Around noon, that same day, a squeaking sound came from the direction of the Growth Point. Curious, Gift and I ran at break-neck speed towards the source of the sound. When we arrived, we saw a grey Land Rover with loudspeakers attached to the roof. A booming voice made an announcement.

'*Lamhla ntambama, kulebhayiskopo yamahala!*'*

Finally, the bioscope was coming to our village! There was so much excitement in the air. We ran home, hoping that Grandma would be back from her errands so we could relay the good news to her. We could not wait for the sun to go down soon enough, because the films could only be shown at night, in the dark.

When we saw Grandma and Bonani approach with heavy bundles of wood on their heads, we ran towards Grandma. She bent slightly at the knees and leaned the pile of wood against the rondavel. The pile stood tall, way above her head, perhaps twice

---

* Tonight, there is a free bioscope or cinema.

her body weight. There was a small crown on her head made from soft cloth, which she placed at the median point along the bundle, to balance it on her head. It formed a buffer between her head and the rough thorny firewood. It numbed the pain, but not the strain on her neck, knees, and lower back.

As soon as she was free, we pounced with the good news.

'Grandma, there is a bioscope tonight. Please can we go?'

She grunted as if annoyed. Understandably, she was in no mood to entertain us.

'Give me some water. I am dying of thirst!'

I ran into the rondavel, filled up a cup with water, and handed it over to her.

She drained it non-stop and indicated that she needed some more.

'I have a terrible headache,' she said, deflecting from our announcement about the cinema.

Grandma's caffeine-withdrawal headaches were like a hurricane. They started out of nothing, caused a lot of destruction, and no one could stop them except the thrice daily dose of very strong Tanganda Tea, thick with sweet condensed milk, embellished with copious amount of sugar. So sweet, in fact, it made your ears itch and toes curl.

I ran into the kitchen and boiled water for her tea.

Grandma had three main addictions: tea, snuff, and violence. If anything, it was the scarcity of tea and tobacco that provoked the latter. Throughout the rest of the day, we ran here, there, and everywhere, and tried very hard to attend to Grandma's every whim. Meanwhile, she gave no indication of her disposition as to the matter of the bioscope.

To our delight, the bioscope van spent the rest of the afternoon driving around the villages Mlomoliwoto, Gongo, Magedleni, and the Growth Point, making announcements through the loudhailers.

'Don't miss it! Free bioscope tonight! Free bioscope tonight!'

Just when we were about to give up, Grandma called me.

'Thabani!'

'Ma!'

'What time is the bioscope?'

'They said it's after sunset,' I responded enthusiastically.

'Good, bring my tennis shoes and jersey.'

I ran and brought back said items with lightning speed.

Excited, I nudged Gift out of the way whilst I announced that we were indeed going to the bioscope.

We made our way to the Growth Point in semi-darkness. Now that the war was over, there was no longer any fear of an ambush.

A big machine cast moving images on the wall. We sat on the bare earth, our eyes trained on the beam as it projected magic on the wall. The films, like our schoolbooks, consisted entirely of Black people, who appeared confused all the time, especially when talking to White people. We watched, to our own amusement, as our lives were projected back to us – *distorted*. People urinated in the river upstream only for others to drink the same water downstream. And, to Grandma's dismay, they showed films about the transmission of venereal disease, and graphic war films intended to deter any aspiring dissidents amongst us – now that the war was over.

The evening ended with the showing of everybody's favourite character, a clown called Tickey. At the start of the film, we counted in unison.

'*Ten, nine, eight, seven, six, five, four, three, two, one!*'

The film was fast-forwarded for added effect. We watched two fat ladies as they chased after Tickey, the diminutive clown, quick on his feet, up drainpipes, through tiny culverts under bridges, over bridges, through washing lines, dragging newly washed clothes through dirt. The two fat ladies probed him with broom sticks up his bottom. He spun round the culvert and crawled in the opposite direction only to encounter a similar fate. When they cornered him, he managed to squeeze through the tiniest of spaces, and escaped. It was the only highlight of the evening.

We returned to school reinvigorated. It wasn't all work and no play. To break up the monotony of child labour, and violence, however entertaining, every Friday afternoon, except on payday, Mr R. Sender convened a theatre group, in which we engaged in the frolics of amateur dramatics as we re-enacted the paroxysm of King Shaka's grief following the death of his mother, Nandi, in which pregnant women were slain, cows with calf slaughtered, and the cultivation of crops forbidden for a whole year. Anyone who failed to shed tears for Nandi, on demand, was immediately killed.

Mr R. Sender was a rarity: a Coloured man who taught in a Black school. He was as close to Whiteness as it got, a discipli-narian who made you so afraid just by looking at you. Yet his class also sang beautifully. Perhaps song and theatre were Mr Sender's attempt to rebalance things.

In preparation, we wore the regalia of warriors: amulets; head-dresses made from chicken feathers; and shields carved out of real cowhide, with small lattices across the face of the shields, which distinguished each regiment. We armed ourselves with wooden *assegais*, almost as treacherous as the real ones, depending on the type of wood used.

The best part of the play was towards the end when all warriors downed their weapons and engaged in song. Military prowess was replaced by chivalry as girls took the lead and boys joined in the chorus. Soon, all was forgotten. Feet rose high above the head, followed by a choreographed and synchronised fall and rise of bodies – hallmarks of a traditional Zulu dance.

UShaka, UShaka wayebusa ngegazi! *
Wasi dumela isalukazana wasibamba ngengalo,
Sathi ngiyekela, ngiyekela, ngamathambo amhlophe!

We sang the song that encapsulated the last words allegedly uttered by Shaka, founder of the Zulu kingdom, as his two half-brothers thrust a spear through his heart – not all bonds are sacred.

Girls ululated as we danced in formation and moved in a circle.

---

* Shaka was a bloodthirsty King, who grabbed an old lady by the arm, and she screamed, 'please let go of my frail old bones', and on the throes of death, he declared that the world hence forth will be ruled by birds.

Solemnity was in the air. We forgot about the past, because right there was the closest we would ever come to being free.

UShaka, UShaka wayebusa ngegazi!
Wasi dumela isalukazana wasibamba ngengalo,
Sathi ngiyekela, ngiyekela, ngamathambo amhlophe!

And so we continued to sing: *'Watsho uTshaka, nyakana efayo, wathi ilizwe seliyobuswa zinyoni.'*

Afterwards, we walked home separately, each one of us caught up in our own little world.

We embraced Friday afternoons as a kind of affirmation, history in our words. Whites had said there was no country here – nothing but trees and animals, just like morning on creation day – and yet here we were.

But instead of song and dance what was required was a cold, calculated analysis of the past, because our wealth was never about the land. It was our consciousness, our language, our history, without which we would never rise to the new challenges.

Many began to ask: who would we be without limitations, without embracing the lies that we'd been taught? But it wasn't just Blacks who needed to do the emotional work to defang the myth of racism and the infallibility of Whiteness. Whites, Indians, Coloureds, all those privileged light-skinned races who had stood by, participated in upholding white supremacy and, ultimately, benefitted from the colour bar, had their work cut out for them.

★

Every Wednesday morning on our way to school, we began to see convoys of White families heading towards South Africa on the Bulawayo–Beitbridge Road. They could not live under Black rule; they wanted to leave because they were unwilling to share with us. Whites, these birds of flight, didn't want to give the new country a chance. After everything that had happened, after all the pain, the anguish, and destruction, they were leaving.

Grandma warned that we mustn't forget that they were running away from the nightmare of Black people as their neighbours. Whites had hidden their own brutality behind the idea of our backwardness. And now they would not give us a chance to show them our humanity. Or embrace our Blackness. How could we ever get back what had been taken away from us?

It was rare to witness this kind of migration. In future, they'd pray for their bleakest predictions of us to come true. They looked from behind their car windows, their cars overladen, but unable to take our land with them. Wherever they went, the ghost of our country would forever haunt them. Like the young men who went to war before them, we would patiently wait for them to come back. They were Zimbabwe's children too. The rivers, the mountains, the springs, were memory too, the coordinates that would lead them home. The land had a hold; Zimbabwe would not let go of them. And they, too, would never let go of it.

At the front, and at regular intervals, between the middle and the rear of the convoy, there was an armoured vehicle at the back of which stood a White soldier on a high swivelling chair, his machine gun aimed at us. He gently swivelled round, as if moved by an invisible ill wind. Now and then, we got a glimpse of his face, hidden behind sunglasses. Without seeing his eyes, we could not tell how he felt about us. But he could see our wretchedness; there was nothing we could do but stand in the freezing cold, in our school uniforms, armed with nothing but blunt pencils and old textbooks with missing pages.

CHAPTER 24

At home, Uncle Sami's physical wounds seemed to be healing, but he was drained of energy. He would go for days without uttering a word, just slumped with a blank, distanced stare. Sometimes I caught him alone, weeping deep sobs, shaking. The war had left behind many like him.

So he left for some quiet corner of the country where he thought he could heal. And yet the war was with himself.

And, with time, Bonani, too, withdrew into herself, her countenance drained of all happiness. She gave Grandma and my sisters a wide berth. The only person she allowed around her was me. A bond developed between us; she told me her nickname: Mamjana.

But I did not foresee where this was leading, because I had preoccupations of my own, unfinished business with Sakhile. I still felt that he had to pay for his crime.

This time I took the issue to Grandma.

'Grandma, I think I have a problem at school.'

And she snapped back at me, 'You think or you have? Which is it?'

I was taken aback, for a bit.

'Yes, go on. I am listening. What kind of problem is it?'

'It's about another boy, Sakhile,' I said, trying to gauge her temperament.

'You mean that little runt? Madlodlo's boy, yes?'

'Yes, Grandma,' I said.

'So, what's the problem?'

'Sakhile is giving me trouble at school.'

'And what are you going to do? This is the same boy who stole your shirt, yes?'

I nodded yes and continued.

'I don't know just yet, Grandma. I've beaten him twice in a fist fight, but he keeps coming back!'

'That still doesn't answer my question. What do you expect me to do? Fight for you? See, when I herded cattle, I used to fight boys regardless. And I never lost a single fight, sticks or no sticks. Now, do you have a knobkerrie? *Unentonga neh?** And do you know how to use it?'

I said yes, because if I had said that I didn't know how to use it there was every chance that she'd volunteer to teach me. And that's a prospect I'd not wish on my worst enemy, let alone myself. But, somehow, she could tell I was lying.

'*Nye! Nye! Nye!*' she said, seemingly annoyed by my placid 'Yes' reply. 'You don't know anything, do you? You can't fight, you don't know how to look after our animals, because every time I leave you with animals for a minute they're gone, before I even

---

* A short wooden club with a heavy knob on one end, traditionally used as a weapon of choice for close combat. It is heavy and lethal enough to crush skulls.

turn my back. The fence is falling apart. And now you're sitting here dangling your balls unashamedly, telling me that you don't know how to use the most rudimentary weapon that every man should be familiar with: a stick! Because if you knew what a stick felt like around your ribs you wouldn't be sitting here procrastinating over fighting with an ill-bred runt!'

'Yes, Grandma,' I said, wishing I'd never started the conversation in the first place.

'Now does he swim, that boy?'

'Yes, Ma.'

'Don't just say *Yes, Ma*! Where, how often, and with whom does he swim?'

'I know where roughly, but I am not sure of the times.'

'It's hot outside, yes?'

I nodded, anticipating her next move.

'The deepest pool is further down the river. Now go and see if you can find him. Wait till there is nobody around. If my memory serves me right, there is only one exit from that stagnant pool. There are rocks this side of the river and a steep bank on the opposite side. The other end is too slippery because of green algae, which means he is all yours. Now, once he's trapped, teach him a lesson he'll never forget! Make sure he gets the message and don't come back here unless you've done a good job of it, you hear?'

I mumbled something as the treacherous plan began to hatch in my mind.

'I said, did you hear what I said?'

'Yes, Grandma!'

'Yes, Grandma, what?'

'I meant to say, thank you, Grandma.'

'Good, now go. Don't come back whimpering like a wounded dog, because you'll have me to deal with!'

And I didn't like the sound of that, but now I was committed after seeking Grandma's counsel. All that remained was for me to execute the plan accordingly. Once again, I turned to Salani for moral support and his first observation highlighted the biggest flaw in the plan.

'What if he dies? Your plan sounds too vicious to me.'

'It's meant to be vicious, but don't worry,' I reassured Salani. 'He won't die – minor bruises and small dents to the head, perhaps. That's all. Grandma said that I should aim for the ribs.'

'And you are going to do all that whilst his head is submerged underwater? What if he sees you and dives under and comes out the other end?'

'Ah, see, that's where you come in. You can cover the other end, no? That way he'll have nowhere to go!'

'What's got into you? You know, it's not too late to abandon your *vicious plan*, as you call it? And I am not convinced about small dents and bruises on his head. You just want to kill the boy and I want no part of it. And you know his older brother will kill you when he finds out, right?'

'But you can help me with the training?'

'*Thabani*, I am not letting you throw stones at me!' said Salani, alarmed at the prospect of being the next moving target.

Undeterred by Salani's concerns, I resorted to hunting for Sakhile at the weekend. I even sent feelers through a few friends to establish his whereabouts. But, unbeknown to me, he had been stalking me. On the final day of my search, feeling exhausted, I sat down under the shade of the acacia tree, with its drooping branches weighed down by the nests of the yellow-and-black weaver birds. Their spherical nests swayed to and fro in the slightest breeze. It was a hot day and I'd dozed off in the slumber of the hot afternoon. As I drifted into a light sleep, something heavy but also surprisingly light bounced off my head. I suddenly felt dizzy, I could not see clearly and within seconds realised that my white T-shirt was soaked in blood. I wiped the blood off my face with the T-shirt and, when I turned round, I saw Sakhile as he made good his escape. I tried to run after him as fast as I could, but I was bleeding heavily, and my strength started to wane. With that, I decided to head home.

When I tried to explain to Grandma what had just happened, she chastised me for sitting where I could be ambushed in the first place. Besides, she despised self-pity. With that, she dragged me closer and examined the back of my head. She ordered my sister to heat up some water. Meanwhile, she shaved the area around the wound with a blunt razor blade that she used for cutting everything else. And when the water was ready, she added a pinch of salt, cleansed the wound, dried it, and added potash to it. It was the cure-all medicine that she used on everything. Afterwards, she bandaged my head with a recycled bandage, which she kept from her old wound, and warned me not to rest, but to go and seek revenge, even before the headaches subsided. And, she warned me, if I didn't seek revenge, I'd have to face her. And she meant every word.

I left the room and stood outside, contemplating what to do next. But I was not ready to fight, yet.

*

On the days that followed, I lied. I told Grandma that I had sharp, throbbing headaches. I was embarrassed to go to school with my head wrapped in a bandage. Besides, there was not only the humiliation to contend with but Mr Gola's wrath also. So I decided to stay away from school whilst I recuperated.

Meanwhile, Grandma decided to excuse Bonani from all extraneous work. She believed that she was pregnant, and she was excited by the prospect of her first grandchild. Each morning, as soon as Grandma and my sisters left, I observed Bonani as she bathed, changed clothes, and walked towards the Growth Point. She wore the same outfit and carried a small plastic bag. When I tried to follow her, she strongly insisted that I should stay behind, what with my head still sore. Wearing the same clothes and using the same route daily was a kind of reconnaissance, to make everything seem normal in order to avoid any suspicion.

I had a deep suspicion that something was up, but I wasn't quite sure what.

So I decided not to tell Grandma, but continued to observe Bonani's routine. It was a Friday; Grandma had already gone early to the fields and my sisters were at school. I sat at my usual spot, on the side of Uncle Sami's bedroom, basking in the early morning sun. Bonani walked past, all dressed up in her favourite white dress. She was also carrying a small suitcase with her belongings. She didn't see me as I was shrouded from view by the wall. Somehow, I knew she wasn't coming back. After everything that had happened to her, I watched her go – she was free at last.

When Grandma got back from the fields, she went straight into the kitchen. There was nothing cooking.

'Where is she?' she asked with thunder in her eyes.

'Gone,' I said.

'Gone? What do you mean gone? Gone where?'

'Gone!' I repeated with a hidden satisfaction. 'She took her things, and she's gone.'

Grandma rushed to Uncle Sami's bedroom and when she came out she mumbled something about whores.

'Why didn't you tell me she was leaving? What is your job around here?'

'But you were far away, Grandma,' I said in my defence.

'You mean to say she didn't say anything to you?'

'No,' I said. 'She just left without even saying goodbye!'

With that, Grandma resigned herself to the fact that Bonani had finally escaped.

Strangely, I thought a lot more about her now that she was gone. She'd arrived like a stranger, sat in the corner, and said very little about herself. She only came to light when she'd forgotten to do something. And yet she was there all along, for nearly two years, and we didn't know who she really was, except as Uncle Sami's wife. And when she left it was as if she'd never been there at all.

CHAPTER 25

Bonani's departure, and the lengthy recovery from my head wound, gave me ample time to reflect on things. The more deeply I thought about how negatively violence had impacted our lives, the more I began to detest it. I reconciled myself to the idea that I was never going to avenge myself against Sakhile. The way in which he had ambushed and struck me with that rock meant only one thing: that he'd meant to cause me the most serious harm, if not kill me. The dispute over a shirt and school playground horseplay had taken a nasty turn: it was no longer child's play. Just recently, an older cousin had been stabbed and nearly died. And every weekend there was a violent incident at the Growth Point. Mawabeni was slowly becoming a hothouse of violence. When I returned to school, I avoided Sakhile. I kept my resolution secret from Grandma.

It took a while, but when Uncle Sami heard the news of Bonani's disappearance, he arrived straight from the mines, still broke. He didn't ask much about her, but continually harangued Grandma for money. Again, the little money that Ma gave to Grandma went straight into his pocket. When Grandma made me write more ransom notes to Ma, as a precaution, I added a line right at the bottom, to warn Ma that Uncle Sami was back – she knew what that meant.

When the money failed to materialise, Grandma suspected foul play, but she wasn't sure who amongst us had betrayed her. Her disposition towards us, particularly Gift and me, suddenly became frosty.

To forget the situation at home, every school morning, Salani and I ran to school together. Mostly, we pretended to be small aeroplanes, the ones we'd seen during the war, dropping leaflets. And we were super excited because Christmas was round the corner. With our arms spread out, we flew all the way to school. We also had the habit of kicking everything that was in our way: cardboard boxes, abandoned home-made plastic balls, cans, cobs, and defenceless smaller boys on their way to school. Occasionally, we slapped those with shaven heads, and we were long gone before they even thought of retaliating. It was all harmless fun unless you were the victim of our pranks.

As we approached the school gate, I saw Sakhile with his newly formed posse. I quickly took note of the faces of his co-conspirators: Nqobile, Nathaniel, Alfred.

Just then, I noticed a home-made plastic ball sitting enticingly on the verge of the grass. My earlier resolution of non-violence forgotten, as soon as I saw it, something inside told me to launch the ball at Sakhile and his co-conspirators as a warning. I had my Bata canvas Tenderfoots on, tied tightly, so everything was perfect. I lunged at the ball with all the force that I could muster, but the ball did not move.

Instead, a sharp searing sensation shot up my big toe and spread up my leg as the most excruciating pain engulfed the rest of my body. I grabbed my leg and spun round on the spot and when I finally let it go it was as if my big toe had acquired a life of its own. Sakhile and his friends fell to the ground, laughing. All I could see from the corner of my eye was a cluster of fingers pointing at the stone football.

And Salani calmly said: 'By why did you kick it? Did you not see me skip over it?'

'No,' I said, my body still riddled with pain. 'Why are you lying? I didn't hear you shouting, nor did I see you pointing at the ball!'

'Look,' he said, 'I am not the one at war with you. I just think that right now we need to go to the clinic and get that foot seen to!'

Luckily, the clinic was a stone's throw from the gate. It was a small blue building, unassuming, the size of one of our classrooms, with a veranda that acted as a waiting area. The two nurses at the clinic were only able to deal with minor ailments, and those with serious injuries had to be transferred to Essex Vale. After my last experience there, I was petrified that I might end up there again.

When we arrived at the clinic, the smell of methylated spirit evoked the terrifying memory of injections. As soon as we entered the main reception area, Sister Bhebhe's large cow's eyes greeted us. Her half-moon glasses hung precariously over her broad nose, and her heavily starched white nurse's uniform just about managed to contain her reels of midriff flesh. A silver fob watch dangled just above her left breast, beneath which a gold-rimmed badge announced her name: S. N. Bhebhe.

Worryingly, her countenance was bereft of any hint of kindness.

'Name?' she said, without even looking at me.

'Thabani,' I answered with trepidation.

And, with the same hostility, she continued her line of questioning: 'And whose child are you?'

'MaMoyo's,' I said, hoping she might recognise Grandma's name. But she didn't.

'Which one? There are many women in this area with that name!'

'Muvu's!' I retorted with glee, this time using Grandma's *nom de guerre*, hoping it might jog her memory.

'Oh, I see!' Sister Bhebhe looked at me as she lowered her glasses even further, before continuing: 'And what were *we* doing today?'

'Not sure what you were . . . Sorry, I kicked a stone football by the school gate.'

And she looked at me again, but this time with such incredulity.

'*Ibhola lamatshe* – a stone football? There is such a thing now, is there? And what kind of brain dreams up a stone football and then goes on to kick it, willingly, knowing full well that it is made of stone, huh?'

And then she took her glasses off completely. As I was contemplating what to say, she turned to Salani, who, rather conveniently, had devolved all responsibility for answering Sister S. N. Bhebhe's questions to me.

'And why are you staring at me like a ruminating goat, huh? You people will do anything not to get an education, which is why you're still crafting balls out of stone like stone-age man! And *you* are malingering in my clinic clogging up spaces for real patients, which your friend here is already doing. And I won't entertain it – balls or no balls. Now get going!'

Dejected, Salani shuffled his way out of the clinic and turned left towards school.

'Someone disguised the stone as a ball,' I pleaded, trying to speed things up.

'And you wilfully kicked it, yes?'

I was in no mood to explain further. The pain was becoming more unbearable.

Finally, Sister Bhebhe got off the chair, put her glasses on, and beckoned me to follow her as she wobbled along the corridor, which led us to a small treatment room. I limped all the way behind her.

'Sit down on the bench and take off your shoe.'

There was blood inside my Tenderfoot, and my big toe was completely degloved, the toenail held in place by shredded bits of skin. Sister Bhebhe took one look and shook her head: 'You've done yourself a bit of mischief, haven't you? The only good thing to come out of this, one hopes, is that there'll be no need for further lessons on kicking stone footballs – for you and your accomplices.'

'It was an accident,' I pleaded.

'That's what you all say. You stab each other close to death and break bottles and bricks on each other's heads and call it an accident. I've seen it all before, and nothing surprises me anymore.'

And, without warning, she sprayed a purplish liquid right on top of the exposed flesh and I nearly jumped out of my skin.

'Sit still and put your foot down. I haven't got all day. You come here uninvited and disturb my peace and now you're carrying on like you are the victim of a great injustice! Had you gone directly to school, we wouldn't be dealing with this now, would we? Now, next time we'll think twice before kicking stone balls or whatever the latest craze is, won't we?'

She grabbed my foot with a gloved hand and placed it on a twice-folded green cloth spread above her right knee. She held my foot in a tight grip and with a pair of tweezers she grabbed the dangling nail and bits of skin, before cutting the loose skin with stainless-steel scissors in a circular motion. The cold steel touched the raw flesh on my toe, and I instinctively tried to pull my foot back, but Sister Bhebhe's prohibiting countenance stopped my foot mid-flight.

Once she'd finished cutting the skin, she removed the rest of the damaged toenail, and tossed the remnants into a yellow clinical-waste bag. She then grabbed a ball of cotton wool with her tweezers, dipped it into a dark brown liquid held in a kidney-shaped stainless-steel bowl, and she daubed my wounded toe with it. The pain cut through to the bone and this time I jerked backwards and fell over on the other side of the bench, still holding my right ankle tightly with both hands.

When I thought of bolting through the door, she was already standing there, her big frame leaving no room for manoeuvre. Cornered, I composed myself and sat back on the bench. I tentatively presented my foot to her again. And she hit me with more of the same. Before I could catch my breath, she added yet another layer of a brown caustic paste, on top of which she applied a thick bandage. Finally, just before the bandage ran out, she tore the remainder into two strips and wrapped it round my ankle to secure it.

Just when I thought it was all over, she asked me: 'Have you had your tetanus injection?' All I heard was the word *injection*. And before I even said anything, she said, 'Let's assume that you haven't!' She sighed disparagingly. 'Such negligence! Come with me.'

She made me lie prone on the metal bed while she grabbed a small bottle, fat in the middle, with a surprisingly tiny neck for a medicine bottle, compared to Grandma's concoctions. She removed the silver foil to expose a soft rubbery top and tipped it upside down before piercing it with a green needle, aspirating the contents into a syringe. Her glasses slid, as if voluntarily, towards the tip of her nose as she slammed the syringe with her fat finger, whilst pushing and pulling the plunger inside the syringe to release the air. And then she pulled my shorts down a little, exposing the upper end of my backside. Without warning, she darted the sharp needle into my buttock, and it felt as though she'd hit the bone. She exacerbated the pain by impatiently squeezing the contents of the syringe into my backside, and immediately withdrew the needle as though in a rush. Then she placed a small ball of cotton wool over the puncture site, and said, rather gleefully, 'There now! Compared to your game of stone football, that wasn't too bad now, was it?'

And without placating me with an apology, given her brutish-ness, she continued: 'Now I need not emphasise that you ought not to be involved in more ball games, stone or otherwise, till this heals. You hear me? And don't run around showing off that wound to those ignorant friends of yours who created this mess in the first place! Come back in a week's time so I can check the state of the wound and perhaps change the bandage. Now, tell that grandmother of yours to leave you alone till the wound heals. Oh,

and when you get home, make sure that you clean those *takkies**
before the blood dries and destroys them completely.'

When I got home, Grandma immediately removed the bandage
to inspect the wound herself just in case I intended to use it as an
excuse for malingering. 'Got work to do,' she said, as she looked
at my toe. I thought she was worried, but she didn't let it show
lest I capitalised on her sympathy. Instead, she interred the injured
toe in a forest of herbs and afterwards daubed the wound with a
concoction of her own.

'See,' she said, 'the problem with White man's medicine is that
it is not strong enough. Takes twice as long for anything to heal.
And don't look at me as if I don't know what I am talking about!'

'But Sister Bhebhe said not to disturb the wound, certainly not
to walk on it!' I tried hard to convince Grandma.

'Did she now? Who in the hell does she think she is to tell
me what to do in my own home? Speaking of which, are you a
cripple now? And who is going to be carrying you around, you
blaliswine?'† She reapplied the bandage. Her dressing, although
crude, was comfortably loose; it allowed the wound to breathe.

---

* Tennis shoes or plimsoles.
† Bloody swine.

CHAPTER 26

In the days that followed, surprisingly, Grandma left me alone. It was as if she was waiting for the next big thing, whatever that might be. After all, the scars on my head wound had barely healed.

It was whilst still feeling sorry for myself that Uncle Sami came up with an idea to cheer me up. Besides, he had nothing better to do. 'Let's go into town and visit your father. Just me and you! You are a man now; you need to meet your father!'

Uncle Sami was not doing this out of the kindness of his heart. He was bored and broke.

But I was very excited at the prospect of meeting my father for the first time. He had never entered my mind as someone real, who existed in the world that I lived in. He was the stranger in the black-and-white photograph fixed to the wall with a single rusty nail. His stare radiated warmth: he was immaculately dressed in a grey polo neck, with white stripes running across his chest. It was neatly tucked in under a belt with a prominent buckle. He was a man with a flamboyant style. I was glad, and sad, at the same time. Because I was in awe of the idea of him being my father. But I also found it hard to reconcile his beautifully manicured

255

hands with those of a man who terrorised my mother with a knife whilst she was pregnant with me. I was eleven years old and, for more than a decade, we'd been separated by the price of a bus ticket. Grandma had mentioned his name: Paul.

We got up early Saturday morning to catch the bus to Bulawayo. We had no luggage. This was meant to be a day trip. When we arrived in Bulawayo, Uncle Sami took me to the beer garden first. He bought himself a beer and for me a bottle of Fanta and a small packet of vanilla cream biscuits. It was a beautiful day, the place awash with people drinking beer under big bright umbrellas. It was early in the day. No one was drunk, yet.

We left the beer garden around noon to get an omnibus. Uncle Sami gave our fare to the driver, who was dressed in an immaculate emerald-green uniform, his green beret tilted to the side like a soldier. He pressed a small silver ticket machine, and it spewed out tickets.

I had no idea where we were going. I concentrated instead on the hustle and bustle of city life. Men in starched red-and-white uniforms pushed heavy ice-cream tricycles uphill, and vendors displayed tomatoes, bananas, green vegetables, penny cools, and sweets.

The bus went through townships with cramped small houses without front gardens, beautiful flowers, or lawns. We drove past White City football stadium, and then Joshua Nkomo's house at Pelandaba. Uncle Sami craned his neck through the small windowpane as he pointed it out to me.

We jumped off the bus outside a big cemetery with thousands

of graves behind tall pine trees. Uncle Sami mentioned that my real grandparents, Grandma Annie and Grandpa Dennis, were buried there. But he didn't take me to their graves. We waited instead for a gap in traffic and ran across the busy road.

When we reached the opposite side, Uncle Sami said, 'This is Old Magwegwe, where your father lives.'

We entered long, winding mazes between houses stacked back-to-back, consisting mainly of two rooms, and outside toilets. There were even smaller outhouses for extra accommodation. Like many houses in Black townships, these houses were not built for families, but to house cheap labour. Since the wind blew from east to west, all the dust from the White suburbs, the city, the industrial sites, and the waste-disposal centre ended up there. It was part of the malignant design of the colonial system.

We turned the corner, then up the road, past the butcher's and the grocery stores, and then down along a small tarmacked road. Nearly two hundred feet further, we arrived at a pale blue house with mango, lemon, and orange trees. It had a small patch of immaculately trimmed lawn and a crop of green vegetables cor-ralled into a small corner of the garden. The window had burglar bars on the inside, moulded into floral designs with spirals at the centre, visible through lace curtains with holes.

Uncle Sami knocked on the solid metal green door. The door opened and a man appeared. He was naked to the waist; his belt was not buckled properly. He was barefoot, his toes and feet pristinely manicured as though he had never walked barefoot in his life. He was not much taller than Uncle Sami. He nursed a slightly rotund belly and unlike Uncle Sami he didn't have a single scar on his face.

He recognised Uncle Sami instantly. His face lit up, exposing tobacco-stained teeth. I could tell that, should he choose so, he was capable of doing harm. 'It's been a long time! I wasn't expecting any visitors today, let alone you. Stay there and don't move!'

He vanished into the room behind him, leaving the door wide open. When he returned, he was holding two chairs, which he passed to Uncle Sami. He went inside again and came back with a third chair. We put the chairs out on the lawn. It was a lovely afternoon; there was a buzz in the air. Everything was packed too close. Houses backed on to each other. You could eavesdrop on private conversations without having to sprain your neck and train your ears.

When we sat down, the man turned to Uncle Sami, pointed at me, and said: 'We haven't been introduced?'

'He's your son. He is a man now. I thought you might like to see him.'

With that, the man started to sob uncontrollably. He got up and walked the short distance towards the mango tree. I listened to him heave and convulse. I remained seated, unmoved. I felt no reason to cry. As Uncle Sami consoled him, I found myself thinking, what made it easy for men like my father and Uncle Sami to terrorise women and neglect their children? I sat still and watched them. When he finally turned round, I came face to face with the man Uncle Sami called my father. He extended his right hand, and I did too, by way of a greeting.

'How are you?' he said. I noted that he didn't call me son.

'Fine,' I replied, trying to avoid his gaze.

'Your uncle tells me you are a very bright boy?'

I nodded, cautiously. I was not sure what to feel. So many things that could have been averted had happened to me. And all along he was there. Throughout the journey, I'd had so many questions to ask him, so many things to say. But, now that he was here, I was completely overwhelmed. I had no feelings for him, and with that I withdrew back inside myself. I scanned him for any resemblance between us. I needed to convince myself that I really was his son and that the whole scenario had not been a made-up story by Uncle Sami. Besides, Grandma said only the mother knew who the father of a child was. Something was lodged in my throat, and I wondered why he had never bothered to find us, if Uncle Sami could find him with such ease.

I observed every little thing about him just in case this would be the last time that I'd see him: his mannerisms, the chubby fingers on his hands, the way he laughed, his gait. Because when you're raised in a broken home you learn to mistrust. And I still wasn't sure what to call him; I had never had the opportunity to call anyone my father. Grandma had always been our mother, father, defender, protector, and everything else in between.

'Do you mind if I take the boy for a walk?'

'He's your son – why are you asking me?' said Uncle Sami with a smile so big his mouth could hardly contain it.

I was still suspicious.

The man put on his shirt, tightened and buckled his belt, and plunged his feet into a pair of new shoes. He held my hand as we walked up the road. His hand was too soft, his grip slack, not purposeful like Grandma. He reminded me of what Grandma had said to me: 'Your hands are too soft for a man.' Perhaps there was a resemblance between us.

We walked past the grocery stores, the butcher's again, round a bend and then downhill.

'How's school?' he asked, as if we'd had this conversation before. I had stood, all by myself, so many times on prize-giving days and award ceremonies at school except on days when Grandma remembered to attend. And to think that he had always been there. But I let it go.

'Fine,' I said. And deliberately brought Gift into the frame of our conversation.

'Gift is in Grade Six and I am in Grade Five. She's good at maths, which I am not very good at, but her English is not that good.'

I decided to test the waters further.

'We both need new uniforms and shoes!'

There was no discernible follow-up on his previous question about school; he totally sidestepped the issue of school uniforms, shoes, and books.

Instead, he said, 'I am taking you to meet your cousins – they'll be thrilled to meet you!'

We finally arrived at a house guarded by a single sweet lemon tree under which was gathered a group of young men. On seeing him, they shouted in unison, 'Hey, *ankeli**! How is your hangover?' They passed him a *dagga* joint†. He took a long draw. I remained on the periphery of their conversation. Until, that is, one of them asked, 'And who's the boy?' as if asking about a recently acquired millstone.

---

* Uncle
† Cannabis joint.

'Oh, this is Thabani, my eldest son with Elisabeth!'

I could tell that he was brimming with pride.

'I thought your eldest was Boyson, with the other woman. What's her name?'

The others stifled a knowing laugh as he humorously evaded the enquiry.

'That's another story. This here is my son. He'll inherit everything that I own!'

'No, really? Is this *the* Thabani?' enquired one of them with a slight tincture of incredulity in their voice. I had gleaned from this random reference that I might have a half-brother somewhere. Or more siblings, whom presumably he took care of. Perhaps Gift and I were the only ones he didn't care about.

The man gently nudged me forward, encouraging me to embrace these strangers. I felt exposed and vulnerable as there were no familiar faces.

My father said, 'Thabani, this is Gerry, Stanley, Dee – these are your cousins, my older sister's, your Aunt Gloria's, sons!'

Gerry was the oldest of the three brothers. He was tall, with a round, welcoming face. Stanley was lean, mean, with a lazy eye and a row of rotten upper incisors. Dee was darker, bulkier, than the rest. He had a scar under his right eye. He had his hat pulled over the left side of his face even though he was in the shade. His bottom lip was a crimson red. He was the one left holding the stub from the *dagga* joint. As he continually dragged from it, all I could see was the flame disappearing into his mouth. I was worried that he might inhale the whole thing into his lungs.

Gerry said to me, 'You are a man now. Why don't you come

and live with your father instead of living with women? And we can teach you how to be a real man, huh?'

They all laughed simultaneously, and shared knowing glances – again.

I was not sure what to say.

Stanley cheerfully interjected: 'He is an exact replica of *you!*' as if proof were needed. I thought he was too light-skinned to be my father because my skin tone was much darker. Grandma had emphasised this one thing about me. In a country where having light skin was seen as a blessing, this wasn't something I was bound to forget that easily.

They decided on an impromptu celebration. We walked back as a group and fetched Uncle Sami from the house of the man I'd now resolved to call my father. And I let that sink in for a while. We headed to the shebeen nearby, run by a voluptuous woman, who, on seeing my father, embraced him for far too long.

We sat down and they started drinking. My father gave me money to go and buy biscuits and a soft drink. I came back and ensconced myself in the corner of the small room. It was as if I was back at Kiki's, but without the smoke. I watched men come and go. Some had one drink and left. Others stayed. My father spent the whole night fraternising with the large woman. She was drinking too. The more they drank, the more they let their guard down. But I'd heard that he had a wife back home in his village.

My father had forgotten all about me, us – so soon.

I watched him leave surreptitiously, via the back door, with the big woman. It was dark outside.

★

Uncle Sami had fallen asleep. I got up and shook him awake. He scratched his head and rubbed his eyes. Once he realised that we'd been abandoned, he said to me, 'I have a plan. Let's pay your mother a surprise visit!'

He wanted to take me to where my mother lived with her latest husband. I didn't know much about this person, save to say that when he last visited with Ma, he spent most of his time reading his newspapers, and didn't seem to have much to say. I'd paid him no mind because in our lives men came and went even before we knew who they were.

Uncle Sami was in his element. 'When we get there, I am going to hide you and then – *boom* – surprise her!'

I went along with his plan. I wasn't sure how this would pan out given that he'd been drinking all day. Also, knowing Ma's volatile temperament, things might turn out differently.

We made our way to the bus stop and caught a bus to Lobengula township, which was where Ma lived. All the Black townships were named after Ndebele kings: Mzilikazi, Matshobana, Luveve. Lobengula was the last of the Ndebele kings before Whites took over our country. He was the reason why Ndebele people had always been blamed for selling Zimbabwe to the White men for a mirror and beads. But the truth was much more complicated than that.

As we got off the bus, Uncle Sami went over his plan to make sure that things would go smoothly. We jumped off the bus outside a big church, and walked across a small swamp, with a whiff of sewage, towards houses located on the brow of a small hill, beneath the city's water reservoir.

Uncle Sami led me to a beautiful white house with a big black gate. There was a manicured green lawn and a flowering sycamore tree. Grey granite gravel was spread all round the house. I could feel its crunch under my shoes as we walked towards the rear, which was where the main door was located. At the rear, there was a big banana tree and a small vegetable garden. Although late at night, the air was mild, cool, and welcoming. Uncle Sami was mistaken; our Ma could not possibly live in a place like this. As we turned the corner, he mischievously brought a finger to his lips and whispered: '*Shhhh!*'

He left me in the shadows as he knocked on the door. Ma opened the door. Even in the dull light, I could make out her form. When she saw Uncle Sami, her face congealed into a frown. Without a single speck of joy in her voice, she said, 'Nene, what are you doing here this time of night?'

Nene was Uncle Sami's childhood nickname. It was a generic name for a little boy. Ma only ever used it when she was about to castigate him for some misdemeanour or other. Seeing that Ma was in no mood to play, Uncle Sami beckoned for me to come forward. He dragged me in front of him, but that didn't ameliorate Ma's hostility. Instead, she looked at me as though she'd never met me before. And then she yelled, 'And what is he doing here?'

Before I conjured up an answer, Uncle Sami interjected.

'We thought we'd surprise you, that's all,' he answered, slightly embarrassed.

'Surprise me? How about asking for permission to visit *my house* before turning up on *my* doorstep, drunk? Or at least tell me in advance that you are coming?'

'I thought—'

And she cut him up.

'No, Nene, you didn't think – that is your problem. You always do what you like regardless of the consequences. So, tell me, where are you two going to sleep? What exactly do you expect me to say to my husband when he comes home and finds both of you here? Tell me?'

'But, *sisi**, I brought your son to see where you live. If you don't want me to stay, I can pick him up tomorrow morning. At least let him stay.'

'Don't blackmail me – I know he is my son. I just don't like drunken surprises. What do you think my husband will think of my family, huh?'

'From the way you're acting, does he even know that you have children of your own?'

With that, Ma flew into a rage. She slapped him so hard across the face that the cigarette in his mouth dropped to the ground. He let go of my hand. And then Ma slammed the door in our faces. He grabbed my hand, and we walked in silence back the way we came. It reminded me of that day in Thokozani Flats, when Grandma and I had paid Ma an impromptu visit, and how displeased Ma had been, even then.

We crossed the main road, past the bus stop, and walked towards another township, nearby to the home of Mr Likwa, Phani's father, our neighbour back home. When we arrived, luckily the light was on. Mr Likwa opened the door. He looked surprised but didn't dwell much on the ins and outs of Uncle Sami's pathetic tale. He let us in and motioned for me to join his kids sleeping on the concrete floor in the front room. I found a

---

* My sister.

little space and wedged myself in, but I couldn't fall asleep. As I lay there, I thought that Ma had always seemed sad. It was as if a dark cloud loomed large in her life. She couldn't even see the bright light in our eyes, however close. I didn't think that she regretted having us. It was just that she couldn't start a new life because my sisters and I were the chain on her ankles that she couldn't shake. And, because of us, she couldn't untangle herself from the clutches of Grandma. All her life, she'd always wanted to run from Grandma, to be free of her. Ma's new home was her ring of steel. With it she could set boundaries and decide who visited her and when.

Conversely, Grandma and Uncle Sami saw our mother as nothing more than a means to an end, and we, her children, as pawns in their fraught relationship. In hindsight, Ma had been an orphan for the best part of her life. How could she give what she wasn't given? If her cup was empty, how could she pour into ours? But, as a child, my life felt like a constant debilitating unravelling. And, in my mind, I was unlovable. Love just seemed such a very complex and confusing thing to me. I turned and twisted for the rest of the night, just trying to fix things in my own head.

In the morning, as we folded the blankets, I vowed I'd never miss Ma or anyone again. The meeting with my father felt like a double bittersweet rejection. He didn't want me, either. And I reconciled myself to the idea that people, no matter how close, will always leave. Adults will always lie for the most trivial of reasons.

I returned home to more bad news. At school, two of my

classmates, twin brothers, had lost their mother. She had been raped and decapitated by an ex-combatant. Even after the brutal war, there was still no word for trauma in our language. Most guerrillas and soldiers and those who had perpetrated the most heinous crimes during the war had come back and resettled amongst us as if nothing had happened. Looking back, there were deeds that were hard to conceptualise in our own language, let alone in another's. For instance, what would forgiveness look like in our own language? What would restitution and reparations feel like in our own words, spoken freely? Because peace and reconciliation were White man's words, his respite whilst he planned his next move to retain power over us.

CHAPTER 27

I defaulted back into the daily grind of things. Uncle Sami vanished, again. But this time, when he came back, he was accompanied by three strangers in a car. They brought groceries – bread, butter, sugar, milk, Tanganda Tea leaves and Grandma's snuff. They had been drinking and were in a jovial mood. Uncle Sami instructed me to go and find all our goats and bring them home. I didn't ask why; all I could think of was meat. I took off towards the *kopjes* behind our house, which was where they normally grazed. It wasn't long before I found them and corralled them inside the small roofless barn. I closed the gate and fetched Uncle Sami. Grandma and the guests came along too. When I opened the gate, she selected two goats. Both belonged to Ma. Uncle Sami trussed them up and, with the help of the strangers, he threw them into the boot of the car and slammed it shut. It was a hot, humid day. After a short exchange of pleasantries, I watched the car disappear behind a cloud of dust with Ma's goats trapped in the boot.

Immediately afterwards, Grandma summoned us to the kitchen.

'Listen carefully!' she said. 'I don't want you running your mouths. Those men you just saw are very important friends of your uncle's. If anybody asks about the missing goats, and I mean anybody, just tell them they were struck by *lightning*!'

'But, Grandma, recently there has been no rain, let alone lightning. Besides, they are Ma's goats. We must tell her the truth, that Uncle Sami sold them to those men!' I said, slightly aggrieved. I'd mistakenly thought that Grandma would be in Ma's corner, since she was the main provider.

'Are you calling me a liar?'

'No,' I said, 'but it is true that they are Ma's goats and there was no lightning!'

And, feeling slightly brave, I challenged her even further. 'But why did Uncle Sami give away Ma's goats just like that?'

'What goats?' Grandma retorted.

'Ma's goats!' I added forcefully.

I kept a tab on all our animals. I knew which animals belonged to whom, and which goat gave birth to which kid, and when.

'Go on telling lies and I'll kill you with my bare hands!'

Frustrated, I recoiled and said nothing for a while. Gift, too, said nothing. We knew we couldn't count on Thoko because she was always in cahoots with Grandma. All she did was cast a sideways glance as if to warn us not to say a word. There had been divisions lately. Because Gift and I shared the same father, we'd formed our own alliance.

Grandma broke the monotony. 'For the last time, those goats were struck by lightning. That's the end of that, you hear me?'

But, somehow, I just couldn't help myself. 'There was no lightning. I am going to tell our Ma the truth.'

I had always been prepared to tell contingent lies, but even Grandma had crossed the line.

And she leaned forward: 'Haven't I looked after you? Raised you like you were my own, and wiped your shit with my bare hands? And now you turn against me like I am your enemy, huh? Old as I am, don't cross me, you hear?'

She retrieved a burning piece of firewood straight from the hearth, but my reflexes were too fast for her. Whenever we had a disagreement, I always watched her hands. So, by the time she'd pulled out the still-smouldering piece of firewood, I was already at the door. She smashed it against the door frame, spreading hot charcoals across the room, which made my sisters jump. 'Come back here, you little swine, and call me a liar to my face!'

Grandma's rage suggested that she had long suspected that I warned Ma regarding Grandma's misuse of our upkeep money. As far as Grandma was concerned, my sisters and I were no longer an investment, but a liability. Also, following Gift and my recent reconnection with our father, she wanted us gone. Our older sister, Thoko, had always been her favourite. It was the little things: a thicker slice of bread at breakfast, bombardment with unnecessary praise, and a certain warmth towards her. In turn, our sister fed lies to Grandma about us, which led to more severe punishments, the withholding of food and affection. Gift and I were on our own. Even if we told our ma, what would she do? She was starting a new life without us.

As Grandma ratcheted up her hate campaign by a notch, there was a slow drift into silence – no more verbal lacerations or violent outbursts. Instead, the cold stares, and breadcrumbs after school. Everything colluded to express the end of care, of love.

But the silent treatment was the toughest thing to have to deal with when you were a child. Because sometimes when we saw something amusing or had good news from school, we'd burst through the door into a cold, distant silence. And we constantly walked on eggshells, never knowing when or what would trigger Grandma's violence.

So, in the end, we decided to run away, but we were undecided on the destination. The streets of Bulawayo, perhaps, till we found a job. But we needed to raise money first. Gift, in consultation with her friend Bongani, came up with the idea of stealing onions and then selling them to raise money. I was not sure what Bongani's motivation was, but it sounded like a good idea to me. The other person involved was Sibanga, an older boy and known thief who lived nearby. According to Bongani, he'd done this before, and he was willing to help us. Why, I had no idea. Now, it was only a matter of timing.

We chose a Saturday morning for two reasons. First, it was a market day with ample opportunity for trade and, second, Grandma would be at church for most of the day.

We met outside Bongani's house at dawn. Bongani had transformed from the petrified, mute little girl she once was into a confident, vivacious teenager. Her hair twisted into small clandestine twigs sprouting out of her skull like a juvenile goat's horns. She spoke fluent isiNdebele now, but she never mentioned the war, or talked about the source of the multiple blemishes on her skin.

We made our way towards the irrigation scheme, located on a bend on the Mzingwane River. With rich, fertile soils, and a water reservoir, it allowed farmers to rotate crops all year round: wheat, maize, sugar cane, cabbage, onions, and carrots.

It took us the best part of an hour to get there.

The river at dawn was like asphalt in the rain from which a silky smog arose. We waded in, knee-deep, to cover our trail, and walked in absolute silence. When we reached a small confluence, we abandoned the river and sculpted a narrow path over the elephant grass. We swooped below thorn trees, avoiding hunters' snares and the green river cobras coiled on branches. Only Sibanga knew where we were going. The dense fog played tricks with my mind. I saw strange figures standing right next to tree trunks. When I crouched, they, too, crouched. When I zoomed in with one eye, the squatting figures turned out to be small outcrops of rock.

We broke out of the trees into a sugar-cane field and stumbled upon irrigation pipes. The soil, recently irrigated, was slippery and wet. We walked along the elevated narrow mounds, between canals, until we came upon rows of onions, perched precariously on mounds of red soil, their green flaccid leaves bent to the side as if dying of thirst. The bulbs were the size of a grown man's fist. Before we set to work, we scanned the perimeter and listened out for any sound of movement, the smell of tobacco, a random cough, or the chatter of voices, however faint. Heads tilted to the side, hands cupped ears. When we were happy that there was no one about, we started. My heart was pounding. There was no turning back.

I unravelled the sack from underneath my armpit and grabbed the first onion at the base of its stem and pulled, exposing its muddy, sinewy roots. I could feel its slipperiness on my fingers as my feet got stuck in the red gluey mud. The strong smell of onions evoked the memory of Uncle Sami's special breakfast:

fried eggs with fresh tomatoes and spring onions, embellished with fresh chillies, which he liked to bite with his teeth exposed, so they didn't touch his lips.

When our sacks were full, we regrouped on the side of the onion field. The onions were heavy. We left under the cover of the forest nearby. That way, we would be able to cover our footprints.

As we emerged, a new dawn arose, resplendent in its reddish gown of morning sunshine. Its rays radiated warmth; its glow lighter than my guilty conscience. We entered the river once more. The trees along the riverbed were less concentrated, the air less dense.

I immersed my feet in the water. Life returned to my toes and feet.

We crossed the river and negotiated the steep climb out of the embankment. The sun slowly drifted across the blue sky. We agreed to go our separate ways, that should anyone ask where we got the onions from, we should tell them we'd bought them from various farms.

Gift and I headed home. Luckily Grandma was still at church. After we washed and changed clothes, we headed to the Growth Point. We joined professional market traders who screamed their wares to bus passengers on their way home from Bulawayo. It was cheaper for them to buy vegetables locally than it was to buy them in the city. Since we'd never sold onions before, we watched and observed how professionals did it. So, when the first bus arrived, we rushed to the partially opened windows.

'Onions! Cheap onions!'

A bulbous shaven head squeezed itself through the confines of a partially open window. Keen to make my first sale, I stood on my toes and tried to push the basket upwards so he could choose his preference.

'How much?' he asked sternly.

Before I could answer, a woman with the neck of a bull ingratiated herself in my conversation with the potential customer. She was taller than me and she lifted her basket of onions way above my head, pushing me away with ease.

'Thirty cents each,' she announced. 'Don't be afraid to touch them – go on! What kind of man are you? I said you can touch them only if you want to buy!'

The bald head bubbled with constrained laughter. They teased each other as if they were talking about something else other than onions. I moved away and tried my luck somewhere else. But someone, again older and taller, stole my customers from underneath my nose. I squeezed through a throng of bodies and stood a short distance away. When I looked at Gift, she, too, was struggling. So, when the next bus arrived, I decided to risk it and go inside. As soon as I entered the bus, a fat woman spilling over the sides of her seat called me over.

'How much?' she asked, as if she couldn't be bothered.

'Thirty cents each!' I said, hoping she'd buy one onion at least.

Suddenly, she put her hands on her chest. 'Are you trying to give me a heart attack? Thirty cents for a tiny onion? You need ten of those to make a decent sauce. I am sure, *mkhwenyana**, we can come to an arrangement, hey? How am I going to feed your wife at such exorbitant prices? Look at her!' she said, pointing to a chubby little girl squashed between her and the window. 'She's

---

* Son-in-law

still growing, and if you want to get married soon, you must give us a discount.'

A thin smile dissolved an earlier surliness. With that, she grabbed five bulbs of onions and gave me a new silver dollar coin. Our currency had changed, too, from pounds to dollars.

The coin depicted the stone-carved national emblem of our country, the Zimbabwean bird, and on the reverse, the ruins of our country – *dzimbadzemabwe* or houses of stone – from which the name Zimbabwe is derived. The bus driver revved the engine as the conductor and his assistant banged on the side of the bus, which signalled an imminent departure. I squeezed between passengers as they rushed back into the bus with their recent purchases.

Outside, I shared the news of my recent success with Gift. From then on, she deployed the same tactic too. We also sold our onions cheaper, to the ire of the resident traders. It was not long before one of them approached me.

'Where did you get those onions from?' she asked me, her voice magisterial.

'My aunt's garden,' I replied, trying to brush her off.

'I didn't know you had an aunt. Aren't you Muvu's grandson?'

'Yes, I am,' I answered.

'That's right! And you are my nephew Salani's best friend, aren't you? Now where did you get those onions from?'

'I can't remember,' I said, trying to walk away from her.

'We ordered ours at fifteen cents each. And for you to sell yours for twenty cents each you must have ordered them at a cheaper price. Just tell us where so we can all order from the same place, huh?'

When I tried to walk away, she stood in my way. Soon, a small crowd gathered around me.

'Tell us where you ordered the onions from!' Under pressure, I capitulated. But I didn't divulge that we had stolen them. 'But that's where we got ours from,' said one of them, looking confused. And then another: 'Where did you order yours from again? 'Cause surely Mr Mnyandu would never have sold them at a preferential rate to you, given that we are his regular customers. And trust me when I say we haggled with that man!' exclaimed the lady, her eyes wide with surprise. 'And you are telling us that he sold them to you cheaper? Why?'

With that, I decided to walk away and find Gift. When I found her, she had the same problem. She was surrounded by irate market women demanding to know why she was spoiling their market.

'There is an agreed minimum price. You can go as high as you want as long as you're not undercutting us, okay?'

'Okay, sorry, we didn't know,' said Gift as she feigned an apology.

We had less than half a dozen onions left between us, and we decided to call it a day, and let things calm down. That was our first truly binding secret. But, given Grandma's intricate web of spies, it would not be long before she found out. And, as it turned out, she'd find out in the most spectacular of ways.

CHAPTER 28

It was early Saturday morning. I registered a commotion amongst the neighbourhood's dogs. When I looked up, I saw a policeman approach. He was tall, Black, and bigger than any policeman I'd ever seen. His gun and shiny handcuffs sent shivers down my spine.

'What is your name?' he demanded.

'Thabani,' I replied, my voice quivering slightly as a desperate thirst gripped my throat.

'Do you know why I am here?'

'No, sir, I don't.' I cast my eyes low to avoid any eye contact; to be contrite was better.

'You do know why I am here,' he said, searching for my eyes, because I was doing everything in my power to avoid his gaze. His enquiry was more of a declaration than a question.

'No,' I said as I tried to convince myself.

'Get up!'

When I finally managed to stand, he said to me, 'I am going to ask you one more time: why do you think I am here?'

And I said it again, less convincingly: 'I have no idea why you are here, sir.'

With his hands resting on his knees, he leaned closer to my face and gritted his teeth menacingly. He wore a vicious kind of stare, breathed heavily, and I inhaled his stale tobacco breath. Then he hit me hard across the face with an open hand. And again, from the opposite direction as if to balance things. Suddenly, words spewed out of my mouth.

'We stole onions,' I said as I rubbed my cheeks and tried to regain my balance.

'So now we both know why I am here?'

I nodded, non-committally.

'You said, *"We stole onions."* Who is *we*?'

'Gift, Bongani, Sibanga and me.'

'Where from?'

'Down at the irrigation scheme,' I confessed, and shamefully pointed in the direction of the river. Every time he raised his hand, I flinched.

'And why, may I ask, did you steal the onions?'

'Because we wanted money.'

'Who lives here with you?'

'Grandma and my two sisters.'

'Anyone else?'

'No,' I said as I tried to find a way out.

'And when is this grandmother of yours back?'

'I don't know,' I said, hoping now that I'd told him everything, he'd leave me alone.

'In which case, you'll have to come with me.'

Defeated, I resigned myself to whatever was coming to me. The policeman was in no rush. He paraded me with the pride of the owner of a newly purchased prize-winning bull. Everyone we came across stopped and looked at me. I wished the ground would swallow me.

When we came across Mr Chuma, he asked the policeman rather authoritatively, 'What's he done?'

'He is a thief. Him and his friends have been stealing onions.'

'Thabani, is that true? You are a thief now? What? Onions? Thabani, were you that hungry to want to eat raw onions?'

Between them, they kept repeating the word 'thief'. Somehow, it was beginning to stick.

And then he turned to the policeman.

'Whose onions and what is so special about them? How many exactly to warrant the arrest of a small boy?' asked Mr Chuma as his inquisitiveness revealed incredulity at the whole onion saga.

'Sacks of onions! According to the witnesses, they've been selling them at the Growth Point,' said the policeman as he looked at me for further elaboration as to how exactly this had happened. I kept my mouth shut. 'I am sure you'll agree we can't afford to have thieves roaming around freely in our community!'

From the policeman's revelation, I gathered that this was a more serious offence than I'd thought. Salani and I had committed much more serious crimes than this, including arson, theft on a grander scale, vandalism, but we'd never been arrested.

Mr Chuma turned to me. 'You're in trouble now, aren't you?' He nodded to the policeman. 'Very well,' he said. 'Do whatever you need to do!'

Before he left, he asked me: 'Does Muvu know you've been arrested?'

'No,' I said.

The last thing I wanted to be dealing with then was Grandma's wrath. I was desperately hoping that Mr Chuma would save me. Also, I would have gladly accepted a whipping, however severe, than get arrested.

Women with small children pointed at me, saying, 'This is what happens when you steal!' And the policeman tightened his grip on my hand.

As we crossed the main road into the Growth Point, a crowd gathered around the Puma truck, which up until then had only been used by soldiers for military operations. Camouflage paint had been replaced by a sombre dull grey, the colour of police vehicles.

The policeman lifted me up and pushed me into the back of the truck. I came face to face with my co-conspirators. And, right by their feet, three bags of onions. I felt relieved; it wasn't me, after all, who'd betrayed them. By the looks of it, it was they who'd given up my name. But it didn't matter. Whatever happened, we were doomed.

A man near us with a menacingly deep wound to the right side of this head quivered maddeningly. His teeth chattered even though it wasn't cold. He had coiled springs of short black hair caked in bloody mud. We learned later that he had chopped his love rival with an axe and buried him – all on his own. A crowd had gathered to see that day's crop of prisoners: an axe murderer and four juvenile onion thieves. Suddenly, a man pushed through the crowd and lunged forward as others tried to pull him back. 'Give me two minutes with this animal and I'll show him what a real man can do!' And another man shouted from deep within the crowd: 'You just want to play with him. Just give him to me and I'll show him!'

I really thought they meant it. Meanwhile, a self-appointed town crier of sorts was shouting: 'The onion thieves have been arrested! We wondered why their onions were so cheap. They've been stealing all along!'

The Puma truck had seats in the middle and very small slits for windows. For the first time, we had the view of the soldiers but no guns or targets to aim at. Bongani and Sibanga faced opposite directions on the other side of the divide. Gift and I sat a metre away from the murderer. We exchanged surreptitious glances. There was nothing to say. We both knew that we were doomed.

'Does Muvu know that you are here?' a voice bellowed from within the crowd.

'Does she know you're thieves?' enquired another.

I gazed over the crowd, shrugged my shoulders.

Some voices were more callous than others.

'You should all rot in prison. We don't need people like you around here!'

Just then Grandma arrived. She waded through the crowd like a whirlwind as people dispersed to make way for her. The look on her face said it all. 'You know I don't have the money to come and get you. You will stay there, however long it takes for you to learn your lesson!' Suddenly, it crossed my mind that she'd searched the whole country looking for Uncle Sami with our Ma's money, and yet she would not do the same for us. Just then, her steely eyes held me still, frozen. I wanted to say that I was sorry, that we both were. But her next words cut even closer to the bone.

'Don't come back, you hear me? I did not raise thieves!'

With that, she walked away after disowning us like unwanted baggage. It dawned on me that we really didn't belong to anyone.

281

Suddenly, there was the clunking of the heavy metal doors closing, followed by the roar of the engine. We were on the move; there was no escape. I felt alone, beset by a bewildering light-headedness. The truck picked up speed as it rumbled over corrugated bumps on the dusty road. We were lifted off our seats, landing momentarily before the truck hit yet another bump and we were jolted up again.

I surrendered to the hypnotic dance of the white line in the middle of the road, and the welling up of distress, the intensity of which did not subside. Nothing was said between us, about what we were going to say once we got to wherever it was we were going.

It was the beginning of something new and terrifying. It was hard to digest that we were on our way to prison.

We arrived at the police compound and were led to a room where a surly and overweight policeman sat behind a desk and, behind him, guns stood upright without magazines. He wore a forlorn expression, curiously blank. He was smoking a cigarette from the corner of his mouth, his right eye slightly squinted. Beams of light penetrated the room from a high window with iron bars. When he finally raised his head from his desk, our escort moved forward and relayed something to him. He cast a knowing glance our way; this was a nightmare I'd never forget.

The injured man was taken to a separate room further away from where we were sitting. He had handcuffs on his wrists and manacles round his ankles.

I was summoned first. I moved forward and sat over my hands

to stop them from shaking. The policeman shot a barrage of questions at me.

'What is your name?'

'Thabani,' I said.

'Do you know why you are here?'

'Yes, that policeman brought us here.'

'No, I mean the real reason why the policeman brought you here?'

'Because he said we stole onions.'

'Who's we?'

I removed my right hand from underneath my leg and pointed at Gift, Bongani, and Sibanga.

'Joint enterprise, I see. Well, did you?'

'Yes, we did.'

'Why?'

'I don't know.'

'Where are your parents?'

'Ma is in the city. I don't know where my father is,' I said as a matter of fact.

'So, you live on your own. Is that why you steal?'

'No, we live with our grandmother, who is also our mother.'

'How so?'

'Because we live with her, and I've always called her Ma.'

I could not keep track of all the answers that I'd given. Besides, I had already confessed to the crime.

And then he asked me the most disheartening of questions: 'When is your grandmother coming to get you?'

'I don't know,' I said. 'She has no money for the bus fare.'

He shook his head as if there was something abnormal about what I'd just told him.

'Well, you can't stay here forever. This is no place for children!' And, as he said this, a small wave of kindness radiated across his face. When the interrogation finished, I was ushered into the next room where a man dressed in khakis awaited. The moment I laid my eyes on him, there was something about him that I didn't like. He beckoned for me to sit on a chair. In his hand he held a razor blade. There was a pile of hair on the floor, which indicated that he had been busy shaving heads all day, perhaps using the same razor blade. 'Remember to sit still!' he said. 'Any sudden movement, this goes deep into your scalp!'

He waved the razor in front of me as if to illustrate his point. Then he firmly grabbed and started to dry-shave my head from the crown downwards towards the sides, without even asking me my preference for any hairstyle, the way Grandma did, before leaving a strip of hair right in the middle of my head, resembling the crown of the lourie bird.

'There are lice here and other nasty bugs that can hide in your hair and feed off your blood!' And he smiled, disconcertingly. He forcefully tilted, rotated, abruptly straightened, and jerked my head from side to side.

The man then asked me: 'Is there any hair down there?'

With that, I grabbed my shorts with both hands before uttering a firm, 'NO!' And prepared to scream the whole place down should he try anything.

'Best not take chances, hey!' he said, a coy smile on his face.

When he finished shaving my head, he doused my scalp with methylated spirit. And then he guided me to a waiting area outside and instructed me to wait there. As a warm breeze caressed my cleanly shaven head, finally, I could breathe.

I sat down on the wooden bench and watched the policemen run errands between buildings. I started to think about school and how long we were going to stay. Or if they were going to send us to a real prison as the policeman had threatened us on our way there.

After a while, Gift emerged, bald as an eagle. The corners of her forehead, more pronounced.

She forced a smile, exposing her jagged teeth.

'Where were you when they found you?'

'At home,' I said. 'And you?'

'I was at the Growth Point. It was that nosey Maggie who brought the policeman to Bongani and me. She's the only one who's been asking us silly questions about the size of our onions and why they were so cheap. Why can't people mind their own business?'

'It was your stupid idea. I should never have listened to you and that idiot Bongani in the first place. Now look at us!'

'Spare me the outrage!' Gift said. 'I bet you haven't thrown away the money that I gave you after we sold the onions! Nor did you refuse any of the biscuits and sweets that I brought home to you. Anyway, have you told anyone about the money?'

'No,' I said, 'Besides, I'd completely forgotten about the money until you mentioned it!'

'Good! Now keep your mouth shut. We're in enough trouble as it is. That money is our only way out of this predicament.'

'Where is your share of the money?' I asked.

'The policeman took it. It's in his pocket.'

'Are you going to ask for it when we leave?'

'Stop asking me silly questions. The money is gone. We just need to think about what to do next.'

Bongani came out, followed by Sibanga, heads all shaven.

A policeman led us away from the caged area, across the gravel forecourt, towards a small building with multiple doors. Sibanga and I were ushered into one room; Gift and Bongani were taken to a different section of the compound. The policeman locked the door from the outside. We were on our own.

Sibanga was older than all of us. He was solid, and he walked on tiptoes as though he had a permanent cramp in his legs. He reminded me of an old cockerel stripped bare of its feathers, all muscle and bone. He had dry ashen skin and visible earwax. His fingernails needed clipping, and he reeked of fish. He needed a good scrub and a change of clothes. Unlike me, he didn't seem worried at all. It was as if he had been jailed before. Grandma had always insisted that he was a seasoned criminal, that I should steer clear of him. Now I was stuck with him. Perhaps I should have listened to Grandma because I'd forever regret the moment that I met him.

CHAPTER 29

It had been a long day. The sun was about to set as we prepared to settle down for the night. There were only three blankets, each encased in dry blood and indistinguishable stains. We placed the first blanket on the bare concrete floor, folded the second as a pillow, and covered ourselves with the third. The concrete floor was hard, the room too cold. Hungry and physically and emotionally depleted, I fell asleep.

I woke up in the morning after a dreary night. My body was covered in bites. When we shook the blankets, dozens of bedbugs dropped to the floor, their rotund bellies bloated with our blood. We went into a frenzy, stamping on them with our bare feet and squashing them with the back of our thumbnails and throwing everything at them. For a while, we'd found something purposeful to do.

'And what is all this commotion?' an anonymous voice bellowed into the room.

'Bedbugs, sir!' we said in unison, still holding the blankets in our hands.

'You mean to tell me that you have woken up the whole compound over a farce about bedbugs?'

'But they were biting us all night – look!'

'I don't know why you feel so outraged. You and those bugs are no different: you are all parasites. Bedbugs and lice are standard accompaniments to prison life. Get used to it!'

And then he unlocked the door and said, nonchalantly, 'You'll miss the breakfast, unless of course you prefer bugs?'

'Where is breakfast?' I desperately enquired, bugs forgotten.

'Follow your nose – you're thieves, aren't you?' he said as he pointed at a building a short distance to the right of where we were standing.

'Oh, and make sure you wash your hands properly unless you prefer the taste of bedbugs with your porridge!' And he laughed as he walked away.

Sibanga and I arrived just before the kitchen door closed. Breakfast was rough cornmeal porridge served on battered, twisted aluminium plates. Because we were late, we got the burnt-out crust from the bottom of the oil drum used for cooking prisoners' food. There were no spoons, but we were too hungry to care. We ate with our hands.

After breakfast, our jailer marched us to the communal sink used by the officers. Numerous taps protruded from the wall, along the length of it. On the floor were piles of dirty clothes, including the officers' dirty underwear. He handed us each a cake of green detergent, with the word Sunlight embossed on its smooth surface. It smelt clean, pure.

'Time to get busy; nothing in this world is for free, even for thieves!'

Once he'd gone, we blocked the outlet at the bottom of the sink and ran the tap until it was almost full. We threw in all the clothes and let them soak for a while. Afterwards, we rubbed each garment with a bar of soap until we'd coaxed enough soapsuds to create beautiful bubbles: small spheres of the rainbow in our hands. We jumped into the sink, leaned against the wall, and pounded each garment with our bare feet as if it were an imaginary enemy. We drained the water, repeated the process, until we were satisfied that all the skid marks from the Independence Day celebrations had gone.

And, afterwards, we hung the clothes on the barbed-wire fence to dry.

The girls disappeared into the showers with a bar of soap. We could hear them giggling behind the high concrete wall as they exclaimed how cold the water was. They washed their clothes and showered at the same time. Afterwards, they squeezed each drop of water from their dresses, put them back on, and basked outside in the sun to dry.

Whilst Gift and Bongani were in the shower, Sibanga and I undressed and washed our clothes in the sink. Afterwards, we scrubbed each other's backs with pumice stones made from a slightly rough stone the size of our hands. We then sat on the edge of the sink, facing the wall, and rubbed our feet against the rough concrete base of the sink. When we finished, we, too, sat in the sun while we waited for our clothes to dry, which didn't take long as it was very hot. It was a good thing that our heads were shaven, because we had no Vaseline to keep our skin moisturised.

Instead, we used soapsuds as body lotion, which left our skin very tight, like the thin layer of the porridge that they served for breakfast. When I smiled, my face felt taut.

Once our clothes were dry, we headed back to the kitchen where the stern cook served us stiff *pap* with kidney beans. The *pap* was off-white with tiny black weevils cemented in the mix. We were prisoners, after all; everything about the place was designed to make us feel that way, all the time. When we said thank you, the cook, a tall Black man with a shaved egg-shaped head, never acknowledged us. We grabbed our plates, and headed for the wall where we ate in silence. The thick, oily gravy on the partially cooked kidney beans made the meal palatable.

After food, we were corralled back into our respective areas of the compound for the night. With that, we parted company with Bongani and Gift. As we faced the onslaught of the bedbugs, alone, they, too, had their own unique challenges.

Two weeks passed, then three and four, and there was no sign of Grandma, Ma or Uncle Sami. The only good thing was that we were not locked up all day, because in the day the tiny cell was unbearably hot. We could hear the patter of small lizards' feet as they ran in the sun on the corrugated iron roof.

We established a routine: porridge first thing in the morning, then parade, followed by watching children on the other side of the fence on their way to school. Afterwards, we attended to our daily chores: sweeping the yard, cleaning dishes, and washing officers' uniforms. When the officers were not around, which was often, we wore their big T-shirts whilst we laundered our own.

Sometimes we watched *real* prisoners, barefoot, in their over-sized, dishevelled khaki uniforms, being loaded on to ominous grey vans with small apertures for windows right at the top. Each window, two each side, and one at the rear, was sealed with steel bars. The rear door was locked at two key points with thick padlocks. Mostly, the prisoners served time as gravediggers, or collected and buried unclaimed bodies from suicides. Those who were too old or too frail to dig and lift swept the streets daily, and cut grass on the side of the roads, in the most blistering heat. So that was what they meant when they said, 'I'll kill you and do time for you!' And they said it with such conviction; made it sound as though it was the easiest thing in the world: killing and doing time.

It was a Saturday morning of our sixth week in detention. We had just had our daily dose of cornmeal porridge. We were on our way to the morning parade when Gift and I were summoned to the reception. When we got there, we found Uncle Sami waiting for us. His eyes were downcast. A stifled rage seeped through his taut skin and permeated the room, like the secretions of an angry black fighter ant. He looked at us with a total disdain. But I knew he had done time too. I didn't understand why he'd be so angry with us.

Gift and I looked at each other and exchanged short-lived grimaces. We huddled together a short distance away from him just in case he lashed out. I watched his hand, ready to bolt at any moment.

The policeman tersely said, 'That is all – you can go now!' Which meant we could have gone home five weeks earlier. All we needed was a grown-up conscionable enough to pick us up. We said thank you to the policeman and he put on a shrewd and seasoned grimace of someone who'd heard it all before, as if to say, 'You'll be back soon!' So that was that. We were free, at last.

We didn't have enough time to share our wonderful news with Sibanga and Bongani. Besides, it was inconceivable that we would be allowed to associate with them ever again. As we walked through the gates of the police compound, I wondered what would happen to us. But, at that moment, I looked forward to the bus ride home, and perhaps a cold Fanta and a warm bun or two. Just the way Grandma and I did on our outings.

But Uncle Sami had an entirely different plan. He steered clear of the bus stop as we walked along the main street. He walked so fast that Gift and I frequently resorted to a gentle jog just to keep up with him. He still hadn't said a word to us.

We pressed on in the oppressive, ruminant silence until we reached the Mzingwane River. It was past noon; the intensity of the sun had increased by a notch. We used the smaller, narrower bridge and descended into the river. There was the echo of heavy trucks on the main bridge above us, their shadows caught in the water below. A man sat still whilst watching his fishing line. A kingfisher, perched high above him on an orphaned branch, watched him with a matching intensity.

Uncle Sami sat on a small rock, removed his shoes, and folded his trousers up to his knees. And, as if wary of slippery stones, covered in the silky green river algae, he cautiously waded into the water towards the deep end. He bent down at the waist, washed his face, scooped water into his mouth with his cupped hands and spat it right back into the river.

My feet were covered in dust, my soles hurt from all the walking we'd done in the preceding three hours. Stale sweat had congealed on my face and left behind rivulets of dry salt. Midges continuously harangued me; no amount of waving hands frantically would stop them. I found a secluded area, not treacherously deep, and dived in, fully clothed. I let my skin and bones soak in the soothingly cold water for what seemed an eternity. When I came to the surface, Gift was standing knee-deep by the water's edge. I could still taste the salt and the sweat as the water dripped from my face. I dived under again and rubbed my face with both hands underwater, and when I came back to the surface I saw a man slamming a catfish dead against a rock. Another, completely naked, stood on a rock by the water's edge as he vigorously brushed his teeth with Colgate toothpaste, hoping for a white smile. And another scrubbed his body with a pumice stone over a lather of Lifebuoy soap as if he feared contagion.

Gift smiled. Uncle Sami was still mute.

When we got home, Uncle Sami ushered us into the kitchen. Grandma was as calm as she'd ever been. She plied Uncle Sami with copious amounts of Tanganda Tea, made viscous by the excessive amount of sugar and condensed milk, complemented by very thick, freshly cut slices of Lobels white bread, heavily plastered on both sides with layer upon layer of Stork margarine. But when it came to both the size of the slices, and the amount of margarine plastered on each side, heavy-handedness favoured Grandma's plate.

When she dunked hers into the rich milky tea, a yellowy glint of butter greased the inside of the cup.

As if to warn us of our impending fate, our tea was stingily teased with a very small dose of milk. It was as if the tea leaves had not been allowed to stay sufficiently long enough in the water. And Grandma grudgingly gave us a very thinly cut half-slice each, cut diagonally.

Given the slightly positive mood, I immersed myself in the sweetness of the tea, and momentarily forgot about the events that had preoccupied me for the best part of six weeks.

After tea, she ordered us to go and lie down – we were exhausted, after all. Finally, we were home.

But Grandma was a master of disguise. As we dozed off to sleep, and with our guard down, she pounced.

She looked at us with concentrated anger as if the tiny veins in her eyes were about to burst. With her vice-like grip on our tiny wrists, she sank her sharp, soiled claws deep into the flesh of our arms. She dragged us to her bedroom, which she'd prepared earlier to ensure that not a single obstacle would frustrate her advances. She dragged us in and shut the door behind us. She forced us to strip naked. Inside, it was dark. Only tiny beams of light squeezed through the gaps in the old wooden door. Once I fully understood her intentions, I scanned the area above the wall, and I could see a crop of freshly harvested switches from the peach tree, thick as an adult's thumb.

'Today we'll speak English!' she announced.

That was her favourite expression right before she unleashed terror on anyone. Because English was the language of violence, both at home and at school.

★

The first ten strikes felt as though she was tearing into my flesh with multiple sharp claws.

'Today I'll teach your bodies never to steal again!'

And she picked the tenderest spots: buttocks, thighs, upper arm. But blows frequently landed on our heads, the sharp end of the elbow, and the lower end of the ribcage. Sometimes, she cut across our palms, fingers, as we desperately tried to defend ourselves, which enraged her even more.

Whilst she tore into Gift, I breathed in deeply and pysched myself up for the next wave of her rage. Pain is like a gas, it seeps through small openings, hides in hard-to-find places with raw nerve endings.

Grandma was more enraged than I had ever seen her. Drawing a little blood wasn't going to be enough.

Breathing heavily, she announced, with a contradictory tenderness, 'You are both mine. I'll kill you if I must!'

She locked us up in the room for the rest of the day. In between bouts of rest, she charged at us like a maddened boxer. By late afternoon, Gift and I were both covered in deep welts, cuts, and striations. Where blows had landed, three or four times on the same spot, distinct bulges started to form. A clear liquid oozed out, only to congeal on the surface of our skin.

When it was all finished, the room resembled an improvised theatre: torn garments, broken clay pots, faces covered in soot, a broken door, and frayed edges of the thatch grass from our attempts to climb the wall. It was my conclusion that Grandma's uncontrollable rage called for a prudent seclusion from normal people.

Earlier in the day, she'd fed us to make sure we were strong enough to withstand the beating. That night, she denied us food. We sat around the fire and nursed our wounds.

PART 2

PART 2

CHAPTER 30

For weeks, Grandma retreated behind a wall of silence. She had become brazenly self-righteous about her own demands. She was done raising other people's children, she said. Gift and I could no longer bear being hostages in her war with our mother; we decided to try our luck with our father.

I wrote to Ma to that effect, and, in her reply, she said we should write directly to Pa, see if he wanted us. So, we wrote numerous letters to Pa. And to make our situation sound more urgent, we amplified Grandma's cruelty, expressing an unyielding determination to be with our real family, even though they were strangers.

We posted the letters one after another and waited.

Outside our home, the reintegration of the guerrillas into the National Army dragged on. Frustrated by what they saw as the lack of progress, some decamped from the assembly points and engaged in banditry. Grandma's prediction had come true. Our prime minister, Robert Mugabe, described them as disloyal, desperate hooligans. Later, he would describe it as a thriving, well-funded, well-coordinated insurgency.

But sporadic violence erupted in the vicinity of the assembly points. The political rivalry between different factions of guerrillas, fanned by politicians who weaponised ethnicity to create divisions in our country, had exploded into real violence. As the bodies of dead guerrillas were being transported by the refrigerated Cold Storage Commission train wagons to secret burial sites, we felt the inevitability of another war.

Gift and I patiently waited for a response from our father. School became intolerable. Grandma's stone-cold silence remained intact. We avoided her wrath by making ourselves scarce. We'd given up all hope of ever being rescued.

But exactly one year after our arrest, just before Christmas 1981, a woman arrived. She was garrulous, with the protruding eyes of a bullfrog. Grandma looked at her in her usual curious but cold and distant manner. She was trying to work out who she was.

And so were we.

She introduced herself as our Aunt Margaret, one of our father's younger sisters. She was his emissary; Pa wanted us, after all.

'My brother would like to invite his children for the Christmas holidays,' she announced.

'Is that so?' asked Grandma. 'If he knows they are his children, what has taken him so long to come and get them?'

'Well,' the woman said, 'there was the war. Besides, things haven't been that easy where I come from.'

'We've all had to endure the vagaries of war, but most people didn't shy away from their responsibilities towards their own children because of war. They are here as you can see. Which begs the question, why are you here, really?'

'I am just a messenger. I cannot honourably answer you, but I totally understand where you're coming from,' she responded apologetically.

'He wants his children, now that I've raised them, and they no longer require much attention?'

'It may well be that they don't like it there. In which case, there is nothing to lose. At least they would have seen where they come from. Surely, there is no harm in that.'

Seemingly unpersuaded, Grandma maintained her obdurate posture. 'It never ceases to amaze me that people just abandon their children as if they are going for a shit, never come back for years, only to pretend that they care about the same children that they abandoned. So, you expect me to trust you with my life's work, huh?'

The woman desperately tried to sugar-coat the conversation with titbits of unnecessary pleasantries. 'I think a lot has happened; people make mistakes. It is never a good thing to bring people in your life when you're confused inside.'

'What is there to be confused about? Are you telling me that a grown man has chosen to remain confused for over a decade whilst his children remained fatherless? That brother of yours lives a stone's throw from here. For less than the cost of two loaves of bread, he could've been here a long time ago. He chose not to be.'

Under intense fire from Grandma's onslaught, the woman broke into bouts of nervous laughter, gasping for air. Grandma remained poised, cold, like a snake watching its prey.

'The last time I saw their father, I was desperately seeking my daughter after he nearly killed her with a knife whilst pregnant. With a knife, remember that! Now he sends you to ask for his children as if nothing happened.'

'They were both young,' the woman said, with the timidity of a bride the first time she meets her in-laws. 'And when people are young, they do stupid things.'

'Come home and see for yourselves,' said the woman as she directly extended the invitation to us. 'You'll have plenty of things to do. Besides, you have so many cousins there. It'll be good for you to finally meet your own blood!'

Grandma corralled the stray remnants of her dress under her thighs, leaned forward and looked at her straight in the eye.

'I will not stop you from taking my grandchildren away from me. I've raised them to be decent human beings, the ones that you now recognise.'

She raised her eyes and shoved a piece of wood deep into the fire.

'To this day I haven't forgotten what your brother did. And he has never apologised. He should pay what he owes.'

'That he knows. That he knows, which is why I am here.' The woman repeated herself, trying to ameliorate the tension.

'There are things that I've gone through with these children that nobody else will ever know. All I ask is that you bring them back to me, whole. You hear me? Now you can take them. I've done my work.'

It was the second time I saw her cry.

In the evening, she was even quieter. Afterwards, she took us to Grandpa's grave, to let him know that we were leaving, and to seek his blessings.

'You'll be amongst strangers,' she mumbled more to herself than to us. 'Always remember that no woman will ever love you the way they love their own children. I am a woman; I have a mother's instinct. Watch out for that stepmother of yours! When she gives you food, make sure you share it with her own children first. You hear me?'

Then she gave us each a small packet wrapped tightly in grease-proof paper. 'As soon as you get there, before you eat anything, chew this and swallow everything!'

And she rubbed us each on the forehead with the soil from Grandpa's grave. 'Tomorrow, you leave with your aura intact. Never forget who you are.'

CHAPTER 31

We left for Bulawayo in the morning. I felt a slight panic. Grandma had always been my world. Without her, I would be lost. If only she could take me under her wing again. But both she and I knew that things had changed – irrevocably.

We met Pa on Lobengula Street, and we shook hands. If he was excited, he didn't show it. Besides, it had taken him over a decade to acknowledge our existence. There was the usual pre-Christmas fanfare: loud music and Christmas shoppers everywhere. We followed Pa and Aunt Margaret around as they purchased groceries for Christmas celebrations: bread, butter, jam, sugar, flour, and cooking oil. There were no Christmas presents, but Pa bought cartons of opaque beer for the journey; and, for us, bottles of Fanta, soft buns, and some boiled sweets.

We made our way towards Grey Street behind the prison wall where our transport to Nkayi awaited. When we got there, there was already a small gathering. Our transport was a blue Isuzu lorry. Apparently, it belonged to a local businessman in Pa's village. Aunt, Gift, and I sat towards the rear. Pa joined his drinking companions at the front. We would not see him for most of the journey.

We left at dusk. I was hypnotised by city lights as they dimmed in the distance. It felt as if we were leaving light behind us and venturing into the darkness. Women began singing songs of freedom, their words sanguine.

Woza, Zimbabwe,
Woza, Khayelitsha,
Woza, Khayelitsha,
*Siyakulilela!**

The song was an ode to our hard-won freedom, the embodiment of genuine optimism about our new country.

Ensconced between the softness of Aunt's bosom and shopping bags, and as we slowly drifted into the darkness, fatigue got the better of me. I fell asleep.

When I came to, it was pitch-black, but the sky above was awash with beautiful bright stars. The driver killed the headlights. There was a deafening silence. I immediately panicked, thinking that we were caught in an ambush. But Aunt explained that we were approaching the narrow bridge on the Shangani River. Many a lorry had fallen off the bridge because drivers approached at speed, miscalculated its dimensions, and collided with oncoming vehicles.

There was no vehicle coming from the opposite direction. When the driver turned on the headlights again, a strong beam sliced through the darkness. We started the steady descent straight down a steep slope, and the truck gradually levelled off. When we

---

* Come, Zimbabwe, our new home, we have been waiting for you!

reached the opposite end, it whined into a steady climb. I could feel the crunch of the gravel on the road. The women ululated; the men, who up until then had been quiet, boisterously encouraged the driver to put his foot down on the accelerator.

'If we crash, we'll bear witness! *Itshaye sizakufakazela!*'

They were all very inebriated, Pa included. Truth was, if we crashed, even if they survived, they would not remember a thing. The women picked up another song. I tasted dust in my mouth as I bounced back from yet another rebound, my back pressed against the iron-hard side of the truck, having lost my earlier soft spot to Gift.

The men had gone through gallons of sorghum beer: *Chibuku Shake Shake*. The onomatopoeic name, *Shake Shake*, came from the ritual of first shaking the beer to mix its cloudy contents before you drank it. They banged on the roof of the cabin, demanded yet another pit stop. As soon as the lorry came to a stop, they jumped off and spread along the side of the road, urinated, burped, and farted. Some were too drunk to haul themselves back into the lorry. Multiple hands helped push, whilst others pulled them back up.

It was Christmas. We were free; everyone was happy.

Along the way, we abandoned lone passengers in complete darkness with their luggage.

And, half an hour later, 'We are home!' said Aunt.

Gift suddenly came to life. She'd been fast asleep on Aunt's lap for most of the journey.

'How far is home?' she enquired, as she yawned and stretched.

'Not too far now,' said Aunt as she tried to peel herself off from the lorry. Pa immediately vanished into the nearest bush.

Throughout the journey, he had not engaged with us. I still hadn't conjured enough courage to call him my father. I'd never called anyone *Father* before.

He came back, fiddling with the zip on his trousers, a cigarette dangling from the corner of his mouth, eyes squinted, zigzagging.

Aunt Margaret was excited. 'Welcome home,' she announced again as we picked up our bags and Pa led the way. He, too, was in a celebratory mood.

Nkayi was one of the oldest tribal trust lands. It was dry, arid land, prone to prolonged and debilitating droughts, but it was also renowned for its thick, dense forests – which is why the first ever contingent of ZIPRA guerrillas operated from there. Pa's family had lived there for more than half a century.

We walked, single file, in the dark. A ruckus of neighbourhood dogs barked to welcome us. Less than a mile down the path, we parted ways with Pa and headed to Aunt Margaret's house. Staying at hers would give us a softer landing.

We went through a small wooden gate that opened into a yard dominated by two small rondavels. Aunt knocked on the door to the kitchen, 'Noe, it's me,' she shouted as she peeped through the gaps in the wooden door. A bleary-eyed girl the same age as Gift opened the door. I guessed that she was one of our cousins that Aunt had already told us about. The girl retreated into the rondavel and lit a small improvised kerosene lamp: a jam jar, pierced through the lid with a wick, filled with paraffin. In the semi-darkness, I changed into my pyjamas and wedged myself between the bodies sleeping on the floor and fell asleep.

CHAPTER 32

I woke up to a different soundscape, having completely lost my bearings. Aunt took us to Pa's house to meet our stepmother and step-siblings, Sipho and Lizwe. We took our belongings with us. The homestead comprised two huts, a barn and our stepmother's and Pa's bedroom. Theirs was the only rondavel built from bricks, with a stylishly thatched roof, a red polished cement floor and glass windows. All huts faced west. In the middle was a raised concrete platform, the foundation for a new house. On the periphery, a tall acacia tree dominated the yard. Behind it were Pa's parents' graves – Koko and Tata. The graves were overgrown with weeds, with termites' mounds on top.

Our stepma was a bundle of energy. She was petite, tidy, and smelled clean. She had dark lips, almost teal blue. She was noticeably younger than Pa. She wore a pink dress and black Bata canvas tennis shoes. She had a high-pitched voice; she laughed freely. I thought that I liked her. But as a precaution, I reached into my pocket and surreptitiously chewed on the root that Grandma gave me. I was my grandma's child.

Her eldest, Sipho, was a pleasant little girl, an exact replica of her: the contours on her face, the thick braided black hair, and the big, bright, luminous eyes. At ten she was compact; she had the serious look of a grown-up.

Pa lit a cigarette with a smouldering piece of wood, said nothing for a while. Aunt Margaret babbled away, regaling both Pa and our stepma about her encounter with Grandma.

I observed my new family's dynamic, and wondered where Gift and I would fit in the scheme of things.

When Lizwe entered the kitchen, our stepma welcomed him with a hug and made him sit on her lap. He was six years old, and he was wearing a red T-shirt with the word *Typhoon* emblazoned across it.

'Look who is here! Did we sleep well? And what did we dream of, hey? Look, you've got a big brother and sister now. Nobody is going to pick on you now!'

Instead of looking at us, Lizwe buried his face into her chest. He looked overwhelmed. Besides, he'd barely woken up.

Lizwe was a light-skinned fragile little boy. He was all bone with knobbly knees. Unlike me, there were remnants of Pa in him – his hands, feet, texture of hair and skin tone. I felt an overwhelming jealousy knowing full well that Pa had always been there for him. But I let it pass.

We ate *vetkoeks* and drank sweet milky tea for breakfast, then I stepped outside to get some fresh air. Just then a man arrived. He was Pa's older brother, my Uncle SaDumo. He was darker, bulkier, much more solid than Pa. He grabbed my hand, squeezed it hard, shook it vigorously. Sharp pain radiated up my arm, all the way to the shoulder. When I tried to pull it back, he wouldn't let it go.

'Are you a man?' he asked as he sternly held my gaze.

Pa watched, silent.

I nodded yes, but I was not quite sure what the real question was. Or, more precisely, why he'd even ask me a question like that. Grandma's seemingly strange observation and commentary on the size of my hands reverberated at the back of my mind. Between Grandma's baffling observation and this man's rather trifling question, I was left slightly confused. Was there something wrong with me?

'Then give me a man's handshake!' he insisted.

With that, he crushed my small bones with his big, rough hand. I squirmed a little and totally relaxed my hand, tried to release it.

He squinted at me.

'Your father needs a strong man to take care of things whilst he's at work. We can certainly use a pair of hands!'

But I was only a boy.

'Come with me,' he enthused. 'Let me show you your inher-itance!'

We walked towards the cattle pen located between the two homesteads, slightly to the right. A squadron of flies hovered above the dung and the animals. There were cows, bulls, oxen, and donkeys corralled in the pen. And, right next to the big pen, a small goats' pen, where a herd of goats ruminated, eyes wide open as if they were surprised by something. I knew then what he meant by an extra pair of hands. Bringing me to his home had been nothing but a ruse, a pretext for securing a herdboy to look after the animals and to do whatever else there was to do. Grandma was right: things aren't always what they seem.

From the cattle pen he took me directly to his house, a stone's throw from Pa's. Outside, there were little children of various ages scattered everywhere like a disorganised nursery.

'*NaDumo*, I brought you a visitor,' he yelled.

'Who?' a female voice enquired from inside the kitchen.

'Paul's son,' SaDumo said.

A hunched figure emerged from the kitchen. His wife, NaDumo, although slender, was not quite as well put together as our stepma. After so many children, she looked tired and vacant. Since people did not call grown-ups by their first names, the preposition *Sa* in front of a person's name indicated that the man was the father of the child. Conversely, *Na* designated that the woman was the mother of the child. It was a mark of respect: having children bestowed dignity upon poor people – children were a kind of symbolic wealth, much more significant than money. It also meant cheap labour: children were part of the workforce, whether by assisting at home with chores such as cooking, cleaning, babysitting, or in the fields with weeding, or looking after animals. From a very early age, every child was endowed with a sense of responsibility.

'Oh, is that so?' she said. 'Don't be shy. Come on over here and shake my hand!'

I obliged and shook her hand.

Between them, they had ten children. Small children ran around, all dressed in rags. They had no shoes on, and I thought they needed a good scrub. As we walked back to Pa's, I had the sinking feeling that moving there wasn't such a good idea after all.

★

The next day we visited our other aunt, Gloria; she had arms as thick as my thigh. Although similar in temperament to Grandma, compared to her, I thought Aunt Gloria was lazy. She moved like a sloth. Her laughter was disingenuous; she was hard to please. There was a sprinkling of niceties here and there, but I already disliked her. Perhaps it was the way she looked at Gift and me.

Her homestead comprised two rectangular bedrooms built with adobe bricks, a big round adobe hut and another much smaller hut right next to the granary on stilts. They had a red scotch cart, multiple ploughs and other agricultural implements that suggested industry.

Her husband, Old Chauke, was tall and slender. He was bald, with tiny specks of grey hair just above the temples. Between them they had nine children, including the three cousins I had already met in the city when Uncle Sami and I first visited Pa.

'*Yebo tishala*,'* he said by way of greeting. 'I've heard so much about you. Welcome home. You'll like it here.'

It was as if he could sense that I was very afraid.

A shared bloodline cut through all three homesteads. Pa, SaDumo, and Aunt Gloria were siblings. Aunt Gloria was the eldest, followed by SaDumo, Pa, and then Aunt Margaret. There were four other aunts and numerous cousins a stone's throw away. So far, I had counted twenty-three cousins. I had yet to meet Pa's other siblings and their children. Everything felt new; I didn't know what lay ahead.

★

---

* Hello, small teacher.

For the first time I woke up without any expectations. I followed Pa around, trying to get to know him; we fished in the local reservoir, in silence – it was as if I wasn't there. My biggest fear was rejection. I tried every trick in the book to vie for his affection. But it just wasn't there. It takes much more than a shared bloodline to form a strong bond. After a while, I gave up and let it be.

When the Christmas revelry had died down, Pa and Aunt Margaret returned to the city. Within a month, Pa would be arrested and remanded in custody for battering a man close to death. We didn't know why. If our stepma knew why, she didn't say.

Despite the setback, Gift, and I both enrolled at the local school – Vula Primary School. The school consisted of three buildings, and it was perched on the edge of the forest. Shops and the nearest source of clean water were more than a mile away. There was no clinic or healthcare facility nearby. It was not clear to me why they'd chosen that location for a school.

There were older, mature students in my class – ex-combatants, some with children of their own. It was all part of the government's ambition for an education for all by the end of the decade.

The headmaster, Mr J. Sibanda, was a wiry little man with darting eyes. His right hand was all sinewy from old burns. He had a scraggy beard and a permanent squint in his right eye. There was something about him that suggested viciousness.

I was pleased I had enrolled at the new school, because education was very important to me. I made new friends and took my time to learn the geography of the place, to adapt to its rhythm. Gift, too, seemed happy.

At night, we played under the moonlit sky with bats, sang

childhood songs. During day, we hitched rides on the backs of temperamental donkeys and played football made from rags on makeshift pitches with thorn trees for spectators.

I discovered new fruit, new words, new idioms. The future looked promising, if only for a moment.

As the memory of Mawabeni receded, I found new joy, created new memories, and forgot about the war and Grandma's torment. I could be happy here, at least that's what I told myself.

But there were still rumours of war. On the way to school, I picked up remnants of sun-bleached newspapers, stuck up against thorn trees, fervently announcing that there was to be a new war on cockroaches. Politicians revived centuries-old interethnic hatreds, accompanied by empty sloganeering and sabre-rattling.

But it was the abduction of six White tourists in July 1982 along the Bulawayo–Victoria Falls Road that was to change everything. Rather than yield to the demands of the kidnappers, Robert Mugabe, then prime minister, vowed to crush the dissidents, once and for all. Before, they were bandits, but now they were dissidents, but many were armed with rudimentary weapons, such as axes, knives, and hand grenades, against thousands of well-trained, well-armed soldiers. Above all else, they had no coherent ideological orientation or support base. They terrorised civilians just as the soldiers did. But their presence was too good an opportunity to waste.

By the beginning of September 1982, the first deployment of soldiers, a combination of regular infantry and Police Support

Units, including the dreaded Criminal Intelligence Officers or CIO, had arrived. They rounded up men of a fighting age and sent them to detention centres for screening. Everything was methodical. Soldiers recorded the names of all the opposition party leaders, ZIPRA ex-combatants and influential individuals, including teachers and all the officials.

Occasionally, they beat people up, but the beatings appeared to be random acts of violence, rather than something centrally coordinated.

We called soldiers 'leaves' because there were so many of them. Also, because of the way they suddenly appeared, like new shoots in the early spring.

As more and more armed men roamed our landscape, people found it hard to distinguish between soldiers, real dissidents, pseudo dissidents, and bandits. We referred to them collectively as the Shadows. Soon they entered our homes, making demands for food and girls, money, and clothes, but we could see from their new boots and guns that they were soldiers pretending to be dissidents. Yet they'd come back the very next day and terrorise us for feeding dissidents.

And, much to our chagrin, in December 1982, Robert Mugabe announced that his North Korean-trained militia was ready for deployment. He wanted a politicised partisan army that would operate outside of the law and the human-rights framework to achieve his goal of a one-party state. So, he cleverly manipulated the kidnapping of the six White tourists as a pretext for pursuing a personal vendetta against Ndebele people, because he knew that the world would be much more concerned with the plight of White tourists than it would be with that of Black Africans.

After all, hundreds had already been killed, raped, and abducted, but there hadn't been that level of outrage.

In truth the army, Police Support Units, and CIO agents had already fulfilled their task to gather intelligence in aid of Mugabe's political agenda and the subsequent deployment of his ruthless militia to root out the main political opposition and its support base, mainly in Matabeleland and the Midlands. Similar operations had taken place elsewhere in Matabeleland, Bulawayo included, under Operation Octopus. The octopus symbolised the tentacles of Mugabe's dictatorial power, his ability to reach the far corners of our country.

So, there was a brief hiatus in military operations, as the National Army withdrew to make way for Mugabe's specially trained unit. And, for a while, things remained unsettled. ZANU PF politicians vowed to annihilate Ndebele people as though it were a mundane but necessary chore. Some chillingly evoked Biafra: Ndebele people had simply become scapegoats for a larger political witch-hunt.

After the war of independence, Mugabe had said that we should turn our weapons into ploughshares, let bygones be bygones. But he had already reneged on most of his promises: we had no flag of our own and he knew that. We waited for his brigade to arrive, not knowing exactly what to expect. Although there was a curfew, luckily schools remained open. And that kept me sane for a while.

CHAPTER 33

When Gukurahundi soldiers finally arrived, I was in class. When I looked towards the edge of the forest, I thought that the trees and tall grass were moving. Mounds of anthills morphed into strange formations, heading towards our school like a mirage in the midday sun. The forest kept edging closer and closer like a silent tsunami wave, red berets tilted to the right on multiple heads like scarecrows.

'Soldiers!' somebody shouted.

Just then, an armed man entered our classroom. He was short, stocky, and charcoal black, with a bulbous nose. He rolled up the sleeves of his camouflage shirt and in one fell swoop, the textbooks, boxes of chalk, cane, empty bottle of ginger beer, and blackboard duster fell to the floor, followed by the teacher who crashed backwards like an uprooted tree. The soldier impaled a hunting knife in the desk.

'We've come to flush out the dissidents amongst you and we won't stop until you tell us where they are,' he yelled. His AK-47 rifle leaned against the wall, and on his belt hung an upside-down bayonet. On his boots clung a dusty reddish-brown soil, the colour of freshly dug graves.

There was silence in the room. A beam of light focused its trajectory on the figure of the maths teacher, who was now lying face down on the table in front of the class, trussed up like a trapped crocodile, baring its teeth.

'I am only a teacher, sir. I have never seen any dissidents.'

His tight, reedy voice quivered, as he tried, in vain, to lift his neck and look backwards while he spoke. We all knew there was no right or wrong answer. Whatever he said didn't matter; this wasn't about the dissidents. It was, as Mugabe had said in his most recent broadcast, about the cockroaches and the enemies of the people. That could mean anything; to be an enemy of the people required no proof.

'Don't insult me!' the soldier bellowed back as he caressed a large wooden stick, freshly cut from the forest. 'Did you know that truth lies between the buttocks of a man? I won't leave you until I see flies in the room. We will purge until there is no more blood to purge!'

The soldier beat the maths teacher's buttocks with determin-ation, sucking up all the air in the room, making it difficult to breathe. We were all sweating profusely and flinching with each blow. In the end, all that was left of the man was a big stain on the floor.

When the soldier finally stopped, the main road outside the school perimeter resembled a jungle airstrip. Each convoy that went by generated a cloud of dust, which settled on the trees and flower beds and sometimes on us, like brown snow flur-ries. Female teachers and older schoolgirls were lined up, trucks waiting. No one knew their destination. The belly of the truck opened, and they were pushed inside like cattle. Amidst the wailing and chaos, the trucks left with their bountiful harvest, headed east under the cover of dust.

On the way home, I watched military trucks as they made vertical climbs out of ravines, looking as if they were about to tip over and empty all the soldiers into the gorge below. There was nothing except us and our animals, and yet I could see soldiers carrying machine guns as though there was a real war going on. When I got home, our dog Shisa was resting in the meagre shade from the kitchen wall, scratching her flea-infested ear, indifferent to the world beyond her own wounds. We gathered in the kitchen, not knowing what to do.

It was February 1983. The rains had failed for the third year running. A severe drought had decimated all our crops, dashing all hope, even for a meagre harvest. We had ground millet porridge with sour milk for supper. By sunset, we were in bed.

A dusk-to-dawn curfew had already been declared. Nothing was allowed to move in, or out. Schools, clinics, grinding mill, and shops were all closed. There were roadblocks everywhere. Everything came to a grinding halt. Those caught using bicycles, donkeys or carts were shot on sight. They were accused of feeding dissidents.

That was the beginning of Robert Mugabe's total war against Ndebele people, barely two years after our independence. Whilst his soldiers roamed the countryside – raping, pillaging, setting homes on fire, and killing people as though there was a real war on, Mugabe continued to broadcast his intentions to annihilate Ndebele people over the radio. He said that we were the infrastructure that supported dissidence. And, for that reason, we had to die: 'When men and women provide food for dissidents, when we get there, we eradicate them. We don't differentiate when we fight, because we can't tell who a dissident is and who is not.'

He also said that an eye for an eye may not be enough, in which case his soldiers may well ask for two eyes instead of one eye.

In his eyes, Ndebele people were a putrid boil on the body of the nation, which needed lancing and cleansing. The patient might wince a bit, but the operation was long overdue, necessary even.

'You voted for the father of dissidents, so don't feel sorry for yourselves. All his generals are now rotting away in prison. As for you, no one will save you!'

His soldiers confiscated identity cards and party loyalty cards, and in subsequent operations claimed that those without were dissidents. Now, they could no longer tell the difference between dissidents and ordinary civilians.

No one knew anything about Gukurahundi soldiers except that they were answerable only to Robert Mugabe. They had been trained, specifically for this task, in the remote, isolated valleys in the north, shielded by the beautiful Nyanga mountains in Mashonaland.

Mugabe called them, simply, Gukurahundi: the soft wintery rain after harvest. In isiNdebele we called them *Imbolisamahlanga*: the persistent wintery drizzle that gently softened maize stalks, introducing rot imperceptibly slowly, so that when farmers tilled the land in preparation for the ploughing season, rotten maize stalks fell and disappeared into furrows created by the shares of the ploughs after the first rains in September. The rot nourished the ground for the new crop of maize plants, sweet reed, melon, and pumpkin.

On their passing-out parade, Mugabe issued them with the ominous instruction: 'With the knowledge that you have, go work with the people, plough and reconstruct!'

But it was February. The ploughing season had long since gone. There was nothing but famine, dust, and disease. His government had resorted to starvation as a weapon of war. They could not feed us, they said. What little food they gave us would end up in the mouths of dissidents. So, all the drought relief intended for us was diverted to ZANU PF strongholds in Mashonaland in exchange for votes.

We were on our own.

CHAPTER 34

We prayed for rain and a miraculous reprieve – but neither came.

Instead, Gukurahundi soldiers, in an assortment of camouflage, flooded our homes from different directions. When they spoke, it was as though ten different languages were being spoken all at once, none of which made sense to me. I was in the middle of giving Lizwe a bath. We were standing on a slightly raised concrete slab, Pa's abandoned project to build an even bigger house.

Shisa started barking ferociously. I tried to calm her down, but she was just too agitated to stop. One of the soldiers shouted at me to calm the dog, but I could not leave Lizwe all on his own. I looked towards the kitchen to see if anyone would come out, but I could not see for the sheer number of soldiers around us. In the end, the soldier lost his temper, and he kicked our dog viciously. She whimpered contritely and hid under the barn. From there, she continued to bark, relentlessly. Soon, a sudden burst of gunfire reduced her to a pile of meat. She died under the barn. Nobody explained why they'd just killed our dog. She meant no harm to anyone. And they knew that.

I kept hold of the rag that I had been using to scrub Lizwe. He started to cry. It wasn't a loud cry but a sob. There was nothing I could do except wish for the ground to swallow us.

In between sporadic gunfire, dogs barking, voices yelling, I could hear screams coming from my cousin Dumo's house. Also, from all the surrounding neighbours. The screams were very loud, but they soon waned into muffled sounds: voices begging for their lives, then they died out. Lizwe was still naked save for the rag wrapped around his tiny frame. Not a sound issued from him, except for the chattering of his teeth. I tried to dress him. I whispered for him to go into the kitchen, but he froze right next to me.

It was then one of the soldiers approached us. He was not wearing a red beret but a military cap with a flap rolled up at the back. His camouflage shirt was folded neatly above the elbow. He had a chain of bullets round his waist. He looked different from the rest – tall, broad, and very light-skinned. He was so big that the machine gun slung over his shoulder looked as if it weighed nothing.

'*Kijane!*'* he called out to me.

I clutched Lizwe's tiny hand; I had no intention of letting it go. First, he asked me about dissidents. Although playful, the way adults talked to children, there was something tenaciously serious about him. I told him a truth-lie. I said that I'd seen dissidents in the past, but they hadn't been back for a while. He asked how many, and what kind of weapons they were carrying. I gave him descriptions based mainly on the weapons that the soldiers were carrying.

---

* *Kijane* is a Kiswahili word for small boy.

He also asked me other seemingly random questions. Such as, who was new to the area? Who'd left recently? And where did they go? He also wanted to know about all the important people such as teachers, soldiers, those involved in politics, and all their relatives. I told him the truth: that the old man Chauke was the local chairman of ZAPU, and that my cousin Bobo was an ex-freedom fighter. I also told him that he had a pregnant wife and a little girl, hoping that that would save them. When I told him that, his eye language changed. He smiled at me. He then asked if there was anything else I'd forgotten to mention. I hadn't forgotten anything, I said. With that, he turned round and walked away.

I rushed Lizwe into the kitchen to fetch his clothes. It was getting dark. For some reason, all our neighbours were corralled into our yard. They trickled in one by one, in small groups, in various stages of undress. Most had been caught in the slumber of the late afternoon heat. That included my cousin Dumo's family, my Aunt Gloria, and her family, including Old Chauke. We were forced to sit on the bare earth and to wait. I chose a spot for Lizwe and me right at the front. I wanted to hear, properly, what the soldiers had to say.

When I turned round and looked behind me, I could see our stepma right at the back of the crowd, her distinctive yellow head-wrap tilted forward. I could not see Gift, or Sipho. I started to panic because I didn't know where they were. The rest of the family were scattered around in the crowd. It had been agreed that we should not huddle together, lest the soldiers started shooting. I caught a glimpse of my Aunt Gloria and, right next to her, the old man still wearing his straw hat, and my cousin Bobo, and his wife Zina. Most of the girls were hiding somewhere at the back.

The soldiers ordered all the men to gather wood and build a bonfire. They insisted on big mopane logs. It was going to be a long night. So, the men tore down the fences to get mopane wood for the fire. Soon, smoke billowed into the air and, slowly, the flame rose. I started to think of the fire and the cockroaches, and what Emmerson Mnangagwa, minister of State Security, and head of CIO, had recently said about cleansing the area of the menace of dissidents. With that, I started to feel anxious, over-whelmed by fear.

The soldiers worked the crowd into a frenzy as if the gathering was an all-night religious revival. They encouraged us to sing about our own death as if that was a good thing. They detached the blades from their weapons, and in a sweeping motion, sliced through the air. They said they wanted to sweep our homes clean with their blades. Through their songs, they mentioned all the places they'd been to recently: Tsholotsho, Silobela, Mbazhe, Nesigwe. We knew these places by heart. We had families there too.

The leader of the group was a very dark, short, and stocky man. The broad buckle on his military belt glinted in the light from the fire. He had rolled up the sleeves of his camouflage shirt just above the elbows. There was nothing else on him except his blade. Like Mugabe and all the ZANU PF politicians, he had a penchant for sloganeering. He strutted, like a cockerel, and pummelled his fist into his cupped hand.

He then raised his right fist triumphantly.

'*Pamberi na* Robert Gabriel Mugabe! Forward with the gallantry of our revolutionary soldiers! Forward with the war on dissidents! Down with the cockroaches and sell-outs! Some say the war is finished. Some even say that you are free now. All these are rumours, of course! Now, here is one thing I want *you* people to help me with.'

He stuck his finger into the air as if he was likely to find the answers to his own question there. Suddenly, a malevolence showed in his eyes.

'Now, we all know that you are hiding and feeding dissidents. They are here tonight, amongst you!'

With that, he waved his right hand over us, as though spreading something only he knew.

'We will flush them out! Don't underestimate our determination to deal with the problem of dissidents, once and for all. That's why we're here. We'll stay for as long as it takes. Or until there isn't a single one of you left. If you think that you are hungry now, think again. First, you'll eat your animals, then your children, then your wives. By then, if there are any of you left, you'll eat the soil. You must understand that we are not the National Army that has so far treated you as if your life matters. You don't matter to us!'

Next, the soldier launched into a tirade about their mission. He smiled when he talked about killing: 'The dissidents will come out of the forest, eventually. If they don't, we'll burn the forest if we must!'

Old Chauke stood up, folded his straw hat in his hands and shouted indignantly: 'If you know where the so-called dissidents are, why don't you go and find them and leave us alone?'

The soldier told him to sit down and keep quiet, but the old man refused.

'What kind of men are you? How can you force people to sing

and dance at gunpoint? If we must sing, let us sing our own songs, like we've always done!'

Then the old man snatched remnants of an old liberation song from under his breath. As he sang, others joined in too.

Senzeni na?
Senzeni na, Senzeni na?
What have we done?

A group of soldiers stood menacingly in the shadows. Just then, one of them stepped out into the limelight and interrupted the old man's song. He was very young, but he looked mean like the rest of the soldiers. His small eyes darted from person to person, as if refusing to settle on anyone. I tried not to look at him.

Then he flared up.

'*Pamberi NeZanu! Pamberi Neruzhinji rwedu! Pasi Nemadissidents!* Down with the sell-outs! And who said you can sing?'

No one answered, but the old man continued, unperturbed.

'We are free now,' the old man said. 'It is only yesterday that you were telling us that we were the sea, and you were the fish. That without us you couldn't survive! Now you kill defenceless women and children and call it war?'

'Old man, I said sit down!'

Seemingly undeterred, the old man rambled on as if possessed.

'We knew right from the beginning what Boers wanted. We fought day and night against them. That was war! And this? What is this? I can tell you one thing. This is not what we fought for!'

The taut cast on the soldier's face loosened, tightened, and then loosened again. He adjusted and readjusted the thickness of the fold on his shirtsleeves. He put his red beret back on and waded through the crowd until he reached the old man. He struck Old Chauke very hard across the face with the back of his hand, and then dragged him out to the front. He pulled him hard, and Old Chauke fell forward. There was nothing with which to break his fall. The soldier pinned his head to the ground with his boot. After what seemed like an eternity, the soldier removed his boot from his neck.

'Am I not your father, son?'

'My father is not the father of dissidents,' the soldier replied. 'There is absolutely no truth in that, and you know it!'

He remained prone; his legs splayed apart. The soldier stood back and kicked him hard in the ribs. He then rested his heavy boot on his neck again. The old man dragged blood, air, and dust in through his nose. It was as if he was dying with a rib-cage full of air. Then he tried to make a plea, but it was the wrong kind.

'Even the most vicious of dogs accepts defeat. But I am not a dog. You, my son, are robbing us of our hard-won freedom. You are no different from the so-called dissidents!'

With that he lay still. The blows kept coming; he was floating between steel-toecap boots, inside a cloud of dust.

All he kept saying was, 'That's the truth. I am not an animal!'

Without so much as a word, another soldier raised the butt of his weapon and struck the old man right in the middle of the head. He tried to crawl but failed. They lifted and swung his body like a bag of sand and, finally, they threw him sideways into the fire.

There was a jolt, followed by an incredible howling.

I grabbed Lizwe's hand, closed his eyes, brought him closer to me. There was a commotion amongst the crowd as Aunt Gloria rose. The women held and surrounded her until she collapsed into a heap. In between, there were intermittent screams; there was gunfire.

As I tried to study the outline of each soldier, each one of them remained elusive. Perhaps it was the camouflage. Or the boots. Or the red berets. Red berets circulated, moved into and around each other. Some tilted theirs to the left. Others to the right. For others, they rested loosely at the back of their heads. It seemed that the red beret, much like the soldiers themselves, had been chosen with care. When someone died, we tied a red piece of cloth on the periphery of our homes, so that others could share in our grief in passing. Whoever chose the berets knew what the red colour symbolised to us. The red berets more than convinced us that we were surrounded – they also brought an inexplicable dread and trepidation.

Some of the soldiers remained in the shadows, making it harder to decipher each outline. They dragged the girls, one by one, into the woods. I watched the girls go in and come out. That was all I saw. When they came back, they carried nervous smiles with them. I still didn't know what that meant. That went on all night.

Just before dawn, they took some of my female cousins and my sister. I watched them vanish into the woods; all the adults remained silent.

Our assailants worked tirelessly throughout the night. They had a list of names to go through before dawn. But it was the haphazard way the beatings were carried out that inflicted the utmost terror.

Men tried to hide behind women and children; others pushed and shoved in the darkness to get away, just as long as it was not them. From then on, there would be no story of us without shame.

When they called out my cousin Bobo's name, nobody pointed him out. He had recently come back from the war as a freedom fighter. He was a teacher, and he had a special way of walking. His right arm gave his slim frame a wide berth, as if he was carrying something heavy, that only he could feel. He never walked in a straight line. Or in the middle of the road. They said ex-guerrillas never did, for fear of tripping landmines. After all these years later, he was still afraid of imaginary minefields. That was a rumour that he neither confirmed nor denied. Then again, he never talked about the war. None of them did.

'*Ah heee*, that was the war! Things were hard!'

That was all he ever said.

But the soldiers thought that his kind were all dissidents. They accused him of defecting, but he had never left home since he'd come back from the real war. He used to say that all those years of hunger, spent sleeping under trees in the bush, inside caves in the mountains, made him realise just how much he missed home. He would say that when you fight for it, the idea of home has a different resonance. Home has a hold in your heart that never lets go. Now that he had a choice, he'd never leave. All he wanted to do was teach and stay at home until he died. That was all.

They asked him if he had a wife. He looked away, way above the soldier's head – that's how tall he was. His eyes stayed fixated on something else; not once did he look at his wife. There was movement right in the middle of the crowd where most of the women were. Aunt's big frame had taken much of the space like an immovable statue. She had spread herself out like a mother chicken protecting her brood. Behind her, Bobo's wife, Zina, tried hard to calm their baby, Lethu, to no avail. Desperate, she squeezed the baby under Aunt's armpit.

Lizwe whispered that he wanted to use the toilet. I didn't know how to ask the soldiers. So I let him urinate right where he sat.

The soldier calmly said to Bobo, 'We know your wife is carrying another dissident. As far as we're concerned the child of a dissident is still a dissident. Why wait for them to grow old? I've already said that we're here to deal with the problem of dissidents – once and for all. We'll find her. I know she's here!'

Gukurahundi soldiers had the reputation for slicing open the stomachs of pregnant women to kill the dissidents growing inside them, or out of curiosity.

Everyone held their breath. He looked at his list again. He called out Zina, but nobody answered. He called her again. Again, nobody answered.

'You people think that we don't know anything. For example, we knew before we came out here that the old man was the father of dissidents. That's why we've killed him. Now, I want you to show me where this dissident's wife is. Otherwise, I'll treat all of you as collaborators. You have no idea what that means! Those of you with absent husbands, brothers, and sons, I want to know where they are. They're all dissidents. I won't repeat myself again. Just so you understand, tonight I want to know where all the dissidents are, so I can kill them!'

When he finished talking, he stubbed his cigarette out. He grabbed his gun as if he was ready to shoot someone. Just then, the big soldier I'd spoken to earlier signalled for me to come to him. I dropped Lizwe's hand and ran the short distance between us.

'*Kijane*, remember what I said?'

I nodded, yes, nervously.

'Now, show me this dissident's wife,' he said, pointing at my cousin Bobo.

'I know that she's here. Just take me to her.'

I didn't want to die. I felt I had no choice but take the soldier to Zina. Aunt Gloria tried to plead with her eyes for me to go somewhere else. But, for some reason, just before I pointed Zina out to him, the soldier called me.

'*Kijane!*'

When I turned round, he signalled for me to come back. He handed over his machine gun to one of the soldiers nearest to him. He stepped forward till I could see his face in the full glow of the light. His hands were very big but clean. He spoke in a very funny dialect. I knew that *kijane* was a Swahili word for a boy. Most comrades spoke Swahili when they came back from war. Inside I thought he was a gentle giant. Something also told me that somehow this was not his war. Otherwise, why else would he save Bobo's pregnant wife? But I was wrong.

He stepped forward and said, 'I just wanted to show you all how easy it is to find out the truth. Never lie to me again!'

He smiled at me. Then one of his men shot Bobo dead right on the edge of our home. They tossed his body into his hut and set it on fire. I felt betrayed; I didn't know what else was going to happen because of what I'd told him.

Immediately afterwards, they summoned Dumo to come forward. He got up in such a hurry, as if he had nowhere to sleep that night. When the soldiers had arrived, he'd been playing his guitar. Since then, he'd been holding on to it. One of the soldiers ordered him to play his guitar. Under normal circumstances, Dumo could play his guitar with such an incredible dexterity. But that night, it was as if there was a disconnect between his fingers and ears.

The soldier asked him to dance. He did not tell him, however, whether he wanted him to stop playing the guitar, or dance, or do both those things all at once. That had major implications for Dumo. When he stopped to speak, that was his first infraction of many unwritten rules. There was no right or wrong answer; either way, that was a game he was bound to lose. After an inordinate amount of questioning, Dumo was asked to lie prostrate. As soon as he touched the ground, a full-force boot landed on his ribs. His slight frame lifted off the ground. He sucked air into his lungs and held it somewhere inside, as if for an eternity. When he finally landed, one of the soldiers placed his boot on the back of his neck and pressed it hard to the ground. So much so that when Dumo exhaled, he created furrows in the sand. Another cut his belt with his blade and pulled his trousers down, leaving his buttocks completely exposed.

They beat his back and buttocks with a thick, freshly cut piece of mopane wood. Dumo tried to put his hands on his back. That only infuriated his assailants.

'*Usabate mnfana, iwewe usabate!* Remove your hands! I said remove your hands!' the soldier yelled.

But it was impossible not to try to save himself. Anyone could see that. When they tired, the mopane stick changed hands. They worked at Dumo with such a sustained ferocity that he drifted in and out of consciousness. None of them, not even the leader of the group, had said anything about why they were killing him. Dumo was not a dissident. That was just the same old tyranny wrapped up in a new flag.

It was his father, SaDumo, next. They struck his head with a shovel. He fell. There was a dull thud, then silence. It was a dream – vivid, disturbing – only it wasn't.

We could have run, scattered. But where would we have gone? In the end, we turned inward, listened to the blows and the desperate cries for help. There wasn't anything I or anyone else could do.

CHAPTER 35

Military trucks left early morning, laden with all the men and older boys they hadn't killed or maimed the previous night. Those left behind, like Dumo, were seriously wounded. He had been badly beaten and could barely stand. He was now totally confused and had been urinating blood. There was nowhere to take him because the local clinic was closed.

Miraculously SaDumo, too, had survived: only just – the cuts to his head weren't too deep, but he was very weak, and incoherent.

The soldiers had left explicit instructions that nobody should be taken to the hospital. There was a rumour that they always returned to finish off survivors. Adults hid Dumo inside the barn at Aunt Gloria's house.

Gift came back dishevelled and disoriented. Her head was a swallow's nest: specks of grass, fragments of leaves, and caked reddish mud from nearby fields. She looked at no one and her hands were clasped into a nervous ball, holding her blood-soaked rag of underwear.

'Here, drink this. It will do you good,' said our stepma as she gave her a glass of milk – all we had. And she looked away as if sheltering from her own rain. Gift dropped her underwear, grabbed the aluminium cup, and embraced it with both hands. She drank the milk in small, desperate gulps, peering into it as if searching for answers. Our stepma took her away, bathed her, and let her sleep in her bedroom for the rest of the day. It was hard to make sense of things; everything felt surreal.

Bobo's hut had burned out hollow. All that was left was a charred metal bed frame and the remains of enamel cups hanging on the wall. I watched his wife, Zina, sift through the ashes, hoping she'd find a part of him to bury, however small. Somehow, I thought that he was still in there, mixed up with all the ashes.

The older women were gathered next to Koko and Tata's graves, digging the grave for Old Chauke's remains. During ordinary times, this was men's work. Women gathered the stones to place on top of the graves. They stayed with the body of the deceased until the grave was ready for the burial to take place. Afterwards, they prepared food and traditional beer. They sang and wailed too; that way, nobody mourned alone. But these were no ordinary times. They had to endure the most terrifying anguish alone.

My stepma was waist-deep inside the grave. She was digging with a heavy pickaxe. Occasionally, she stopped and swapped the pickaxe for the shovel. The grave seemed too narrow and too shallow to contain the magnitude of the old man.

As the women swapped places, Aunt Gloria kept walking around the empty grave with her hands above her head. There was no wailing, no singing – just sadness. When they tried to gather the ashes, a whirlwind scattered them. Aunt sent me to fetch a bucket of water, which she poured over the ashes. Then they used shovels and buckets to transfer the black sludge into the open grave. Aunt said that she didn't want to lose any more of the old man. She wanted to bury him whole – what was left of him. Somehow, it already felt too late.

Nearby, homes had been completely abandoned. Others had been burned to the ground, with the remains of the dead still inside. For those found dead on the outskirts of the forest, the women had to bury them where they found them, to prevent dogs from eating them. They buried some of the bodies inside termite mounds to aid their memory. Aunt Gloria said that when the war was over, they'd have to dig up their remains and bring the deceased's spirits home.

We had always believed that we were human beings first, born with dignity. But Gukurahundi soldiers changed all that. They disrupted the very order of things, from the way in which people tried to memorise everything, to the way in which they related to each other. And then there was the fear, which forced us to discard everything that we knew, and all the precious things that we held dear, including the way we buried our dead. So many things were missing, so many people too.

By the time the women had finished, it was past noon. They withdrew indoors, the way they were supposed to after a funeral. They sat around the hearth as though it was a cold winter's night.

'What will people say?' asked Aunt Gloria. 'Were these soldiers not our sons only yesterday? Did we not cook for them? And allowed them to kill on our behalf just as long as they were not killing us? Can we say, hand on heart, that they were not killing innocent people then? And did anybody intervene? I mean, did any of us intervene? Did we?'

Bobo's mother brushed dust off her clothes that was no longer there. She'd been doing that ever since she'd sat down. And when she began to speak, her voice quivered slightly.

'I waited for my son to come back from war, like any mother would. And, each night, I prayed to God to bring him back to me. And, when he finally came back, after six years in the bush, with all his limbs, body, and face still intact, I thanked God for his beneficence. And I slept for the first time! Yeah, that's true. I slept peacefully for the first time in six years, because, finally, I was convinced that the nightmares were over now that the spirits were watching over him. And I remember how we celebrated, like it was yesterday. There was even a greeting, right here in this village: *Nkululeko! Nkululeko!* Which meant, simply, that we were free. That, finally, the Boers would leave us alone so we could raise our families in peace and watch our children grow into decent human beings. That the time had come for us to see all the good things that we'd been denied by the Boers become manifest in our children's lives. And I never thought that I'd be afraid again! Never! Not under Black rule! And they shot my son in front of his wife and child. His only crime? To fight to liberate this country! What hurts me the most is that the very people he fought with have killed him. They've taken my son's life for nothing. I don't even know how I'll survive this.'

And, pointing at Zina, she said, 'Now, what am I supposed to do with this child who no longer has a husband?'

And she looked at Aunt Gloria, who in turn cast a glance over the dying flame, as if looking for a way out. She agitated the firewood gently, as if after everything that had happened this was the only thing that she had a right to do.

Her tears came effortlessly.

'But that was war,' she said. 'And we didn't expect these soldiers, our sons, to come back like this!'

It was then that my stepma, her feet still covered in red soil, leaned forward. A half-smile, half-frown stretched across her face.

'Somehow, they make life feel so miniscule,' she observed. 'Now, our lives do not mean a thing. We'll never be free from this. Never! Mark my words, the young will inherit this madness!' She continued. 'In the last war, we slaughtered our animals, raised the young, and looked after comrades, while men hid in the cities and drank beer all day. We carried weapons on our heads and backs; and sometimes hid food in the most intimate parts of our bodies, just to feed our sons! We suffered humiliation at the hands of White soldiers. We gave of our sons and daughters, our most treasured resource, to fight for our freedom. Even as they cut our lips to silence us, we kept all their secrets. We ignored the fact that they abused our bodies all in the name of freedom. Because there was a belief that being generous with our bodies was the bare minimum we could do. That we could not expect others to shed their own blood to free us without us contributing to the war effort. They took everything from us. Everything we had. But we survived. We watched people forced to dig their own graves before being killed. We told ourselves that it was war. And yet still it is us women who continue to bear the burden of the last war. They have the temerity to come here asking all these ridiculous questions about dissidents!'

And she stopped as if to breathe momentarily.

'Did we not clothe and feed guerrillas even as they brutalised us for things not even dogs deserved to die for? They're doing the same now. They desecrate the graves of our loved ones by forcing us to dance on them. They ask for blankets and take our daughters with them. Yet we cannot ask what happens to our daughters under our own blankets.'

She pointed towards the door as if there was someone tall standing there.

'There are still things that happened during the war that our own husbands, fathers, and brothers won't talk about. Since we carry this burden alone, how are they ever going to understand us? Then this? The same cowardly men, like my husband, will come back and start asking silly questions: "What happened to so-and-so? Whose grave is that over there? What happened to my animals?"'

Just then the cattle bells started ringing. The little ones grabbed an enamel cup each and exited from the kitchen. They were heading for the *kraal*, lured by the promise of milk. But that day there was no one to milk the cows.

SaDumo sat with his back against the wall. His head was covered in improvised bandages and purple gauze. He looked dejected, defeated. He ran his finger along the contour of each wound as if trying to find the source.

And the vast, dry land was now filled with anxiety. Its sandy loam soils, which were in abundance, were very shallow. Rainwater vanished as soon as it rained. The road to the Shangani River was deserted. Because of the war, those who went to the river to fetch water sometimes never came back, so we had not seen water carts for a while.

In the midst of drought, the memory of water lingered the most. Sometimes I saw birds hovering above dry wells, as though they too were beginning to doubt their own memory.

We had yet to receive the drought relief our leaders had promised us. But Mugabe vehemently denied that he was deliberately starving us to death. He said that everyone was well fed, that the violence and the hunger existed only in our imagination. Truly speaking, we were on the brink of starvation.

People were already praying for the past to come back. Things were better then, they said. That, yes, there had been killing and starvation, but there had been hope too.

Unlike other parts of the country, development had been slow in Matabeleland. It had been three years since our independence in 1980. There had been much talk of relocation to more fertile lands, but we were still waiting. The Whites wouldn't sell their farms for redistribution. There was more talk about their rights than there was about our plight.

When we ran out of food, we gathered baobab fruit pods, smashed them open and poured water over the white powder to create a nutritious, sweet, and sour milky drink. We ate nuts from the marula tree, foraged for wild fruit and berries, and ate small sun-dried raisins the size of hungry deflated ticks for sustenance. We slept out in the open. That way, when the soldiers set fire to our homes at night while we slept, we wouldn't perish in the flames too. Our survival, our very existence, depended on small acts of resilience.

But it was inevitable that we would develop relationships with soldiers. Girls fell in love with them too. Besides, how could they say no to men of violence, who forcefully took what they wanted? Casper, the light-skinned soldier who'd first spoken to me on that fateful night, would sometimes visit me with Chico, his pet monkey. His platoon had established their base camp next to the water reservoir and from there infiltrated deeper into isolated villages. Work on our village had been completed. We patiently waited for those kidnapped to come back, however deformed.

I got up at dawn just to see Casper's platoon set off, his camouflage shirt neatly folded above the elbows, his combat trousers tucked inside his boots, and the laces on his boots pulled tight. It was as if all body parts had been reassembled, harnessed, and set in motion. Arms swung, and legs moved at the same pace.

They sang in beautiful soldierly voices, as if the songs would somehow ameliorate the bitterness of war and assign, in its place, new beginnings. They killed to a rhythm; the song galvanized effort, ironed out the clumsiness of the blows, added purpose to mindless killing work, and absolved their conscience.

Through song they did work that they had to do diligently. They smoked human beings like wild game; they pruned, cut, and splayed bodies open, as if working in a cane field. Inside the war song, terror was reconfigured and passed on.

The songs would echo long after they'd gone.

Amai nababa, musandicheme,
kana ndafa, nehondo,
Ndini ndakazwipira kurwira Zimbabwe,
*Kana ndafa, nehondo**

Casper's machine gun pointed ahead menacingly. But Chico, alert on his right shoulder, was a much better hunter of people. When he found them hiding in their lairs, he sought them out, bared his teeth, and remonstrated with them till they came out.

And when they came back from their patrols, Casper sought me out. Sometimes I would be out in the forest looking after our animals. Somehow, he always managed to find me. Together we entered inside the shade of the tree whose branches swept the ground. From the outside, you could not see inside. Mostly, he wanted to know what had been going on. But I didn't ask where he'd been; I already knew.

Casper fell asleep with his left hand clutching the belt of bullets that fed into his machine gun. I studied all of him, right down to his giant fingers. And I watched him breathe – in, out, in, out. His chest rose and fell. Under his spell, I felt very small, irrelevant. I prayed for myself to grow quicker: if every man in our village was a liar and a coward, I dreamed of becoming a remorseless killer, because there was so much power invested in the gun.

He was amiable and kind. When he played with Chico, when he relaxed, he folded his camouflage trousers just below the knee. Every so often, he removed his bayonet from its scabbard, looked

---

* To my mother and father. Do not mourn for me when I die. I volunteered to serve my country, and if I die, do not cry for me.

at it, only to replace it without saying a word. But I noticed a pattern – whatever I disclosed to him determined what happened next. So I had to be extremely careful with my words.

On the surface of things, he appeared to enjoy my company. But I was thirteen years old; I had no idea why. Perhaps I was the only source of intimacy he had. Inside the madness of war, intimacy was the most persistent of longings. It was inside forbidden tenderness that we knew that we hadn't lost everything. What happened between us stayed under the solitude of the tree. Afterwards, it was hard to feel places in my body with raw nerve endings. Everything felt numb like an overused arm that was no longer part of me.

Sometimes, I tried to figure out who he really was, but of what use would it be to know the full extent of his monstrosity beyond what I already knew? I could also see, in small glimpses, that he longed for peace, but I didn't ask him to account for the heaviness on his shoulders. When he drifted into a deep sleep, he slept like an ordinary man and not a killer. It was as if he walked through an invisible door, beyond which no sound could reach him. There was something remarkable about his kind of tiredness.

Chico sat above us in the canopy of the tree, fastened to a leash that was tied to a branch. He, too, was tethered to the violence. He came down, sat right next to me. We shared his monkey nuts from a small pouch attached to Casper's ration pack. He fell into fits of agitation. He pulled and rattled the bullets and jumped on the tree branches above us, causing a fracas to Casper's consternation. It took time for Chico to calm down. When his fit of rage was over, he came back down. Between us three there was a connection. Perhaps I, too, possessed the power to hurt, maim, and kill.

'He goes mad for no reason. One day I'll let him go, but where will he go when I release him?' Casper said.

I did not know what Chico had witnessed. After everything that had happened, I could never afford to fully trust men like Casper. In war, no bond was sacred; every relationship was contingent upon prevailing circumstances. It was all about survival.

Later in the day, military helicopters traversed the sky, their whirring blades disrupting the slumber of the afternoon. As Casper and I emerged from our hiding place, a man stood across the field, watching us. It was SaDumo, still dazed. He knew that I could not disclose to him what went on between me and Casper. So, he pretended that he could not see things as they were. And that, too, was survival.

Inside, I felt isolated; I had witnessed, first-hand, the power-lessness of the adult world.

But, looking back as an adult, I could not say – hand on heart – that Casper had coerced me into doing anything. Or that he molested or sexually abused me. Somehow, it felt as though subconsciously I had willed for it to happen. But I also felt a deep sense of shame because silence in war is a double bind; it protects as it betrays: how could I avoid betraying others, when betrayal meant protecting myself and those closest to me? Conversely, to what does a thirteen-year-old boy consent under duress? Because consent implies freedom of choice, and a full understanding of that to which one is consenting. But the silence – mine, the adults', and the state's – was a kind of wounding too. And, even after all these years, it is still hard for me to think that I was a brave little boy who risked everything just to survive.

After the whirr of the helicopters and the distant rumble of the machine guns had ceased, everything stood still – sky, trees, homes burned out hollow. Nearby, donkeys took a dust bath and afterwards retreated under the meagre shade of the mopane tree. Even that momentary peace seemed fabricated.

CHAPTER 36

In a place not too far from where we were, Gukurahundi soldiers had taken fifty-two men and women to the river, shot, and killed them. Only one young man survived, by hiding under the warm corpses. His own father had to amputate his arm, pulverised by machine-gun fire, with an axe just below the shoulder to save his life.

In another village, they corralled whole families into buildings and set them on fire. It was said that there were human remains in pit latrines, in mineshafts and shallow graves. These were rumours of war, of course, with each person painting their own versions of terror.

Within six weeks of their deployment, Gukurahundi soldiers had killed more than two thousand people. Some put that figure closer to three thousand. The exact figure will never be known; no official survey of the killings was ever carried out.

In the end, the secrecy surrounding the massacres could no longer hold. News of the atrocities crossed borders with refugees who had walked hundreds of miles all the way to Botswana to tell the world what was happening in our country.

On being questioned, Robert Mugabe said that he understood the people's concern over military action in war zones. That whenever there was military action there was bound to be casualties. He put it down to the overzealousness of the people's army. He denied and derided the notion that his soldiers had committed gross human-rights violations in Matabeleland at a time of peace.*

Meanwhile, prominent ZANU PF politicians took international journalists to areas where there had been no military presence as proof that Gukurahundi atrocities had been nothing but a fabrication.

Still under pressure, Mugabe relented. He said he had already spoken to his military commanders, and they'd agreed that 'the Brigade', as he called Gukurahundi soldiers, needed retraining and reorientation, since they'd already met and exceeded their objectives: *to work with the people, to plough and reconstruct.* As a country, we'd had an unprincipled fight. We needed to exercise a little restraint: let bygones be bygones.

We were willing to accept the temporary reprieve, however disingenuous, because we had been wounded by so many things. In response to the clamour for a ceasefire and, as a gesture of goodwill, in April 1983 the curfew was lifted. In July 1983, Gukurahundi soldiers were withdrawn from Matabeleland North, albeit temporarily.

There was a scaling down of military activities, but there was also the nagging feeling that the war had not finished. Mugabe's

---

* See *Gukurahundi in Zimbabwe: A Report on the Disturbances in Matabeleland and the Midlands, 1980-1988* (London: Hurst Publishers, 2007).

announcement that his Brigade needed retraining and reorientation was unsettling.

And for a while it appeared as though he had listened. But what the media attention and his own inquiry had highlighted was the recklessness with which the Brigade had carried out its operations. Armed with this new information, his commanders changed tactics, which was what Mugabe meant by '*retraining and reorientation*'.

We had waited for so long for a permanent reprieve – but it never materialised.

They were back within a month. The beatings and the interrogations started all over again. The violence escalated to an intensity that far exceeded what we'd previously witnessed. What had also changed was the removal of people from their homes to makeshift detention centres – abandoned mines, dip tanks, schools – for interrogation and subsequent mass murder. This time, they made sure that there was no evidence of the massacres and no witnesses. People left in the night, never to be seen again. Desperate, many spent weeks in forests, dodged roadblocks, and walked for months just to get to safety.

But the cruellest, most inhumane thing that Gukurahundi soldiers did was disappearing people. See, we believed that blood had an echo, that the spirits of the unburied would come back to haunt the living. Also, seeing the body of a loved one, however decomposed, charred, or mutilated, offered closure. Apart from the sociocultural beliefs, there were more practical aspects to it. War orphans could not obtain birth certificates or their parents' death certificates, which ultimately deprived them of the citizenship of the country in which they were born, a land in which their forebears had lived for close to a century. Like the hidden bodies of the dead, they were held hostage by the memory of Gukurahundi atrocities. That way, and for generations to come, its victims could never forget.

As politicians goaded us to provide proof of the massacres, state-sponsored newspapers were replete with the statistics of those killed and raped by dissidents. But there was not a single official statistic on how many people had been slaughtered, raped, and abducted by Gukurahundi soldiers.

Most Whites were silent; speaking out did not serve their interests. This was even though dissidents had killed more than thirty White farmers and their families and laid to waste more than 200,000 acres of prime farmland.

People in Mashonaland just didn't care. Many believed that we deserved everything we got. It seemed we were on our own. But conscientious doctors in hospitals across the country took huge risks and bravely reported an upsurge in the number of victims with gunshot wounds, many exhibiting signs of torture. Some were detained and hospitalised themselves. In the end, the Catholic Church, too, became involved. And, presented with incontrovertible evidence of the massacres, Mugabe capitulated and agreed to withdraw his troops.

CHAPTER 37

It was late 1984. There was a scaling down of military operations. We could see trucks laden with soldiers heading towards Bulawayo on the main road, and for the first time there was a glimmer of hope. But it was such an unnecessary waste of lives; Gukurahundi was nothing but a pyrrhic victory. Following both domestic and international pressure, they were recalled under a cloud of ignominy. And to this day, they'll always be associated with the darkest part of Zimbabwe's history, especially by the people of Matabeleland.

Gift and I had agreed that as soon as the buses started running, we should leave and try our luck with Ma in Bulawayo. We didn't want anyone to know that we were leaving, but if anyone should know what was going on, it would be Casper.

So I decided to pay him a visit to see if he could help us with money. When I arrived, there was a hive of activity in the camp. All the soldiers were packing their belongings into oversized military backpacks. Those who had finished packing were busy writing letters. Casper was playing with Chico. When he saw me approach, he beckoned for me to come into his tent. I sat down on his folding military chair made from green canvas looped round a silver metallic frame.

'*Kijane*, it's good you came by. I have something to tell you.'

He looked away through the small plastic window on the side of the tent. He was not smiling as he often did when he saw me. So, I waited for him to continue as I had no idea what he was going to say. But, judging by the amount of activity in the camp, I surmised that he, too, was leaving.

'I have been thinking of home,' he said. 'Taking a stroll by the river, having a wash, watching the world go by whilst waiting for my clothes to dry on a rock. Silly little things like that, I've missed all of that.'

I listened, wondering why it was taking him so long to tell me whatever it was he wanted to tell me.

'You're very clever,' he said. 'When all this is over, and as soon as schools open, make sure you get back to school, finish your studies, and maybe we can meet again under different circumstances?'

But I wasn't sure if our relationship would survive under different circumstances. Remove the war, there'd be nothing there. I could see it in his eyes – he was looking for a way out, and that was all.

Then he finally managed to say it.

'*Kijane*, I am leaving early tomorrow morning. I was going to come and say goodbye to you. I am going to miss you. After every mission, on the way back, I always think of you because you make me laugh and make things easy because you don't judge me.'

And for the first time he genuinely talked about the war, and he left his machine gun and blade out of it.

'The idea of holding a gun as a remote possibility is always enticing. But when you have it in your hand it has tremendous power to change you. But your hands and your heart are still clean. They're not as tainted as mine, so please keep them that way.'

Everything he'd just said made me believe that he cared deeply for me. But I soon recoiled when I thought about Bobo, his pregnant wife, Dumo, the old man Chauke, the girls, the rape, and everything else in between. Strangely, I didn't hate him. For me, our relationship was purely about survival. I had no choice in it; if what he said was true, that he thought about me after every violent encounter, then he, too, depended on me for his own survival. And there was nothing wrong with that.

Besides, he had given me food and protected me. And all I did was tell him about the comings and goings in the village. At least that's how I liked to think about it.

The heat inside the tent was becoming unbearable.

Casper broke the silence.

'Let's go for a walk,' he suggested.

All three of us exited through the tent. Chico, unbound, hopped on to Casper's shoulder. We walked in silence, save for the rattling of the machine gun and bullets.

Further down the road, Casper put his hand in his pocket, retrieved a brown envelope, and gave it to me.

'I wish you the best of luck, *kijane*. The war is almost over; things are changing. Remember what I said about school?' And then he smiled.

But he didn't say sorry about all the things he'd done. I watched him disappear towards the camp. He didn't look back.

When I got home, I went to Gift's hut. We opened the envelope together. Inside, there was enough money for our tickets to Bulawayo. There was also a small piece of paper, and it read: *Lt. Wilfred Casper Chibonyongwa, 5 Brigade, C-Coy, Gweru.*

CHAPTER 38

Although we'd lived close to what had been a slaughter camp, there was a kind of ecstasy in the air. People recited incantations that banished the horror of Gukurahundi to the past. We searched the camp for answers. Any clue, no matter how small, would do: pieces of cloth, abandoned shoes, human remains, teeth, jaws, T-shirts last worn by the disappeared, earrings, identity cards, wedding rings, and handkerchiefs with love messages stitched in love motifs. But all that was left were tyre marks, empty cans of pilchards, cigarettes packs, stubs, beer bottles, all corralled into an abandoned fire pit.

In the aftermath, we sang Gukurahundi songs of our own volition. They were the only gift they left behind. That and the children from the rapes that they committed. People called them Gukurahundi children – they were the embodiment of the violent legacy of our country's history. Like guerrillas and soldiers who raped and impregnated girls during the war, nobody knew their real names, their totems, or what madness flowed in their veins. And yet they were now an intrinsic part of our genetic make-up.

But the storm had passed; the ill wind that was Gukurahundi, gone. There were no death songs or rampant gunfire to serenade us to sleep. The air was no longer suffused with the smell of death. In the morning, there was no stampede of feet as girls found their way home after an all-night *pungwe** – sleep-deprived, tired feet finding the path home in a daze.

We gathered our animals, those that had survived the massacre and the drought, and watched them feed. It was October, the beginning of the rainy season. The grass was surprisingly verdant. It was as if all the blood had been washed away.

In the days that followed, ghostly, emaciated figures appeared on the horizon, their clothes torn, dirty. They were the last survivors of the detention camps. Up until that moment, we had no idea that they were alive. When my cousin Khaya came back from detention, he could barely walk. The soles of his feet had been totally stripped. His back was deformed, splayed into rivulets of cuts, small mounds of pinkish-brown earth. His buttocks pulverised into a big, soft purple bruise: plump, ripe, torn to shreds. His tongue was swollen too. Soldiers had used detainees' mouths as ashtrays. He was in so much pain that it was hard to watch him breathe.

I sat outside the kitchen wall and eavesdropped on the conversation between him and my other cousin, Themba, who had also been released from detention.

'By the time we got there, they already had freshly dug graves,

---

* An all-night political meeting popularised by guerrillas during the war of liberation.

waiting. All I could feel was the cold steel blade on my throat. And, strangely, the mud: slippery, wet in between my toes. Soft but repulsive. Just a visceral feeling, you know. All I could do was stand still. Just a stillness, you know. And then there were the muffled sounds: not howling, but soft, placid screams. In complete darkness. Right inside freshly dug graves. Still, they came, one after another after another. I lost count. Afterwards, they used our mouths as ashtrays. When I smell cigarette smoke, I feel a complete revulsion. And the thing is, you know . . .'

And then he hesitated as if he'd just remembered or stumbled upon something he wasn't expecting. Something trivial, but a detail that was important, nonetheless.

Themba interjected whilst Khaya retrieved his words.

'At night they put us in an underground container. All I could hear was the sound of footsteps underwater. And grown men wailing for their mothers. Alone. And the soft splashes of water; *ta ta ta ta ta*. I never knew that the sound of water alone could be so terrifying.

'In the morning, they buried us right up to our necks and left us in the sun. And you know what they did? They urinated in our mouths to keep us cool. I couldn't breathe, you know. The funniest thing is that all I wanted to do was scratch my nose so badly, but I couldn't. Don't you think that's funny? That of all the things I could think about, scratching my nose became the most important preoccupation right in the throes of death. The worst thing is that I can't simply walk away. It's in me now. All of it!'

There was some detail he kept stepping over. I wondered what he meant when he said, 'It's in me, all of it.'

And when Khaya suddenly woke up from his slumber, he

wondered out loud, 'I don't even know how long we were there for. There were so many of us, but I felt alone. The only consolation was that when they started on someone else, it gave you a temporary reprieve, time to breathe again, you know. Just to breathe. And the screams: "*Mai babo, voop! Mai babo wambulala! Voop!*"*

'And then they forced us to fight against each other like it was a spectator sport. Just like that, they just pitted us against each other like bulls. If you don't believe me, just look at me,' he said, desperately trying to convince Themba by pointing at his face. His face had ballooned. It was pockmarked. His eyes were partially closed, and his lips swollen from cigarette burns.

Themba looked, and simply remarked, 'There are parts of my body I still cannot feel. I am not sure if I ever will.'

I walked away just to calm down. Because when I sat still for too long it felt as if I was caught up inside the endless loop of a recurring nightmare. And that's what Gukurahundi did to people.

---

* A plea for mercy: you are killing me!

CHAPTER 39

After two years in prison, exactly two months after Gukurahundi left, Pa finally came home. It felt as though a burden had been lifted off my shoulders. I wanted to tell him about everything that had happened in his absence, but it seemed there wasn't enough room in his heart for all of us.

After seven years of primary-school education, despite all the obstacles, I had finished top of my class. Which meant that I had the highest probability of securing a place in some of our country's best secondary schools. But when I broke the news to Pa, he said there was no money. When I suggested that perhaps he should sell one or two of his animals to pay for my education, he told me that they were strictly for emergencies only. That infuriated me, because it was me who had spent all my precious time looking after his animals. Also, after the war, what other emergency was there?

Gift, too, was in a similar situation. Frustrated and demoralised, we just gave up, let it be, and finalised our escape plan. We had sufficient funds for the bus tickets to Bulawayo and our onward journey to Grandma's. We washed, ironed, packed our clothes, and waited for our moment.

It was the first Christmas almost two years after Gukurahundi first set foot in our little corner of the country. Returnees from Kwekwe, Harare, Bulawayo and Gweru descended upon us, rousing our village from its languourous post-war daze.

Those who'd fled the war had come back to see what was left of the old world. But they didn't want us to talk about the war. Instead, they regaled us with the tales of city life, glossing over our pain and the years of hunger.

Silas was there too. He was one of my cousins from SaDumo's small house. He was an exact replica of SaDumo: his hands, feet, jagged teeth, and mannerisms. He was also violent, querulous, disagreeable. He carried a knife wherever he went. Everybody was afraid of him; most people kept him at an arm's length.

But it was Christmas. The war of retribution had just ended, and everyone was in good spirits. Pa, SaDumo, my cousins Shadrack and Khaya gathered outside the liquor store for a drink. Silas came along too. I joined them. They didn't seem to mind me being there. As they downed beers, a heated argument ensued between Silas and Khaya, but I couldn't wrap my head around it.

Khaya was from SaDumo's big house: he and Silas were step-brothers. But, unlike Silas, he was quiet, reserved. He was a cobbler, the only knife he carried was for his trade. He never concealed it, but it was very sharp. It cut through tough leather like a sharp razor blade slicing through thin paper. And I knew that Silas had his own knife too. With the alcohol, frayed tempers, and knives, I listened to my intuition and left.

Later that night, I visited Khaya to see if he was okay. Ever since he'd come back from detention, he seemed very fragile. Somehow, I felt it was my job to save him. I found him sitting alone in the dark. I noticed that the clothes he had been wearing earlier that day had been washed and they were hanging on the clothes line. He didn't say anything to me, but he was visibly shaken.

Also, he was nursing a gaping defensive knife wound on his left forearm, and another on his right shoulder. Those were the only ones that I could see; I said nothing about his wounds even though I feared the worst. I left him there and went to bed full of trepidation.

Early morning on Boxing Day, I felt cold even though it was warm outside. There wasn't a single cloud in the pale blue sky. But something was off-kilter with my body; I had no idea why. Just then I heard screaming coming from SaDumo's house. I ran the short distance between our homes, so I didn't miss anything. It was Silas's mother; SaDumo was desperately trying to hold her back, to contain her rage.

'Where is that cowardly son of yours?' screamed Silas's mother. 'Tell him to come out here and do the honourable thing and confess to his dreadful crime!'

'Please calm down!' SaDumo said. 'What are you talking about?'

'Khaya, that's who, that shrivelling, evil excuse of a man!'

And NaDumo strongly interjected: 'Please stop spouting nonsense and tell us what this madness is all about. You can't just come into my home, after sleeping with my husband all these years, and start yelling obscenities at my son for no reason. What has my son done?' she asked, gesticulating as if ready for a fight.

'He killed his own brother that's what. What kind of a man

preys upon his own brother? Come out here and tell us why you've brought this evil on your own family!'

'Who has he killed?' enquired SaDumo, seemingly confused.

'Silas, that's who. I've seen my son's body with my own eyes. Even though he's mutilated him, I know it's him. I gave birth to him. He carved him up like a wild animal and left all his entrails hanging out. After everything that's happened, why now, Khaya? Why didn't you just walk away and let my son live? Just let him live so I can look at him one more day!'

'*Khaya! Khaya!* Come out here right now and explain this to me, and it better be good!' shouted SaDumo, now angry, puzzled, but with the most dreadful fear plastered across his face.

'He slaughtered him like a wild animal, and he could have simply walked away!' reiterated Silas's mother, who was relentless in her quest to make her accusation stick on Khaya.

'And how do you know it was him?' asked NaDumo, who was as puzzled as everyone else.

'Somebody saw them fighting right where Silas's body was found this morning. Let him come out and explain why he is still alive, whilst my son's dead. That's what I want to know.'

SaDumo continually banged hard on Khaya's bedroom door. When the door finally opened, it was his wife, who, from the looks of it, had been asleep.

'He came home seriously injured last night,' she announced, eyes cast to the ground. 'He said that it was Silas who stabbed him first. He was up early like he always is. He doesn't always tell me where he's going.'

She elaborated by shrugging her shoulders, seemingly lost, and confused.

When there was a lull in the shouting and screaming, Dumo said, 'I think he's gone.'

'What do you mean he's gone?' asked SaDumo.

'He grabbed a long piece of wire, a snare, and headed towards the forest this morning. I think he's gone trapping.'

It was always the small things, the seemingly trivial, unresolved familial conflicts that people carried until one day they exploded, and nobody knew why. But all along the signs were there, from the little things that they said, to the way they treated animals and other people, to the way they whispered curses under the tongue.

Khaya was quiet and reserved, but that didn't render him incapable of killing. Silas must have done something that crossed the threshold of what he was willing to tolerate. And that was all it took.

I said nothing about Khaya's wounds.

We traced his footprints as they made their way towards the edge of the forest. An hour later, we found him dangling from a wire high up on the bough of a tree. He had taken all the answers with him; he had also opened a wound for which there was no balm.

And the adults had the unenviable task of guarding the bodies whilst they waited for the police.

When the police arrived, they loaded the bodies into the truck. SaDumo sat at the back with no canopy shielding him from the sun, as he guarded the bodies of his two sons. Khaya's bruised neck was slightly twisted, hiding the wire in the fold of his skin. SaDumo tried to loosen the wire, but the policeman instructed him to leave everything as it was. It seemed such an unnatural thing to do, to let him continue to hang like that. A thick green liquid trickled from underneath Silas's body into the small furrows on the floor of the police truck. Everything was gone except the residues of lives that might have turned into something wonderful. Even though the Gukurahundi war had ended, the rage it had created was still here.

CHAPTER 40

Gift and I escaped at dawn on New Year's Eve. The once clogged arterial road network had been reopened. Old, familiar sounds of buses marked the end of trepidation and debilitating hunger, and a thirst for peace was here. Over time, sections of the road had fallen into disrepair. Small corrugated gulleys traversed the surface of the dust road.

We boarded the bus and sat right at the back. There was every possibility that the bus was nothing but a fire trap. Rogue elements of Gukurahundi were still operating in remote areas: mopping up, tidying up loose ends, and disappearing survivors just to be sure that there were no witnesses left.

Years later, Mugabe would say that Gukurahundi was a moment of madness, which wasn't true. It was no different to Operation Hurricane, Chimoio, Nyadzonya, and all the other tragic massacres of innocent Blacks by Ian Smith's racist regime. In Zimbabwe today there are still new discoveries of the remains of those massacred and buried in secret mass graves by Smith's illegal regime. And none of those involved were ever held accountable: impunity wasn't Mugabe's invention; it persists even after his death.

The austere landscape was littered with burnt-out homes, overgrown fields, schools swallowed by tall weeds. Carcasses of hollow buses stared at us from the side of the road. There was the noticeable absence of the voices of women and children too. Small boys wandered aimlessly behind braying donkeys and emaciated cattle, the kind you never saw on White farms.

As we approached the first roadblock, there was an air of bewilderment and trepidation inside the bus: red berets had been replaced by green berets. When the bus came to a halt, a soldier entered the bus. His rubbery lips peeled back to reveal stained, mossy teeth. He had no gun; I calculated the dimensions of his blade from a distance. It was the same size as Casper's. Only the soldier was of a diminutive stature compared to the man mountain that was Casper, wherever he was.

When you're afraid, time is never in a hurry.

So I held in my breath, lest something exploded. Besieged by a debilitating fear, suddenly outlines blurred and the soldier's uniform and smell triggered the memory of the massacres.

'Who are you travelling with?' a voice bellowed.

Gift promptly answered: 'We are travelling on our own to visit our mother in the city. We'll be back in a couple of weeks in time for the new school term.'

At seventeen, she looked and sounded much more mature; she knew how to handle soldiers, however menacing the look.

Although serious, his question lacked sincerity, like a whirlwind that starts and stops for no reason at all, except raise dust. He could see we were trembling, and he shrewdly tried to exploit our nervousness.

'Is there anything you want to tell me about the dissidents? Anything at all?'

'No, not really,' we answered in unison as we vigorously shook our heads.

'All the men outside, ID cards in your hands!' the soldier commanded as he walked along the aisle.

The men trembled as they exited the bus. Outside, I watched them raise their hands in the air. They spread their legs apart as soldiers searched them for weapons. Miraculously, most of the men returned to their seats, except for a handful of unfortunate souls detained for further interrogation – they came close to escaping.

The bus hiccupped and threw dust in the air as we headed towards Bulawayo. I went further ahead, imagined Grandma welcoming us with a warm embrace. We hadn't seen her for the best part of three years. For the first time in a long while, I thought about her. I had missed her terribly.

As derelict villages gave way to pristine farmland, there was less tension in the bus. It was as if everyone had exhaled at the same time. The transition to a tarmacked road restored our composure. We were there, still alive. But the memory of Gukurahundi was most intimately felt in the heart, the rampant heartbeat, the fear that paralysed every muscle in your body every time we passed stationary military vehicles, or men in uniform.

We arrived in Bulawayo in the late afternoon. It was the rainy season. A deep red clay provoked the scent of an imminent downpour. A cool breeze greeted us as we exited the bus. But since we didn't have Ma's address in the city, we caught a connecting bus to Grandma's place. Hers was our only home;

it had been a long, arduous, and very emotional journey; we slept most of the way.

We arrived at Grandma's just before sunset. She was old; her red moist eyes scrutinised us disdainfully, and she remarked, 'You're darker and much uglier than when I last saw you. What did they do to you?'

We had no answer to her question, but if only she knew the significance of her words, because we were broken beyond repair. Besides, memory is no timelessly valid thing.

I felt restless, but mostly ashamed; I could no longer face Grandma. After all, everything that she'd said had come to fruition. So, a week later, armed with Ma's latest address, I made my way to Bulawayo to find her. Luckily, my arrival coincided with Aunt Gladys's visit from Harare. It was the first time that I saw her in real life: tall, gangly, forthright, her cheeks blemished by dark Ambi patches. She laughed more readily than our ma.

After considering my dire circumstances, it was agreed that I should go to Harare with her. Besides, she had no children of her own; I would be the surrogate son that she never had.

Two weeks later, Aunt Gladys and I took an overnight train to Harare. I sat quietly right next to her as she intermittently brushed off imaginary dust from her clothes. The train moved at a slow pace. Everything ground along to a slow, steady rhythm as people brushed their teeth from enamel cups, spat out of the windows and prepared to sleep. Aunt fell asleep still clutching her handbag even as the train swerved and rattled over crossing points. For a while, I could not fall asleep. I was busy imagining my new life. Aunt had promised me that as soon as we got to Harare, she'd see to it that I was enrolled into one of their best schools. As I didn't know much about Harare, I had no idea what the best schools there looked like. I envisaged them as resembling the Whites-only schools that I knew: Sacred Heart, or perhaps Falcon College. But I was excited, all the same, by the thought of going to a new school in the city, in the absence of war – a new beginning.

INDEX

ACKNOWLEDGEMENTS

I was born and raised in a country where intimacy was forbidden between races; where racism, in its broadest implication. disrupted the capacity for linking. Where violence was, and still is, a mode of communication, a way of relating; where the brutalisation of women through political violence continues to mark the tension of a nation in crisis. I came of age in a devastated and devastating landscape.

Therefore, this memoir is a re-memory of things past, as I remember them. It testifies to the fact that memory is not just one, but a set of recollections attached to oftentimes irreconcilable meanings, conditioned by, but also conditioning, the interpretations available in the present. But I hope, at least for those who survived, that this memoir paints a recognisable portrait of the past, because memory is no sure-footed thing.

But a work of such magnitude would not have been possible without the help of remarkable individuals, because no one heals alone. I am eternally grateful to my dearest friend and mentor, Russell Celyn-Jones, for his kindness, patience, and generosity with time; to Jacqueline Rose for saving me, even though she might disagree with that sentiment. And to Polly Clark, whose generosity changed the trajectory of my writing career

But my sincerest gratitude goes to Jon Riley, editor-in-chief at Quercus, whose unflagging belief in this project made it a reality; to Jasmine Palmer, commissioning editor at riverrun, and to Samantha Stanton Stewart, for their due diligence and scrupulous editorial skills in smoothing out the clumsiness of my writing. Although certain names and places have been changed to protect the living, the work is my own and I take full ownership of all the mistakes.

Finally, I would like to thank Emilia Bila-Sayi, my wife and companion for the past twenty-seven years, for the gentle nudges, and for saving me from the grip of night terrors. But most of all, for keeping the home fires burning, even when I had the most crippling self-doubt. Here is the love poem you've so patiently waited for: *Ďakujem za všetko!*

Acknowledgements to:

Yvonne Vera's *The Stone Virgins*; Christopher Mlalazi's *Running with Mother*; Alexander Kanengoni's *Echoing Silences*; Shimmer Chinodya's *Harvest of Thorns*, and Wole Soyinka's *Aké: The Years of Childhood*.